Global Minstrels

Global Minstrels

Voices of World Music

Elijah Wald

Routledge
Taylor & Francis Group
New York   London

Routledge is an imprint of the
Taylor & Francis Group, an informa business

Routledge
Taylor & Francis Group
270 Madison Avenue
New York, NY 10016

Routledge
Taylor & Francis Group
2 Park Square
Milton Park, Abingdon
Oxon OX14 4RN

Printed in the United States of America on acid-free paper
10 9 8 7 6 5 4 3 2 1

International Standard Book Number-10: 0-415-97930-7 (Softcover) 0-415-97929-3 (Hardcover)
International Standard Book Number-13: 978-0-415-97930-6 (Softcover) 978-0-415-97929-0 (Hardcover)

Library of Congress Cataloging-in-Publication Data

Wald, Elijah.
    Global minstrels : voices of world music / Elijah Wald.
        p. cm.
        Includes bibliographical references (p.   ) and index.
    ISBN 0-415-97929-3 (hardback : alk. paper) -- ISBN 0-415-97930-7 (pbk. : alk.
    paper) 1. Musicians--Interviews. 2. World music--History and criticism. I. Title.
    ML394.W33 2006

    780.92'2--dc22
    [B]   2006022760

Visit the Taylor & Francis Web site at
http://www.taylorandfrancis.com

and the Routledge Web site at
http://www.routledge-ny.com

Contents

Preface and Acknowledgments

The interviews that make up this book were conducted over the last fifteen years, most of them while I was the world music critic for the *Boston Globe*, but a few for other publications or specifically for this project. While my *Globe* editors were remarkably accommodating, a daily newspaper has obvious space limitations and I often bemoaned the fact that I had to chop interesting conversations down to fit the requirements of the medium. This book gives me a chance to present the interviews as I originally would have preferred, and while many retain the basic form in which they were first published, they have all been expanded, and some have been entirely rewritten.

The selection of artists involved a lot of difficult choices. I tried to maintain some balance and variety, and to avoid pieces that focused on a particular tour or album. However, I did not exclude artists simply because they are no longer active, nor did I include all the biggest stars I have spoken with. There are excellent world music surveys available, and I hope to provide something different: a chance to meet interesting musicians from many cultures, and to hear what they have to say about their lives and work. So when less-known artists were more articulate than their more successful peers, I included them in the hope that their stories would be illuminating or entertaining even though readers were unfamiliar with their music.

The concentration on good conversations led to some admittedly quirky decisions. Interviewers are at the mercy of chance much of the time, especially when we are seizing moments in someone's busy tour schedule. Some people I would have loved to include were not feeling talkative when I happened to reach them—I spoke twice with Cesaria Évora, and both times was treated to grumpy, one-word answers— and there were other impediments as well. Being reasonably fluent in English, Spanish, and French, I could talk directly with almost all the performers from Europe, Africa, the Americas, and much of Western and Central Asia, but when it came to East Asian artists I usually had to use whatever interpreter happened to be on the tour, and that often meant that I couldn't get any flavor of the performer's own speech or manner. So this book has been created from a confluence of choice and happenstance, and the omissions are not all voluntary.

That said, over the years I have managed to talk to hundreds of fine musicians, and I want to thank all the people who made that happen, and made this book a reality. Most of all, I am grateful to the performers themselves, both those included here and the many I could not include, who did so much to educate me about their world and their work.

At the *Globe*, I had a uniquely free hand for a freelancer, being allowed to choose my subjects and interview artists who often were completely unknown to my editors and my readership. For making this possible, I must thank the editors: Scott Powers, Jan Shepherd, and Mary Jane Wilkinson. For commissioning other stories, I thank Matt Ashare and Jon Garelick at the *Boston Phoenix*, Bettina Gram at *Zapp*, Mark Moss at *Sing Out*, and Jeffrey Pepper Rodgers at *Acoustic Guitar*.

I would also like to thank the promoters, club owners, tour organizers, record companies, and community organizations that brought these artists to the United States and facilitated my conversations with them. There are too many names to include all of them, and neither my memory nor my files are complete, but I must single out Maure Aronson of World Music, who was uniquely important in making Boston a major stop on the international circuit, expertly assisted by Susan Weiler. Others who were helpful over the years include Siddiq Abdullah, Alex Alvear, Obain Attouoman, Sue Auclair, Nili Belkind, Cindy Byram, Marlon Catao, Reka Chitre, Jacob Edgar, Bill

Eliopoulos, Debbie Ferraro, Ellen Friedman, Frank Ikero, Rafael Jaimes, Desiré Mondon, Flo Murdock, James Nyette, Claudio Ragazzi, George Ruckert, Wafaa' Salman, John Stifler, Dmitri Vietze, and Dana Westover. Many people also were helpful in chatting with me about the various styles and steering me away from egregious errors. Their names are too numerous to include, but I cannot omit Banning Eyre, Julia Goldrosen, Fernando González, Perry Lederman, and Ned Sublette.

Introduction

In the 1990s, world music began to sell in mainstream American record stores at a rate that was comparable to jazz and classical music. The stage had been set by a series of high-profile pop collaborations: Ry Cooder, Peter Gabriel, Paul Simon, and Talking Heads made recordings with artists whose names seemed strange to most of their fans, and whose playing added an exotic flavor to the standard rock lineup. As interest grew, some of these foreign artists had their own records released in the United States and were booked on national tours, and others followed their lead. In a surprisingly few years, Cesaria Évora and the Cuban old-timers of the Buena Vista Social Club were being heard in homes that had never before listened to anything more foreign than the Beatles, Mahlathini and the Mahotella Queens turned up in Decatur, Illinois, and the religious chants of Nusrat Fateh Ali Khan appeared as atmospheric music in big-budget films.

While all these foreign artists are filed in the "world" bins of record stores, they often have little in common. So it seems reasonable to ask, What is world music? Or, more to the point, what *isn't* it? The bluesman Big Bill Broonzy famously responded to a question about whether he was singing folk songs by saying, "I never heard a horse sing 'em." In the same way, a lot of people argue that all music is world music, and that the term is ridiculous.

The world category recalls one of those medieval maps on which all the details of Europe and the Holy Land are clearly marked, but the rest of the planet is full of blurred or unmarked borders, drawings of people with two heads, and warnings that "here be monsters." Record stores separate their wares into the Euro-American mainstreams—rock, jazz, classical, folk, country, R & B—neatly divided and filed by artist, and what is left over ends up in the world section, mysterious sounds from "out there," filed only by country or continent.

This view of the world seems particularly odd when one compares it to the way those mysterious foreigners regard us. Given a constant diet of American films and television, the average person on the other side of the globe may be more familiar with the streets of Los Angeles or a Beacon Hill barroom than with the people living across the next mountain range, and American styles have dominated the international pop scene for decades. As a result, while Americans find fusions of rock and foreign styles quirky and exotic, for much of the rest of the world they are the norm: Indian pop stars sing a blend of ancient court song and Madonna; Arabic bands combine shawms and techno rhythm tracks; and African dance orchestras have been blending traditional drums, James Brown-style vocals, Cuban horn sections, and rock lead guitar for so long that it is considered rather old-fashioned.

Some critics will therefore argue that the whole concept of world music implies a blinkered, Eurocentric view of the world, at best ignorant and at worst racist and colonialist. Most of those critics, though, are now listening to more music from a wider range of regions than ever before. Which is to say that, irritated as they may be, they are at the forefront of the "world" trend. And to counter their grumbling, one can point out that the whole spirit of the world music scene has been to counteract the ingrained provincialism of Westerners.

Whatever one's ideological take on the situation, there is more music now available to more people and from more different places than at any other time in human history. Because of that, people like me have ended up with the peculiar job of trying to sort it out and make it more accessible to American listeners. I landed in this position more or less by chance: back before the world music boom, I was writing on folk and blues for the *Boston Globe*, and since I spoke Spanish and French and was curious about other styles I was handed the occasional foreign offering by default. Then the trickle of foreign music grew to a river, and eventually a flood, and I was doing two or three pieces a week.

Like pretty much all the writers, musicians, and producers who have immersed themselves in the new wave of international musics, I was coming from a position of appalling ignorance. Fifteen years later, I have attained at least a basic knowledge of many styles from around the world, but on the grand scale little has changed. Even with genres I came to know quite well—flamenco, Congolese acoustic guitar—my knowledge remains that of an outsider. The fans on the street in Spain or Central Africa have a familiarity with their music that I could only gain by spending years specializing in one particular style. I received most of my education from recordings and tours that happened to reach the United States, and it has been as spotty as it has been fascinating. In some cases, I am convinced that I have heard the finest artists alive, while in others I doubt whether I got a representative example of the style I was supposedly hearing. But always, I had to learn as I went along. And I think that in a way this helped me as an interviewer, because I was trying to get answers to the same question my readers would be asking: "What is this stuff?"

One thing I learned, and what to me is perhaps the most compelling thing about this book, is that there really is something universal about music, and about the lives and attitudes of its players. Many of my questions got almost identical answers whether the performers I was talking to were from Asia, Africa, Europe, or Latin America. Musicians face similar challenges all around the world, and tend to fulfill similar needs in their societies. Some are more deeply rooted in their local styles, some more eager to reach a foreign audience; some are folk musicians and some are regional pop stars—but all are trying to balance the demands of tradition with the need to keep their music relevant in changing times. In a way, this is the real meaning of *world music*—that it is simply the large-scale version of what on the American scene is called *roots music*, those styles that are clearly rooted in a particular place or culture rather than being an indistinguishable part of an ever more homogenized global pop scene.

If, at least in the context of the United States, there really is such a thing as world music, there remains the question of who is listening to it. The answer usually provided by critics and concert promoters is that Americans (and Europeans) are more conscious than ever before of being part of a global economy and more interested in learning about foreign cultures. There is some truth to this. Albums like Paul Simon's *Graceland* and Ry Cooder's *Buena Vista Social Club* reached audiences that had never listened to African or Cuban music before, and many of those listeners were soon showing up at concerts by Ladysmith Black Mambazo and Compay Segundo. Some dug very deep, and over the years I met quite a few people who had become true "world" listeners—the sort of fans who might dance to Zairean *soukous* and Cuban *son*, and then relax to Brazilian *MPB* and Japanese *koto* records.

Indeed, in some ways international folk and pop styles have been replacing classical music as the favored listening of people who consider themselves cultured. There is a feeling that, by being a fan of this music, one is demonstrating a healthy intellectual curiosity and separating oneself from one's more provincial neighbors. Like a certain sort of classical fan, there are even world music listeners who are quite happy to be bored by, say, the Turkish Whirling Dervishes, because the sense of boredom just makes the experience seem more educational and uplifting.

As I covered the international music scene, though, I became aware that there is another component to the boom that the media tend to miss. While English-speaking Americans are indeed hearing more foreign music than ever before, the United States is also experiencing the greatest influx of immigrants in its history, and the varied audiences of newcomers are supplying much of the power behind the world music market. For example, a new wave of Portuguese *fado* singers has been reaching an American audience that never heard the music before, but when someone like Mariza or Cristina Branco comes to Boston, roughly half the audience will still be Portuguese; when Kayhan Kalhor sells out Disney Hall in Los Angeles, that is due to the city's immense Iranian community. It is no accident that many of the better-known Brazilian, Cape Verdean, Indian, Iranian, Lebanese, North African, Pakistani, and Portuguese musicians have had a relatively easy time breaking into the American concert market, since they are singing largely to their home folk.

This is not to say that large immigrant populations can necessarily be equated with world crossover success. Haitian dance bands, Mexican *norteño* acts and Chinese, Russian, and Vietnamese pop singers are all filling halls in American cities, but without reaching more than a handful of listeners outside their own communities. Meanwhile, Tuvan throat singing and flamenco have captured good-sized American audiences without having a significant immigrant constituency. Still, any attempt to understand the current flood of global styles must take into account how many of the records are selling to the same people who would be buying them back home.

This book includes conversations with some of the biggest crossover stars, but also with musicians who continue to be heard almost exclusively by their core audiences. Notably, this seems to make little difference in the way they talk about their work. Whatever their personal tastes, all are working performers who have to balance their desire to play the music they love with the need to find a market. The singers who are reaching a broad audience of English speakers continue to insist that they are remaining true to their roots, while the ones who are playing only for their conationals are eager to reach a broader range of American listeners.

Another thing that almost all the figures in this book share is that they are leading their own groups and making their own music. Though a lot of American listeners have heard world styles as exotic flavoring to rock and pop projects, I must admit to something of a prejudice when it comes to fusion experiments. The best fusions are wonderful, but in my years as a world music critic, I have received far too many phone calls from publicists who explain that, while the record they are promoting is by a jazz, folk, rock, or classical artist, it has world elements that should interest me.

The conversation typically goes something like this:

Publicist: "It has kind of a world feel."
Me: "As opposed to what?"
Publicist: "What?"
Me: "What else could it be if it wasn't world?"
Publicist, laughing pleasantly: "Oh, you know what I mean."

But I usually don't, and neither would anyone else. Sometimes they mean a Japanese flutist, sometimes a talking drum played by an American who studied for two months in Nigeria, sometimes a band that has added a guest musician from a foreign country, sometimes a jazz saxophonist improvising on ancient Sumerian scales extrapolated from notation preserved on clay tablets discovered in the seventh stratum of a recent archeological dig.

Or, to be fair, I know exactly what they mean. They mean that they need some press, and they are trying to find a hook that will interest me—which I completely understand, but as a general thing the fusion projects leave me cold. I am interested in music from around the world, and in genuine, well-developed attempts at cultural interchange—but not in the fact that somebody has added a couple of exotic instruments to an otherwise standard jazz, folk, rock, or classical album.

Basically, I feel that writing about international music is a lot like travel writing. Where people read about rock or hip-hop because they are fans and want to know more about their favorite songs and performers, a lot of the people reading about world music are doing it at least in part because they want to get a sense of how people live and think in other parts of the world. I would hope that the voices in this book will not only tempt readers to pick up some CDs, go out to concerts, and discover unfamiliar styles, but will give them a better understanding of other cultures, and of what makes music truly a sort of international language.

1

AFRICA

Africa is the obvious place to begin any survey of the world music scene. The world boom was to a great extent sparked by the quest of musicians like Peter Gabriel, Paul Simon, and Talking Heads to reconnect their music with its roots, and for a hundred years quests for the roots of pop have tended to lead back to Africa. Ragtime, jazz, blues, rock, salsa, reggae, hip-hop—the rhythms of Africa and the African diaspora have been the engine of virtually all modern international styles.

The search for roots, though, has sometimes reinforced stereotypes and led to misunderstandings. After all, modern African music is both African and modern—no continent has gone through more changes in recent decades, and no musicians have been more innovative and open to new fusions and technologies. One result is that the African music that has most appealed to international listeners is often very different from what has been most successful back home. In the 1980s, when Simon went to South Africa to scout collaborators for *Graceland*, the country's most popular recording artists were generally disco stars like Brenda Fassie and Sipho Hotstix Mabuse, whose records were hitting throughout sub-Saharan Africa. The fact that Simon bypassed these hot, young stars in favor of Ladysmith Black Mambazo and the accordion bands of Lesotho is neither a criticism of him nor of them. For Africans, the disco beat was a thrilling new sound; for a New Yorker, it wasn't a reason to leave town.

This divergence of taste and experience means that an overview of African music on the international scene is necessarily quite different from a survey of what is played in Africa. Folkloric artists like Stella Chiweshe and Ephat Mujuru enthrall halls of foreigners, but in Zimbabwe most people are surprised that anyone could make a living by quietly telling stories and playing the thumb piano. Conversely,

European and American audiences have shown little enthusiasm for the synthesizer-driven *soukous* bands that have ruled the African club scene. The difference is cultural as well as musical: the concept of a concert hall, where listeners sit quietly and listen to a performer, is unknown in most of Africa, where music has never been separated from dancing and social situations.

There is also the issue of authenticity. Just as Americans did not find Talking Heads less authentically American when they used African drummers, Africans do not find their stars less authentic when they use a drum machine or wear a brilliantly cut Italian suit. Foreigners, by contrast, tend to want to hear and see something that feels "African"—just as Africans, when they see a country-and-western star, want him to strum a guitar and wear a cowboy hat.

That said, today's world music listeners have acquired a very broad view of African music. One of the most important things about the *Graceland* album was that Simon chose to highlight choral singing, accordion, and electric bass rather than traditional percussion. Since then, artists like Youssou N'Dour, Tarika Sammy, Oumou Sangaré, and Ali Farka Touré have further expanded the international perception of African styles to the point that young listeners may not even remember the time when all African music was stereotyped as jungle drumming. Nonetheless, for many people, drums remain the defining feature of African performance. If a European or American band adds one African collaborator, it is usually a drummer, and when most foreigners think of African styles, drums immediately leap to mind.

This makes some sense, considering the the intricate rhythms and central role of drumming in so much African music, but ignores the fact that Africa has as wide a range of instruments and styles as any other continent—by some counts, far wider. All the basic families of instruments have been present there for centuries, if not millennia: wind instruments, from tiny reed pipes to trumpets that are bigger than their players; stringed instruments, from the Ethiopian lyre to the twenty-three-stringed kora; keyed instruments from the thumb piano to all sorts of xylophones; and the list keeps growing, with electric guitars and keyboards, synthesizers, and turntables each being adopted as they became available.

This highlights another fact: Euro-Americans need to remember, when they hear African music, that African audiences have been listening to our records for far longer, and generally with far more attention, than we have been listening to theirs. From "Negro spiritual" groups to the Trío Matamoros and Louis Armstrong, cowboy yodelers to the Beatles and James Brown, American and European artists have profoundly influenced modern African styles. That is part of what makes African music so appealing to outsiders: so much of it is already a "world" fusion, its exotic characteristics balanced with aspects that are instantly familiar.

African compositions and musicians began to surface on the American pop scene long before the world boom. Zulu harmonies hit the charts in the 1950s with the Weavers' cover of Solomon Linda's "Mbube," under the name "Wimoweh," which resurfaced in 1961 as the Tokens' "The Lion Sleeps Tonight." The 1960s brought Babatunde Olatunji's *Drums of Passion*, Mariam Makeba and her "Click Song," and Hugh Masekela's "Grazing in the Grass," and the 1970s gave us Manu Dibango and "Soul Makossa."

In 1982, King Sunny Ade's *Juju Music* LP and his subsequent American tour provided a lot of non-Nigerians with their first taste of a full-scale African pop orchestra, and his marathon shows became an instant legend. Around the same period, Talking Heads and Peter Gabriel added African drummers to their records, and in 1986 Simon released *Graceland*, which set a new standard for world fusion success.

People began talking about "world beat" as a promising new genre, but at that point "African beat" might have been a more appropriate name, since virtually all the early projects consisted of fusions of European, American, Asian, or Oceanian styles with African percussion. As the rubric shifted to "world music," that emphasis was diluted, but African players have continued to be ubiquitous in international fusions, and African stars among the most consistent concert attractions.

Naturally, the international stature of African musicians has changed their musical approach. Some of the artists in this section have continued to work almost entirely for African audiences even when they travel abroad, but others have become true world artists, shaping their music and performances to reach not only the home audience but millions of foreigners for whom they are the voice of modern Africa.

South Africa

Ladysmith Black Mambazo

If one had to pick a date for the beginning of the world music boom, an obvious choice would be 1986, the year of Paul Simon's *Graceland*. There had been plenty of earlier experiments in international musical fusions, but Simon's album arrived at a moment when listeners in the United States and Europe were feeling starved for new sounds, and it opened the music industry's eyes to the market potential of foreign styles. The timing was perfect. South Africa was in the news almost daily, and with the release of Nelson Mandela and the end of white minority rule, the deeply rooted but ebulliently energetic styles of the township bands felt like the voice of a new era. Along with giving a huge boost to Simon's career, the album created an instant international fan base for the South African artists he featured.

The most popular of these, by far, have been the singers of Ladysmith Black Mambazo. Though their a cappella sound had largely run its course as a pop style in their homeland, it was one of the most immediately recognizable elements of the *Graceland* project, and blended the progressive optimism of the new South Africa with the old-fashioned appeal of gospel and choral music. Ladysmith soon had a fan base that could be relied on to pack their yearly American concert tours, even if many of those fans never went to another African show.

A key component in Ladysmith's success is the savvy and charisma of the group's founder and leader, Joseph Shabalala. As befits a man whose music has deep roots in spiritual traditions—both African and Afro-American—Shabalala's language often has the flavor of a biblical parable, flavored with the distinctive accent and grammar of the South African countryside. For instance, take Shabalala's story of how he came to name his group: "I take that name from the span of oxen. When we were working on the farm, plowing the land, there were three different types of span: the red one, the colored one, and the black one. The black one was the most powerful, and I was the leader of that black span. So, when I started the group, I called them, 'This is my black span from Ladysmith.' Ladysmith is the place where we come from, and black is those span of oxen."

As for Mambazo, it is the Zulu word for axe: "I was hoping that they can have a powerful voice like an axe, to cut all those trees from our way. Also, at the time when we were young, from nineteen fifty-something to sixty, we used to compete with another young ones, and we always warned the competition: I said 'Yes, I have a black axe, just paving the way with their voices.'"

The trail Shabalala's singers have cut since then is longer and broader than he could possibly have imagined. In the early 1970s, they rocketed to the top of the South African pop market. In 1986, they moved onto the world stage with their appearance on Simon's album, and the next year a solo album won them a Grammy. In 1993 they opened on Broadway in *The Song of Jacob Zulu* and accompanied Nelson Mandela to Norway for his Nobel Peace Prize acceptance. Later albums would mix traditional Zulu song with band cuts featuring guests like Dolly Parton, Bonnie Raitt, and Lou Rawls.

Shabalala says that when Ladysmith became nationally famous in South Africa, audiences were startled by his combination of traditional music and youthful energy. "When people heard this music, they think they are going to see an old man with white hair. But when they invite me to Johannesburg, they were surprised. That time was 1972. They said, 'This young man, oh, he knows everything! He might be a graduate!' And I said, 'Yes, I'm a graduate. Because my mother, my father, my grandmother, they have told me about these things from generation to generation.'"

Often, writers describe traditional musicians as untrained or self-taught, but as Shabalala emphasizes, there is no deeper form of education than what people have received for centuries in their own communities. "Those people who are at the rural areas, they were there doing something," he says with obvious pride. "And they were professionals of that thing. But all along people were saying, 'Aw, forget about the old things.' That changed because of these young men, Ladysmith Black Mambazo. I always praise them, because I was just like a sick man, and Black Mambazo healed me.

"They loved to listen, and they had that patience to sit down after work—after the whole day, working nine to ten hours. In the beginning they said, 'Why are you so serious?' And I said, 'I feel like I have something to present our people. They are all away from their music, and they don't like even themselves, they don't like even their color. But I think we have something good we can present them.' And the guys were serious after that."

While Shabalala always stresses his style's deep roots, he points out that he also added new ingredients and brought a fresh approach: "The music was from the people on the farm, but the way to develop it, that was an idea which came to me at night in a dream, an idea to take the music to the market. In the dream it was just like somebody was teaching me that you can put this harmony and this melody and then you're going to do many things."

Ladysmith's choral style arrived on the national market at a time when the South African pop scene was dominated by township jive and fusions with everything from jazz to rock 'n' roll. The group became national stars by recalling the countryside. "The township music is for the people who mix it and copy it from the records, from the foreign music," Shabalala says. "But we have our own music on the farm, and this type of music now, here in South Africa, you can hear even the trumpet trying to sound like that, because Black Mambazo reminded them. We told them, 'Don't throw away all your good things. It's good to have your good things—and then you can have some other good things from your friends.'"

Over the years, Ladysmith has added some of those "other good things" to their own music, in their collaborations with Simon and other foreign celebrities, and by recording songs like Bob Dylan's "Knockin' on Heaven's Door" and Billy Joel's "River of Dreams." Some fans have questioned whether such ventures add anything of value or just dilute Ladysmith's sound, and Shabalala admits that at times he has had doubts, especially when it came to adding instruments to the group's basic a cappella style. Still, he wants to keep up with the times and please his international listeners, and he also has been influenced by the younger singers who joined his group as original members died or retired. By the mid-1990s, three of his sons were members, and he says that their tastes had a particularly strong effect: "They were teaching me how to blend with this music; it was easy for them. To me, I have another way. But these young men, they are very active. When I look at them, I see myself at the time when I was young: I was active like this. Because I'm getting old now."

Shabalala laughs as he says that last sentence, and his voice sounds anything but old or tired. He refers often in his conversation to "the new South Africa," and takes obvious pleasure in the level of respect he is now getting from his compatriots. He is being invited to appear at schools around the country, not only as a singer but as a sort of Zulu elder, passing on traditional ways and wisdom to the younger generation and helping to set them on the path to adulthood. For him, this is the ultimate accolade, the justification of a life's work.

"When I was just beginning, I remember an old man who came to Durban to work," he recalls. "He said to me, 'Boy, you're so serious about these rural things. We have been doing those things years and years, but nobody cares for this. You are so young; just go and play football, do another type of music.' But I just laughed at him and said, 'Don't worry about this.' And nowadays, he says, 'This boy, I know him from his early time when he begin this. He was serious.'"

Zimbabwe

Ephat Mujuru and Stella Chiweshe

While the most famous African musics have emerged from dance traditions, the continent has also spawned plenty of quieter styles based on solo singing and gentle accompaniments that put lyrics at the forefront. The best-known of these are the epic court songs of the West African griots, but there have also been village minstrels and traveling troubadours like Zimbabwe's Ephat Mujuru and Stella Chiweshe.

"From ancient times there were people who used to travel from place to place with their instruments, playing music and telling stories," Mujuru explains. "They would go from village to village, bringing the news to another area. My family has done this for generations; they are even written in the history books."

Stella Chiweshe. Photograph © Jack Vartoogian/FrontRowPhotos.

Like bards throughout the world, such musicians have served not only as entertainers but as historians and educators. Among the Shona, Eastern Zimbabwe's dominant ethnic group, their main instrument is the *mbira* (also known as the *kalimba,* or thumb piano). A mbira is made from a hollow wooden box with from five to forty wooden or metal keys that the player plucks with his thumbs and forefingers, while loosely attached shells or bottle caps add chittering rhythmic accompaniment. In the hands of a good player, the mbira produces light, rippling melodies, and its sound has influenced guitar and keyboard styles from South Africa to the Congo.

"The mbira is one of the ancient instruments of Africa, but it was most highly developed by the Shona people of Zimbabwe," Mujuru says. "My great, great ancestors from the very ancient time, they had an empire of Mbire, and from there it has been handed down thousands of generations. There are many people, but they are all from that same family; it is like a tree with so many branches. And all of those branches, they have got mbira. We have mbira with diatonic and chromatic scales, and also major and minor. It is unlimited. It can play almost any music, from anywhere in the world."

Mujuru was born in 1950, in a country village near Zimbabwe's eastern border with Mozambique, and says that at that time there was little contact with foreign music or culture. "We didn't have any radio or television, so we grew up entertaining ourselves. If we wanted to see something like a TV we just had to see people dancing. It was all live." In those days, the urbanites dancing in Harare's nightclubs had little interest in the gentle sound of the mbira, and the style was actively discouraged by the colonial government. "Now they are playing African music there," Mujuru says, "but in that time those people who owned those clubs were coming from the colonial time, and they were suppressing the African traditions, so in those clubs they didn't want to hear African music."

In the 1960s and '70s, mbira—and Shona music in general—was associated with the guerrillas who were fighting to overthrow the white minority government of what was then Rhodesia. Mujuru and Chiweshe both attained national fame as underground artists, producing songs that through metaphor and parables carried the message of rebellion. The most famous Zimbabwean revolutionary singer, Thomas Mapfumo, mixed mbira with electric instruments, creating an Afro-pop style called *chimurenga*, which has earned an international reputation. Mujuru and Chiweshe have collaborated with guitarists and other modern musicians over the years, but they prefer to perform alone or with simple percussion, showing the roots and depth of the mbira tradition, and they see themselves less as musicians or entertainers than as cultural ambassadors.

"I added storytelling because just singing and playing was not enough to share my culture," Mujuru explains. "Mbira and stories, they go together. When you have a story, it helps you to visualize, to create in your imagination. I wanted the people, when they are hearing, to imagine that I would take them to Africa."

Moreover, he feels that the traditional lessons are as applicable in Europe or America as at home. "It is like a university with a music department. And also with philosophy, because every story has a moral it teaches to the people. It's an ancient way of teaching. Of course, our cultures are different. But when we go deeper, we find out that we are all one people. I recorded an album called *Hapana Mutorwa*, and it means there's no one who's a stranger on earth. We are all brothers, and if there are people under the water, they are our brothers, too. The mbira is for unity; it expresses happiness. And what the stories teach for my people they can also teach for your people."

Chiweshe is of the same generation as Mujuru and shares his fame as a bearer of ancient music and wisdom, but she had a much harder row to hoe. "Before, women were not allowed to play mbira," she explains. "When I began, the people said a lot of things to try to stop me. It was hard. It was not easy. At every interview I'm reminded of this painful time when I wanted to learn mbira. But the feeling, the burning desire that I had, made it possible for me to be able to break through.

"My mother's uncle, who played mbira but who was living very far away from our home, saw me struggling. He saw me for a long time trying to learn, until one day I think I convinced him and he agreed to teach me. And after that a lot of other mbira players liked to teach me, because they saw that I could play a little bit. They accepted that.

"Then, to find somebody to make the mbira for me, so that I could own my mbira, that took a very long time. The way it happened was one day I had gone for a football game. There was music going on for the people in the full stadium, and I felt that they needed something stronger, and that was my mbira. Right away I went to borrow an mbira from somebody and I recorded a song which became a hit in Zimbabwe. That was 'Kahsawa,' and even today people still ask for that song."

With her new popularity, Chiweshe soon had her own mbira, and "Kahsawa" was followed by "Chachimurenga," an anthem of the independence struggle, as well as recordings of traditional themes. Other women followed her lead, helping to spearhead the renaissance of the traditional Shona style.

Chiweshe is clearly proud of her accomplishments, but refuses to take all the credit. In Shona society, the mbira is not only an instrument; it can be a way of communicating with the spirit world, and Chiweshe emphasizes that it is the mbira itself that has had the success, acting through her: "I don't say it's me who has made it possible that all the people are playing now. I say, 'It's mbira who has made all the people to play.' You understand? I put mbira before me, mbira first, then me second. So I'm proud of mbira, that it is now reaching a lot of people.

"The mbira player is a medium, who plays for the spirits. Also for the living—when I say 'for the spirits,' it doesn't mean to say that I leave out us human beings. Uh-uh. The spirits live together with the living. This includes us together, this soul, the spirit that we have. Like there was one time when my soul had separated from the body, and it was holding with just one small thread, and the soul was looking down at the body and saying, 'Oh, this was the body I was in.' But later my soul was brought back. I was told, 'There was something that you didn't do yet. So go back.'"

That something was to share her knowledge with the world. "I play for the spirits that are in the human beings, and not only the spirits of Zimbabwe," she says. "For example, when I come here [to the United States], I have to announce to the spirits of this country: I talk to them; I say, 'I have come into your land, I set my foot in your land. I come from Zimbabwe. I bring with me Chidodo, Leonard, and Gilson [her accompanists]. We are mbira players, and we are going to play in this place.' I tell them that, so they will know what this music is. What makes it easier for me to play for the foreign audience is that I imagine that they are the mediums of their spirits. And this mbira music is for everyone; it is not excluding people who don't know it."

Mali

Ali Farka Touré

Like Ephat Mujuru and Stella Chiweshe, Ali Farka Touré represents a solo style that is not part of a dance tradition, and that is intimately connected with the spirit world. In other ways, though, he is very different. For one thing, he is from the opposite end of sub-Saharan Africa, and for another, he is a guitarist. The most popular solo acoustic performer to have toured out of Africa, he was introduced in Europe as a sort of missing link between ancient traditions and modern blues. Early promoters hailed him as "the Malian John Lee Hooker," a description he at first encouraged but grew to dislike over the years. A proud man and a leader in his own community, he feels

Ali Farka Touré. Photograph © Jack Vartoogian/FrontRowPhotos.

that too many people have viewed him as a novelty and failed to appreciate or properly respect the depth of the tradition he represents.

"For some people, when you say 'Timbuktu' it is like the end of the world, but that is not true," he says.* "I am from Timbuktu and I can tell you we are right at the heart of the world." Touré is lounging on a motel couch, chain-smoking strong cigarettes and talking in rich, Malian-accented French. Though he has spent most of his life in the small hamlet of Niafunke, by the banks of the Niger River in northern Mali, he seems completely confident and at home in foreign surroundings. He has the assurance of an acknowledged master, an artist secure in his abilities and his uniqueness, and a respected elder in a culture that traces its history back for many centuries.

Touré first attracted widespread international attention in 1987, when the English World Circuit label released an album with "Amandrai," a song in the Tamashek language that features a guitar accompaniment remarkably similar to Hooker's playing on records like

* This interview was conducted in French.

"Tupelo." Some blues scholars had been arguing for years that the music's source was in Northern Mali, and Touré was put forward as exhibit A, a Malian bluesman who had recognized that kinship and created a style that made it explicit.

These days, Touré dismisses the blues label as inaccurate and annoying. "The journalists always ask me the same questions," he says. "They always want to know about blues. I say, the word *blues* means nothing to me. I do not know blues, I know the African tradition. The music that you call blues, I can call by its proper name. I can call it *agnani*, I can call it *djaba*. I can call it *amandrai* or *amakari*, the music played on the indigenous guitar, the one-string, or the three-string. I can also call it *kakamba*. There are many names for this legendary art.

"The first time I heard John Lee Hooker's music, I recognized it immediately. I argued with people; I said, 'This is not possible, how can this exist in America?' Because these are not Western tunes. Not at all. This music is one hundred percent African, and particularly from Mali. The tunes he plays are some of them in the Tamashek style, some in the Bozo style, some in Songhai style, and some in Peul. John Lee Hooker does not know the sources of his music. I respect him and appreciate his genius as the translator of African music in the United States, but my music is the roots and the trunk, and he is only the branches and the leaves. These are our tunes, and he plays them without understanding them."

That may sound extreme, but Touré is not boasting about his personal abilities; he is describing what he sees as a simple historical truth. He admires the musicianship of the great bluesmen and speaks with pride of performances with Clarence "Gatemouth" Brown, Ry Cooder, Buddy Guy, B.B. King, and Taj Mahal. But he knows that his is an older form and is pleased to quote Brown on the subject: "He is one of the great blues guitarists, and he told me frankly that it was only now that he had discovered the source of what he does. And that is natural, because all of this music comes from my home."

Such encounters have made Touré confident that, after being inspired by blues records, it is now his turn to teach and inspire. He feels that American musicians have lost touch with the original spirit of their music: "They say nothing, they speak only of alcohol or beer or whiskey, and that is not what this music is about. It is very far from that, completely the opposite. It is a very historic music; it has wisdom and knowledge. It speaks of cows, of greenery, of a man with his animals in the wilderness who hears certain sounds which do not come from the animals, but from nature. It speaks of love and of harmony in the family. All of these tunes have their words, their legend, and their story, and it is not beer or whiskey."

Touré's music is among the oldest styles in West Africa, the songs and melodies nomadic herdsmen played when they were alone, to please themselves and the spirits. Traditionally, it was played on small, light instruments that were easy to carry for miles on foot, prehistoric ancestors of the twenty-one-stringed koras and long trumpets of court and city musicians. Touré developed his skills on the reed flute, the one-string violin or *djerka*, and his "little guitar," the one-string *njurkel*.

"I made my njurkel myself in 1951," he says. "It is made with a small calabash, a wooden neck, and a string of horse hair or silver wire. It is not even fifty centimeters [about twenty inches] long, and it is the most dangerous instrument in Africa, because it is an instrument uniquely for the spirits. It can do things that no other instrument can bring out. There are tunes that I play on the njurkel that I cannot approach on the guitar, at least for the moment."

Touré no longer travels with his njurkel, which he gave to Ry Cooder, but to demonstrate the music of his youth he brings out the djerka. It is tiny, with a body like an oval banjo head barely the size of his hand. The bow is a small bent stick about ten inches long, strung with white horse hair, and both bow and instrument look like child's toys. When he starts to play, though, the music is complex and inventive, a keening tune that sounds as ancient as the wind and makes one's whole body sway to its rhythms.

"This is my teacher," Touré explains. "It gives me my melodies. I built this in '54 because the njurkel caused me so much trouble. The njurkel is very genetic [meaning that it is connected to genii and spirits]. When one is playing it at night, you hear it a kilometer away. In the daytime, it does not reach even twenty meters. I could play it here and someone standing in the doorway would not be able to hear it, but at night you hear it for a kilometer."

Touré adapted his njurkel style to the six-string guitar after a visit to Guinea in 1956. "I saw one of the greatest guitarists I have met in my life, and the finest in West Africa, Fode Ba Keita," he recalls. "He was the director of a group called Joliba [later Ballets Africaines], and he was playing traditional Malinke music on the guitar, singing in Bambara and French. I had my little guitar with me, and when I saw him playing African tunes on the modern guitar I said to myself in my head, 'I play the guitar too. Couldn't I do the same thing he does?' Only, instead of playing the songs he played, I wanted to play the music of the njurkel, to tell our stories and play our tunes. And that was how I began."

Touré says he learned guitar entirely on his own: "It is very easy for me; it is a gift. I was never at school. Never. I have always made my own way." It was an unusual path, made more so by the fact that his people had never been musicians. "I am from a very noble family, from a very great tribe," he says. "So it was not at all normal that I should be an artist. But one cannot go against a gift, so although they tried to change my mind I never accepted it. Still, I have never adopted music as a profession. I have many professions: I am a shoemaker first; all my people are shoemakers. I did farming, fishing, raising animals, and I was a mechanic and a driver. So it is only after I have done all my necessary work for the year that I can give myself to music, and then it is like a vacation."

As a sort of gentleman amateur, Touré is scathing in his contempt for the griots, the traditional bards and court musicians who continue to dominate the Malian scene. While Touré's predecessors were playing for their animals and the spirits, the griots developed some of the most sophisticated music on the African continent, and in modern times griot innovators like Toumani Diabaté and Mory Kanté have achieved international acclaim with their astonishing kora improvisations. Many musicologists have also focused on the griot tradition as a source of blues and jazz.

Touré, however, regards the griots much as American music purists regard Kenny G or *NSYNC: as facile and soulless pop musicians. "Griotism is done for flattery and exploitation," he says. "It has nothing to do with my music. The music I do is a music of education, to influence people and bring them to reason. It is not only a music of peace and prosperity. It is a music that fights against idleness. It has the teachings of the spirits, messages that one must bring to people, so that they can remain on the right road. This art, it has love and says you must love those around you. Griotism is only to flatter someone in order to get something from him."

Touré considers himself a teacher rather than an entertainer. "I take the tradition, and I translate all that I can of the music of my country. I find an indigenous guitarist who gives me the tunes, and I learn them and practice. The words are already there; they are legends that I know. So I only adapt, I translate that which has been dictated to me by the old people. I speak nine languages, because I am there for everybody, not only for one individual. Honey is not good in only one mouth. And that is what has made me popular and successful, because I play for everyone."

Even for those who cannot understand his lyrics, Touré onstage is an exciting performer. He laughs easily, and takes an obvious and infectious pleasure in the music. "I am as transported as those who are listening," he says. "Because this is what I live for. This music goes deep into my heart and if my fingers give me satisfaction, if I like what I hear, then I am very, very contented. Of course, there are moments when one cannot feel like that, but then one only has to wait a little while and one will get that feeling back."

He adds that the feeling is everything: "If one gives this music to a professional he cannot play it, because this is very different from what he does. There is no music theory about it. I may play it in a certain way, but there are many different tunings. One can tune the guitar like the indigenous guitar; one can tune it like the indigenous violin. All to get the same sounds, but differently. Because sounds are like that. That is what makes the melody, and melody is the reality of the road we are making. For us, this is the tradition. Every tune means something; every tune has a story that is deeply part of nature, not invented by X or Y. These are things that are very, very deep in the legends. And they are things that we are not allowed to speak of beyond a certain point."

As that final comment indicates, some questions that seem natural to a Western interviewer lead in directions that Touré is not willing to follow. Asked about a certain song, he will say that he knows the meaning but cannot explain it, because it is something that should not be revealed except to those who are ready for the knowledge. He is friendly, but also careful, speaking like a man who knows that he is always being watched by powers that must be respected. As he explains, "Spirits exist, just like people. All the entire world was made with the earth, and man came from the earth, but the spirits came from fire. The spirits are all around us, but to know them one must be a believer and understand Islam. He who does not understand will not believe me, because it is not the same culture, the same tribe, the same earth. But the spirits exist in my country and they exist here. When we walk out on the street here, you do not see the difference, but I can see that some of the men are men, and some are spirits."

And the spirits are at the root of all art. "They are dreams which have been there forever," Touré says. "It is not we who created them, it is reality, it is nature. But they must have love for a person to give him power."

One is reminded of the Mississippi Delta blues legend about musicians going to meet a mysterious man at the crossroads, and being given a supernatural mastery of their instruments. Told of this, Touré nods in recognition. "It was almost the same thing for me," he says. "Music is a gift. So, when one says *blues*, that means nothing. It is the African tradition. In Haiti, in the Antilles, there is a thing you call voodoo, and it is real. It exists in Brazil. And where are the roots? In Mali, and on into Niger. A little in Benin. All the rest now, they only copy. These are roots that go out and that reach all over. But the holder of all the secrets is one person, and that is a secret one can never reveal. And it is that which makes music."[*]

Oumou Sangaré

In Africa, as in Europe and the United States, traditional-sounding acoustic musicians tend to have relatively small, specialized followings. Ali Farka Touré is more famous in Mali for his popularity in the West than for his music and has nothing like the audience of the electric urban dance bands. There are exceptions to this rule, though, and one of the most exciting to come along in recent years was the wave of young Wassoulou women who set the West African music

---

[*] Ali Farka Touré died in 2006.

Oumou Sangare. Photograph © Jack Vartoogian/FrontRowPhotos.

world on fire in the 1990s, led by a singer named Oumou Sangaré. Like Touré, Sangaré was deeply influenced by older styles, but backed by a band of superb acoustic players, she became a leading voice of a new generation.

"Tièbaw," a typical track on one of Sangaré's records, starts off with the loose rhythm of the *kamalngoni*, a sort of five-stringed harp. Then her voice comes in, a warm, soaring lead answered in call-and-response by her backing singers. The music is mostly acoustic and deeply traditional, with the lead line taken on an ancient wooden flute. The message, however, is something quite new: "Women of the world, rise up," Sangaré sings, in her native Bambara. "Women of Mali, women of Africa . . . let us fight together for our freedom / So that we can put an end to this social injustice."

Sangaré's debut recording, in 1989, rocketed her to overnight success. It reportedly became the biggest-selling cassette in West Africa, beating out established stars like Youssou N'Dour and Salif Keita, and startling prognosticators who thought electric bands owned the future of African pop music.

"I think people were missing something," Sangaré says.* "And that was the tradition. I think my success is because of that—because otherwise, there are plenty of other people who sing well and who make good music. People missed the tradition very much, but they didn't know what it was they missed. And then, when they heard it, they recognized it."

Sangaré comes from a long line of singers in the Wassoulou region of southern Mali. Her grandmother was a local star, and her mother still occasionally performs at traditional ceremonies. She explains that their style of singing started as a sort of cheerleading for local farmers: "Since we do not have the money to buy cultivating machines, we cultivate by hand," she says. "So, to help the cultivators, we bring music into the fields. The young women sing as a sort of encouragement for the young men who are working."

Sangaré's own career started not in the fields, but in the capital. "I began singing in the streets of Bamako," she says. "People would invite me, and I would sing at marriages, baptisms—at ceremonies." Despite the urban environment, though, she stuck to the Wassoulou tradition, choosing not to fuse her sound with the music of the professional musicians, the griots, whose tradition is carried on by modern stars like Keita.

Sangaré always saw her music as more than entertainment. She is from a tradition of ceremonial, religious singers, and while she now composes original songs around contemporary themes, she continues to use her music to instruct and educate her listeners. Non-Africans are often startled when they read the lyric sheets to African pop records and find that a bouncy soukous number or a tender acoustic ballad is talking about political or social issues rather than being a love song or an exhortation to get up and boogie. "Music is very powerful in Africa," Sangaré says. "It is listened to very carefully, and if you are a bit successful, you can really get your message across."

Sangaré's message has centered on women's issues. "I speak very much of the women of Africa," she says. "And the women of the whole world. I fight for the improvement of women's situation. Because African women do not have the same rights as men. It is the African

---

* This interview was conducted in French.

woman who is tired in the society; it is she who is responsible for the house, the children, everything, but if that woman wants to speak in the society, she is not listened to. That is what bothers me, so I defend the cause of women; I sing their cause."

As a musical activist, Sangaré has become particularly associated with the crusade against polygamy. "I am not trying to change the society as a whole," she says. "But I do not like injustice, so I do not like that men marry whenever, marry up to four wives, and the women suffer. So I sing a great deal about that, about what I see in the society, and everyone hears me. And almost everyone likes it. All the young people are with me. The women, naturally, are with me, and certain men who already have three or four wives don't like me, because they cannot like me, but there are many more who like it than who don't."

When it is suggested that there might be conflicts in using traditional music to convey modern and perhaps antitraditional ideas, Sangaré says that at times she has actually quoted the tradition ironically to drive home her points: "The lyrics to 'Sigi Kuruni,' for example, are the advice that the old women give to the young bride before you go to your husband's house. They say, 'You must truly obey your husband to have a strong child; you must do this, you must do that.' This is something which is completely untrue for me, but I sing it as they sang it before, to show the young women of today what they used to say—that you have to obey your husband, your husband's mother, his family, his friends. It is something that has no rapport with our lives now."

Sangaré feels that her use of older forms has given her views special force, though, and in general she treats them with respect. "There is a great deal that is very positive in the tradition," she says. "Things that I defend, and that I want very much to keep. And there are also facets that I want to remove. So to fight against those facets, if I use modern music, then only the young people will listen to me. But if I want *everyone* to interest themselves in this, whether they are old or young, in the bush or in town, I have to use a music that everyone will take interest in.

"If one puts on a cassette, one first listens to the music. Afterward, the words come, but the music has to be compelling; if it is just 'bam, bam, bam,' then people go, 'Oh, that's not good music,' and they make no attempt to understand you. So, I first attract people's attention with the traditional music, which is very highly respected in Africa, and very well liked. Then, with that as my arm, I launch my words."

Not that Sangaré is afraid of experimentation. On her *Worotan* album, she added a Western horn section, including James Brown veteran Pee Wee Ellis, to several cuts. To her way of thinking, though, this does not constitute a musical fusion: "Even when I use modern instruments, I use them in African ways, with a truly traditional approach. We have wind instruments at home as well, and they serve the same function as the horns here." It is all part of her plan to broaden her audience while retaining her basic sound: Africa has been won over, and Europe and America are providing more fans every year.

"To many people, my music seems very simple," she says. "But really, it is the true source, it is really Africa. Africa has a different musical ear than Europe; the cultures are not the same; the music is not the same. But we listen to European music and Europe must also listen to our music, so that we can understand each other. Of course, it is better if you can understand the words, but it is not necessary. For example, when I listen to the voice of Bob Marley, I get goose bumps, though I don't understand a word. Words are interesting, but I think the voice is what is essential, and the rhythm. So for me, it is the same whether I play for Europeans or Africans: those who understand the words will like them; those who don't understand the words, they will like the African performance, because it moves so much, it is such a show. Music is universal."

Congo

Tabu Ley Rochereau

One of the tricky things about the international music scene is that the tastes of outsiders—for example, the typical American and European audiences—are often very different from those of people that are from the same background as the performers. The African scene has been particularly polarized, to the point that it sometimes seems as if any act that has major pan-African success can be relied on to excite little or no interest among Western fans, while any performer who can fill concert halls in New York and London will have no credibility with African clubgoers. While Westerners thrill to the ancient instruments, clothing, and dance movements of an Oumou Sangaré or Salif Keita, African dance clubs—whether in Africa, Europe, or the United States—will be playing hip-hop-influenced styles like East African *bongo flava*, or hot modern dance beats like Ivory Coast's *couper decaler* or Congolese *ndombolo*.

For the last fifty years, the Congo has been Africa's pop music powerhouse.[*] As Tabu Ley Rochereau puts it,[†] "When you travel all over Africa, even back in the time of Jean-Bosco Mwenda [an acoustic guitarist and singer from the southeastern Congo who began recording in the early 1950s], in almost every street from South Africa to Mauritania, when you enter a house you will find at least ten Zairean records there." In part, this was due to the infusion of Cuban styles that became popular in Kinshasa in the 1940s and 1950s. A Cuban-Congolese fusion developed, which swept all of sub-Saharan Africa, and by the 1990s soukous bands were touring regularly in the eastern United States, filling clubs with African dancers eager for a taste of home.

Some of these bands were also presented at "world" events, but never with the success of West Africans like King Sunny Ade or Youssou N'Dour. As a result, soukous shows provided a unique opportunity to feel as if one had entered another world. There would generally be a handful of white faces, along with maybe some Haitians and other people from the Caribbean, but the core audience was overwhelmingly African. As one entered the crowded room in some downtown hotel or suburban nightclub that had been rented for that evening's dance, it was like being instantly transported to a bustling city in Central Africa. And the pleasure was not just the thrill of an exotic experience: African music at its best is a shared interchange between per-

---

[*] Confusingly, there are two countries bordering the lower Congo River, and they are currently named the Republic of the Congo and the Democratic Republic of the Congo. To avoid confusion, they are often referred to with their capital cities attached, as Congo-Brazzaville and Congo-Kinshasa, respectively. Congo-Kinshasa, which for twenty-six years was called Zaire, has produced most of the great music, though Brazzaville has spawned some fine performers.

[†] This interview was conducted in French.

formers and listeners, and seeing a band playing for a crowd of people who understand the words and know how to dance to the rhythms is utterly different from sitting in a theater seat with your eyes glued to the stage.

Rochereau is the grand old man of soukous, and he helped lead the shift from rumba in the 1970s. He was born in 1940 and grew up in Kinshasa during a particularly exciting time. Country people were coming to the city, and the busy port was also acting as a conduit for records from the United States and Latin America. In the early 1950s, Congolese guitarists and bands brought these sounds together, laying American country-and-western and Afro-Latin vocals on a background of traditional drumming and Cuban instrumental breaks. Called rumba—though it was actually less influenced by Latin rumba than by what Cubans call *son*—it was the music of a new age and served as a soundtrack to the glory years of African independence.

Rochereau grew up surrounded by the rich musical variety of that time. "I lived in a quarter that was very active musically, like Times Square in New York," he recalls. "My grandmother on my mother's side and my father himself were musicians, so I was always in contact with performers and there was music playing all the time. That was how I was influenced very young. And when I was fourteen, I won first prize in a great contest of composition and song in the King Baudouin Stadium. That was in the colonial period, 1954."

That same year he received the nickname Rochereau, though not for musical reasons. "Tabu is the name of my father, Ley is the name of my grandfather, and my Christian name is Pascal," he explains. "They named me Rochereau in school, in the *sixième première* [middle school]. We were studying world history, and in particular French history, and were asked who was the general who had won the Swiss campaign. The whole class didn't know, because we were more familiar with the history of Belgium and the history of the Congo. But because I knew a bit by chance, I said, 'Denfert-Rochereau.' The teachers punished the whole class and didn't punish me; they gave me good points. So the whole class was against me, and they called me Rochereau, not to congratulate me but to make fun of me. Me, I didn't want the name, but everyone called me that and I got used to it."

Rochereau finished school in 1959 and got a job as a government functionary, but meanwhile he was becoming well-known as a singer and songwriter, working with Kinshasa's top bandleader, Joseph Kabasele (also known as Le Grand Kalle). Rochereau soon realized that he would have to make a choice and decided to devote himself entirely to music, first as lead singer and artistic director of Kabasele's African Jazz, and then by forming his own group, Afrisa International.

Many of the great Congolese bandleaders were guitarists, but Rochereau never played an instrument, and he says that, oddly enough, this was one of his group's advantages: "If one doesn't play, one can find musicians who are very strong, and they don't compete with the boss. If one is oneself an instrumentalist, one doesn't want to engage guitarists or pianists who are stronger than you yourself, so that makes problems. That made difficulties for a lot of orchestras. But I always engage guitarists who are very strong, soloists, because I am not jealous of them and they are not jealous of me. And I am the singer, author, composer, and arranger."

By 1970 Rochereau had helped to spread Congolese music more broadly than ever before, with an extensive African tour and a smash run in Paris. At the same time, he was leading the changeover to soukous. "In 1968, I went to the Ivory Coast," he remembers. "We gave concerts and the people just looked at us; they didn't dance. But we were not dancing either, and they couldn't understand the words, and the songs were slow. So I said to myself, 'If I started to dance, I think they would dance, too.' That was the first time a singer began to dance, and it became a new fashion.

"With that, it was necessary to create songs that went very fast, the opposite of rumba. Rumbas are very pretty, very beautiful, and one dances quietly, but one doesn't sweat. So I created a moving, shaking music—*secouer* [shake], *soukous*. First I called it *bouger* [move], but the people pronounced it *boucher* [butcher], like the guy who does the meat. That wasn't good. So I said, 'Okay, when an airplane shakes, that's *secousse*, so we'll call it that.' It is not an African word, but I Africanized it to *soukous*."

For the next twenty years, Rochereau shared the soukous crown with the guitarist-bandleader Franco, and since Franco's death in 1990 he has been the music's grand master. However, for most of that time he has had to rule his empire from abroad, moving between Paris and Los Angeles. Mobutu Sese Seku, who ruled Congo-Kinshasa from 1965 to 1997, turned it into one of Africa's most notorious dictatorships—as well as changing the country's name to Zaire—and forced many of the country's finest musicians into exile.

"We cannot play in Zaire," Rochereau says. "The living conditions are difficult, the money is not international, so one cannot travel with it. And there is no security; they kill people. Someone like me, who is a name, if you sing for the regime, the people kill you; if you sing against it, the regime kills you. All the great musicians have died curiously, from diseases or what have you. I am the only master left. So all my family, my friends, my fans, they tell me to stay away. It is not to avoid dying, because death is everywhere, but it is possible to be a little bit more secure."

Fortunately, Rochereau's years of exile saw African music reaching new fans around the world. Asked why he thinks this happened, he gives a response that highlights the differing perceptions of Africans and Westerners. In the West, we are used to thinking of European and American music as divided into many disparate genres, but of African music as to some extent a single category. By contrast, Rochereau knows the variety of African styles and considers Western pop overly uniform: "Western music is two musics: the classical music of Beethoven and all the great academicians, and then Western popular music, which is called jazz, blues, punk, rap. All of these resemble each other. When a song begins, you don't know which it is—except a bit for country music—they are all playing the same thing. So when African music came out, I think that captivated the ear of Western people, white people. And furthermore, the spectacles that we present, our way of dancing, sits very much between primitive dancing and modern dancing. It is original.

"I continue to develop my music. I am working with American producers, for example. But with uniquely Zairean musicians, because I don't want to destroy the authenticity of this music, the originality. If I use a couple of American musicians, that is a pleasure, but not so many because then the music won't be Zairean or African any more. Our music is not faked, it is not invented. It is spontaneous music of the African soul. It is music of the heart, music of suffering, like the music of African-Americans who came here [to the United States] and have made the blues, soul, jazz. It is a music of lamentation, of amusement, of distraction, of the heart and the spirit. And even if you cannot understand the words, you can understand it and like it."

Lucien Bokilo

In the United States, with its relatively small population of African immigrants, the club scene rarely has presented soukous superstars like Rochereau, Kanda Bongo Man, or Papa Wemba. These figures have tended to appear at major festivals, or in concerts in New York or Los Angeles. Meanwhile, club crowds have been treated to performers like Lucien Bokilo, who—often for reasons of management as much as music—have not attained as much international fame.

Bokilo is from Brazzaville, across the river from Kinshasa, in the Republic of the Congo, but he grew up with the same music, and his description of its evolution echoes Rochereau's: "Before, in Congo and in Zaire, we danced rumba, and soukous was the logical next step. The structure of a rumba song begins with an introduction—it can be simply a voice with a guitar—and then you have a languorous part, which is sung. One sings and sings, and then comes the dance part, the part that is nothing but instrumental music and *animation* [shouted party exhortations from a man known as the *animateur*]. Soukous is just the dance part. It was an evolution; we began to work much more on the musical section, the part that made people move."*

Bokilo became a popular singer in the music's second generation. "I started very young, at the age of twelve," he says. "I started singing in the choir, at the mass. Afterward, I had a little amateur group, then went professional. I worked with all the great musicians of Congo-Brazzaville. I worked with Youlou Mabiala, who is called the prince of Congolese music, and I was hired by the biggest group of the Congo, Bantous de la Capitale. Then I had my own group, Moziki la Juventus, 'Music of the Young.' I was still a young teenager—in all the groups, I was always the youngest."

---

* This interview was conducted in French.

Bokilo became an international name through his work with two innovative soukous groups, Loketo and Soukous Stars, and also toured with Kanda Bongo Man before deciding to go out on his own. "I wanted to express myself more," he says. "In a group, it is always a matter of each person bringing what he has and working as a team, while as a soloist, it is really my own artistic and musical orientation. I write my own songs, in Lingala and sometimes in Kikongo or in French, and do my own arrangements."

Bokilo's music combines a grounding in classic soukous with the innovations of the Paris scene. He explains that he first came to France in order to broaden his musical knowledge: "I went to study at the conservatory. But I was a bit distracted by touring, because I was very much in demand, so I had to do both. The first three years went well, but the fourth year I began really to tour a lot and it became too difficult to combine the two. But I got all the necessary basis that I had hoped for. The rest was work that I had to do on my own, because if one really has the desire one can also learn without going to the conservatory. But I learned how to structure my songs, to write them better."

He remained for the same reason so many other Congolese players have made Paris and Brussels their homes. By the 1970s, life in Brazzaville and Kinshasa had gotten so tough that musicians tell of having to collect old records and bring them to the pressing plant so that they could be melted down to make new singles and albums. "In Africa, we have all the cultural riches, the talent is there, but the working conditions are hard," Bokilo says. "In France, I had a better opportunity to make records; the conditions were better."

However, for all but the most successful bands, the European scene also has its shortcomings. Instruments, technology, and recording facilities are available, but prices are high, and there are fewer first-rate musicians willing to work for what a second-tier bandleader can pay. As a result, most bands have shifted away from the horns and orchestras of the older Congolese sound to a more electronic, synthesizer-driven approach. The guitars are still out front, but the music has less of the sinuous, soulful feel that first made it an international sensation.

Bokilo is quite open about the reasons for this change. "To make a really good soukous record, that demands a lot of resources. Why? Because, for example, a drum kit, to play it live, one needs a really,

really good studio. Otherwise, the sound is not good. And at the moment, it is very hard to find producers who believe in this music, who want to really invest in it. If someone comes along who is prepared to support us so that we can work in very good conditions, at that point we will revive all of that live sound, the drums, the guitars, and everyone will gain from it. But with the current economic conditions, there is less and less chance to give concerts, or to find producers who will invest the kind of money we need to show the live side of the music. So people prefer the ease of being able to program certain sounds; one saves money and one saves time. That benefits the producer; it benefits the artist. The one who it possibly does not benefit so much is the public. But it is an economic problem."

However, he insists that the music is gaining as much as it loses: "Everyone doesn't accept that things change; that's why you have conservatives and progressives. But I think it's good not to stay nailed to something which doesn't evolve. Of course, that makes some people gnash their teeth, those who miss the old style. But it is more interesting, because it evolves; it conquers a new public which is outside the borders of Congo and Zaire. That is very important, because music can be, in my opinion, an extraordinary instrument for transmitting messages, to educate, to give advice."

Though he is known as a dance-band vocalist, Bokilo follows the African tradition of socially conscious songwriting, and he says that he does not really feel comfortable singing the sort of romantic lyrics that dominate Western pop music. "What interests me when it comes to messages is the human condition," he says. "Man is always conditioned: To live, he must eat, he must do many things. He must work; everything is a challenge to be overcome. I don't think I am likely to become a protest singer, but I am against injustice. People live in difficult conditions—not only in Africa, but everywhere—and I am very sensitive to what touches people. The daily life of a person is extraordinary: to see him wake up, go to work; there are others who look for work, who don't find it; others who find it but do not want to go. And all of that fascinates me.

"I believe that, while we are living in a world in which there is suffering, one is obliged to denounce that suffering before speaking of love. For example, in Africa our living conditions force us to shout for help, to say, 'This is not right! We are suffering here!' In the United States or Europe—in France, for example—they have hundreds and hundreds of years of written history. It's incredible. The United States is the largest democracy in the world. But in Africa it's the opposite, it's dictatorships. It is a matter of, 'You do what I say, and if you don't, either I eliminate you or you leave the country.' People are not free—culturally, politically, or economically. And that plays on them, and influences the artists, their way of thinking, their way of writing songs."

Bokilo adds that this is yet another reason to keep evolving, and to welcome the collaborations and changes that have come with his move to Europe: "I, personally, place myself on the side of promoting African music and at the same time African culture. I want this music to be valued, and I want to make it grow. And for this, I want to mix things together, to bring in new sounds. Because it is important that it be accessible to the four corners of the world."

Kenya

Fadhili William

One of the oddities of the world music boom has been the relative absence of East African performers. There are quite a few Ethiopian players living in the United States and playing for the large immigrant community here, but none has crossed over in a substantial way, and the country's music remains familiar only to its core audience and some aficionados. As for the musics of Kenya and Tanzania, they have been almost invisible. This is all the stranger because Kenya has such a long history of interchange with the English-speaking world, and its music would seem particularly accessible to Western sensibilities. Perhaps that is just the problem: Westerners come to African music in search of deep roots and powerful rhythms, but the most successful Kenyan styles have relied on lilting melodies and relaxed singing, much of it influenced by American country-and-western—in the early 1990s, one could still hear programs of Kikuyu cowboy yodelers on Nairobi radio.

It is probably due to this accessibility that, despite the lack of East African artists on the touring scene, the most popular African song in the world is still "Malaika," a Kenyan hit from the early 1960s that was brought to South Africa and the United States by Miriam Makeba and went on to be recorded by such disparate artists as Harry Belafonte, Pete Seeger, the Afro-German disco group Boney M, and the West African R & B star Angelique Kidjo.

I was in Nairobi in 1990, and went in search of Fadhili William, who first recorded the song, only to be told that he was working in a gas station in New Jersey. On returning to the States, I found that the address I had been given for him was no good, and gave up hope of finding him. Then, in 1997, he turned up as a guest star at one of Boston's short-lived African nightclubs, appearing with the Kenya-based soukous band Virunga. He had not made his living from music for many years, but his voice was as sweet and gentle as ever, and he was happy to talk about the old days and his connection to one of African pop music's most enduring hits.

"I guess the school choir inspired me to music," he recalls. "It came to a time that I could hear the notes, the staff notation, better than the choir master, so he had to choose me to be the choir conductor. And on my school vacations—because I had my schooling in Nairobi—I used to go back to my place of birth, which was Mombassa. When I went there, I used to go around and see people playing music, and mostly I was interested in guitar. I used to look at what they are playing, and when I came back from the vacation I asked my mother to buy me a guitar, and she bought me a box [acoustic] guitar and I started learning by myself, without a teacher, just by going to a place where they are playing and sitting quietly and looking how he is running his fingers. And when I go back home I try to imitate the same by myself until I got the way."

This was in the 1950s, when Nairobi was one of the most active recording centers in Africa. William was hearing local artists on records and the radio, and even though he was still a schoolboy, he was ambitious to join them: "Every weekend I used to go to a certain record company, AMC, African Mercantile something. By that time I was composing my own music, and I went into a studio and they said, 'Okay, play us what you know.' I played a few songs from my country, because I'm a Taita by tribe and back there people love music. So I started recording those traditional songs and ones I composed by myself. After they were released, they were hits, but I didn't know exactly what I was doing, I was just doing it for people to know who is Fadhili."

William had to leave school after fourth form (the British equivalent of tenth grade), and after playing for a while in Mombassa, he moved to Nairobi to live with his mother. As he recalls, "I kept on practicing, practicing, trying to buy books to guide me, and that's the time I composed 'Malaika.' Because this song has got a meaning: When I was in school I had a girlfriend, and to me she looked like an angel. Her name was Fanny, but I nicknamed her Malaika ['Angel' in Kiswahili]. I wanted to get married to her, but you had to pay a dowry to get married and I didn't have that kind of money; my father passed away when I was two years old, so he could not help me. So she was married by somebody else who had the dowry, the parents. And the only thing I could do to make her remember me is by playing that song.

"The song says, 'Malaika, I love you, my angel, but the only thing I'm lacking is money. Because if I had money, I could have got married to you. I keep on thinking about you every now and then, but there is nothing I can do since now you are married.' And even though there was her husband at home, listening to the radio, she could hear that song, because she knows her nickname, and the husband won't know who is this Malaika. So I wrote this to portray that message to her, that I still love her.

"Now, during our independence celebration—that was '63—Miriam Makeba and Harry Belafonte were invited to come and celebrate, and when they came, they sang that song, 'Malaika.' I gave them the lyrics, and we shared the stage—people thought it was funny for the foreigners to sing Swahili. After that, they came back to America, and Miriam Makeba recorded the song and put her own name on it. Me and my producer, whose name was Charles Worrod, he sued

Makeba, and eventually she started putting my name, F. William, on the record."*

While his song traveled around the world, William's own recordings have rarely been heard outside Kenya and its surrounding countries. However, his career was by no means limited to that one hit. Before "Malaika" he was already a popular singer and one of the pioneers of the lightly swinging electric band style that swept the region in the late 1950s. "I made a band called the Jambo Boys, which made a hell of a success in the country. We traveled as far as Ethiopia, and when the Beatles came to do their concert in Kenya, we went around with them. When the late Louis Armstrong came to Kenya, we traveled with him all over: Nairobi, Mombassa, Nakuru. The other one was Roger Whittaker—we used to play with him everywhere he go." (The Beatles never played in Kenya, so there is clearly some confusion here, but Armstrong certainly did. As for Whittaker, the British easy-listening balladeer was born in Nairobi and recorded a live album there in 1982.) Along with his performing, William also worked for many years as a talent scout and producer, and was one of the best-known figures on the Nairobi music scene.

Both as a musician and a producer, William was involved in the evolution and fusion of older Kenyan styles with new influences from throughout Africa and the Euro-American pop world. However, he tends to downplay such innovations. For example, although he was in Boston with the Congolese bandleader Samba Mapangala, and recalled meeting the old Congolese masters Jean-Bosco Mwenda and Edouard Masengo when they were based in Nairobi in the late 1950s and early '60s, he says their style had no effect on his own work. "I didn't go too much on Zairean music, because Zairean music is somehow Latin American music," he explains. "The Zaireans were near Brussels, so they could get this Latin American music; that's why they started developing that beat on the other side, and we didn't get that beat until recently. Mostly,

---

* Evocative as this story is, other Kenyan musicians have disputed William's authorship of "Malaika," and he never received either legal credit or royalties for the song, though he pursued both until his death in 2001.

because we were under British rule, we played like English music."
That included American styles, especially country-and-western,
and he is quick to add that he also picked up some rock and soul
when they were in fashion.

However, he emphasizes that he always felt most comfortable with
his own sound: "In Mombassa, where I was born, there are beats like
chakacha, and that's what I like to play—'Malaika,' 'Taxi Driver,' those
are the songs which made me famous. I can play the other music now,
but it doesn't get into my nerves."

Nigeria

Sir Victor Uwaifo

Another musical style that has never gotten its due on the modern
international scene is West African highlife. Like "Malaika," the
highlife sound attracted fans in America and Europe back in the
1950s and '60s, with its infectious blend of jazzy horn sections and a
rhythm that recalled calypso. Since the 1980s, though, the Nigerian
styles that have been most successful are King Sunny Ade's rootsier,
heavier *juju* music and the soul-funk afrobeat of Fela Kuti, rather than
the lightly swinging guitars of highlife stars like Prince Nico Mbarga
and Sir Victor Uwaifo.

As a result, the concert engagement that brought Uwaifo to Boston
was sponsored by a group of Nigerian businessmen rather than by an
international music promoter, and though it had excellent advance
press, there couldn't have been more than a half-dozen non-Nigerians
in the hall. (Estimating the ethnic sample was easy, since the whole
audience consisted of only about sixty people.) Uwaifo did not seem
bothered by the turnout. Leading a crack twelve-piece band, he strode
the stage like a wild man, playing guitar with his teeth and behind
his head and tossing it spinning into the air between solos, while fans
showered him with handfuls of one-dollar bills. (Every few minutes,
an assistant would gather the bills off the floor and take them to the
side of the hall, where audience members were waiting with tens and
twenties, ready to buy another handful.) The concert ended only when

Boston's concert curfew laws kicked in and the policewoman on duty threatened to pull the plug on the sound system.

Uwaifo (who, since receiving a doctorate styles himself, Sir Doctor Victor Uwaifo) says the excitement was typical, whether he plays at home or abroad: "My show is a phenomenon. It is beyond human explanation. You have to see it to believe it, and every day it's different. You know, I don't drink, I don't smoke, I don't take drugs, I don't do anything like that, but the music is my intoxicant. So when I get onstage, it sends me to the high heavens."

Between the high-energy floor show and his dapper, youthful appearance, it is hard to believe that Uwaifo had his first international hit in 1966. That was when, with his Musical Maestros, he recorded "Joromi," which sold over 100,000 copies in its first six months and was heard throughout West Africa. Uwaifo built on its success, becoming one of the most popular stars on the highlife scene. In 1970, he took his music to the world, touring Europe, the United States, and Japan, and seemed poised to bring highlife to a wider audience than ever before.

Instead, for most of the next twenty-five years he stayed home in Benin City. He cheerfully explains that he was simply too busy to tour. "I have so many different functions that I hardly even want to go out now," he says. "The other [stars], basically they depend on music, but I have an empire of people that are looking up to me. I am an artist and writer, I am a justice of the peace. I have property here and there. I have a school of music. I have an art gallery. I have a whole world of my own."

What links all of Uwaifo's efforts is his commitment to the culture and history of Benin. The Benin Empire (geographically distinct from the present country of Benin) was by many measures the most advanced of West African states, famed as far back as the thirteenth century for its bronze sculptures. "Benin was known as the capital of the whole world," Uwaifo says. "We never even knew that there were people on the other side of the hemisphere."

Uwaifo's mother was a member of the royal family, and though many of his relatives played music as a hobby, his parents were troubled by his excessive interest in the guitar, an instrument that was considered low class. "It was feared in the Benin royal circle that anybody who played the guitar would probably end up in the palm wine bars," Uwaifo remembers. "But I said I would prove them wrong."

When he was twelve, Uwaifo built a guitar out of plywood, using bicycle spokes for frets and "trap rope" (fishing line) for strings. That period was the heyday of "palm wine" guitar, a rippling, melodic style played on acoustic instruments and somewhat similar to the string-band music of Trinidad and the Bahamas. Soon Uwaifo was going into town to take part in *copetee* (competitions) with older players. "They would say, 'Let's play copetee,' and then one man would play in the background, I'd take the solo, and at a time he would say 'change,' then I will play the background, he takes the solo. It was a duet."

He was also bringing his guitar to school, where he became a legend among his classmates: "I was a good sportsman: I set the high-jump record many, many years ago and it still stands today. Nobody has been able to break it. I used to take my guitar to the high jump pit, and before I do my high jump I would play the guitar, to stimulate myself. I would look at the crossbar, and I would bring it down with my eyes, and when I'd see it down, I'd take off. My style was the western roll: I would jump and roll over with an angle parallel it to the bar, and land with one leg, two hands, and one leg up in the air. I'd be bouncing, and until they stop applauding I wouldn't get up. That was the beginning of my showmanship, and I transposed that showmanship into art, into music, in my later years."

Back home, Uwaifo organized his brothers and sisters into a musical group that he named the Uwaifo Quartet, and as his parents got used to the idea, they began making recordings for Nigerian radio.

By the late 1950s, the electric guitar was taking over from its acoustic forerunner, and amplification was changing the face of popular music. Just as electrified country and blues combos jolted big-band pop in the United States, amplified Nigerian guitarists revolutionized the horn-driven highlife orchestras. Smaller bands could now be loud enough to fill a hall, which made it easier and cheaper to put a group together, and helped Africanize a music that had drawn much of its impetus from recordings by American and Cuban orchestras.

Uwaifo explains that big-band highlife had been associated with the ruling classes: "I traced in one of my books how the name even came to being. It was a time after the Second World War, and all these veterans who went to Bombay and other parts came back to West Africa to settle, and some of them were musicians and they formed some bands, with brass instruments. Once in a while the white colonial masters would hire them to play in a ballroom, and they hardly will admit the black people into the ballroom dance hall. So some of the people who cannot go in, because maybe they don't have enough money to pay or they are not admitted, would stand outside and start peeping through the window to see how they dance and know what's going on in the ballroom. After each dance there is a very loud ovation, applause, and so on, and then those people behind the window would say, 'Oh boy, this is high life! These are highlife people.' It means the world, the life beyond their own reach."

Back then, Uwaifo says, the trumpeters were king. "In those days, the bandleader must be a trumpeter. Not even an alto saxophonist, no, because everybody was looking up to Louis Armstrong. Some of them would hold a white handkerchief in his left hand to show off, to say how much he can play the trumpet. So every other instrument took its cue and guitar was just one of them."

When electricity came along, Uwaifo helped lead the revolution. "I had formed my band, I could play guitar well, and I thought, why should I play second fiddle? I said, 'What's in trumpets? Single notes. And I can play single notes. But I can also play chords, whatever. So why should I subject myself to this kind of an imposition?'"

Guitar-band highlife became the new, hot sound in West Africa, paralleling changes throughout the continent. It was perceived as a modern style, but just as in the United States, the guitarist-led outfits brought an injection of old rural rhythms and melodies that had been played for centuries on acoustic string instruments. Uwaifo says that he was particularly drawn to these traditional styles, and while other electric players imitated rock, soul, or Latin licks, he reworked the old palm-wine and ceremonial melodies. "I integrated Western music in my development, but I knew where to draw the line," he says. "I can play you waltz, quickstep, blues, jazz, and classics, but I was able to evolve my own style by looking at the culture of our people, the homogeneous ethnics of Benin City and Nigeria and other parts of Africa."

Along with his musical fusions, Uwaifo adapted the tradition in other ways. He had become involved in visual arts, earning a degree in graphic design, and found a surprising overlap between his interests: "I discovered the relativity between colors and sound, how to represent the notes in the scale with colors: do—black, re—red, mi—blue, fa—green, so—neutral, ti—violet. Then I was inspired by a kind of cloth woven in the eastern part of Nigeria called *akwete*, a beautiful woven pattern. So I was able to transpose akwete music."

He followed akwete with a string of other unique fusions—*ekassa*, *mutaba*, *gbadagbada*, and *titibiti*—producing a string of hit songs in both his native Edo and the "broken English," or pidgin, spoken throughout Anglophone West Africa. He says that, as with akwete, many of his melodies came from nonmusical sources: "Sometimes when I am driving in a car, songs whisper into my ears, and if I like the song I write it down or put it down on tape. There are some other occasions when I just close my eyes, then I think of a scenario when I'm taking my solo. If I see lightning, I transpose it into sound: *rrrrap!* The lightning strikes and the thunder rolls. You hear such feelings. Or the waves in the sea. I can think of an accident—it's raining and you apply your brake suddenly and it swerves and hits the shoulder of the road. All those things I have at the back of my mind. And so I create a scenario, some picture with my guitar.

"Then there are some other occasions when you just feel that you want to write on a particular subject, on the contemporary scene. That's when you sit down and write in rhyme or in alliterative form, and then you start to work out the melody. That's the most serious work, because I am touching the minds of people. If I make a million records, that means I've touched the minds of a million people at the same time."

Over the years, Uwaifo has had several records in that class. "Guitar Boy," which came to him one day in a vision, was even adopted as the code name for a Ghanaian coup, apparently because its speedy guitar lick sounded like a machine gun. Uwaifo's popularity was fueled by his wild stage antics and quirkily eye-catching guitars. For example, in 1967 he developed his own double-necked instrument. "I had played all the notes on the guitar, and I wanted something else, to transport me to space," he explains. "So I built a guitar with a second, shorter neck an octave higher." That was followed in the 1980s with his "magic guitar," a cordless instrument that incorporates a keyboard and is attached to his belt in such a way that he can spin it.

Uwaifo's inventiveness spiced his shows, but also left him with less and less time for music. He wrote three books: an autobiography, a musical history, and a volume of poems and philosophy. He designed and built an ornate car that he named "the Vision"; a cement house in the shape of a Boeing 747; and a variety of bronze sculptures, from abstract pieces to a statues of historical figures like General Logbosere, who fought against the British expedition that destroyed the Benin Empire in the late nineteenth century.

"They looted the artwork and so many things," Uwaifo says of the British. "But one thing they forgot to take away." He looks quizzically at his listeners. "You know what?" Getting no response, he laughs. "That thing is me. Because I'm still there, propagating the culture and the history of Benin."

It is indeed a full life, playing music, making art, and writing books, and who knows what the future may bring? "I have multifarious talents, and I want to explore each one to its fullest," Uwaifo says. "Because I regard it as a sin if I allow any one to fade out. There are many people who don't have talent, and I don't want to be in a situation where I will be asked by posterity, 'Why did you waste that talent, which would have been given to somebody else?' I am so privileged to be able to generate my feelings to other people, and I feel that there could be nothing better than what I am. And if I had to come back to this world and do it all over again, I'd do it the same way."

King Sunny Ade

Of all the great West African innovators, King Sunny Ade was the first to make a major impact outside the African continent. Before *Graceland*, before most Euro-Americans were aware that Africa was producing some of the most active and vibrant pop music on the planet, before there were terms like *global beat* and *world music*, Ade brought his Nigerian *juju* orchestra to England and the United States. It was 1983, and Island Records was trying to find an artist who would maintain the audience it had built up with Bob Marley. The

King Sunny Ade. Photograph © Jack Vartoogian/FrontRowPhotos.

label settled on Ade, and for a few years he became the world's best-known African bandleader. Later albums failed to equal the success of his first two Island releases, and he was somewhat overshadowed by a wave of other West African stars, but he has continued to make occasional tours and his shows remain among the most powerful and exciting on the scene, featuring up to twenty musicians playing hours of high-energy, fiercely polyrhythmic dance music.

"I'm still there, the way God put me," Ade says. "Doing the same and even more than before. I keep on because I am always thinking that my best is yet to come. I owe the world everything that I can put into music, and I'm just lucky that my band members love me, they love the kind of music we're playing, and they love their profession. We are together for twenty-something years, and I am lucky to have people like that."

Juju became the popular dance music of Nigeria's Yoruba people around the period of World War II, and in the 1970s Ade emerged as its new star, battling for primacy with the somewhat older Chief Commander Ebenezer Obey. Ade's band blends intricate, hard-edged percussion, talking drums, guitars, bass, keyboards, and pedal steel guitar, an import from Nashville that became one of his trademark innovations. With the exception of the pedal steel, all the instruments tend to play a largely percussive role—even the guitars and keyboards function essentially as tuned drums—creating some of the most complexly polyrhythmic music on record.

"Rhythm is the basic music of all Africa," Ade says. "African people dance to rhythms, they listen to rhythms, they are from the rhythm land. The rhythm is in everything, and no matter how the songs are and how the guitars or keyboard go, you have to first find the rhythm."

Although he is the main composer and bandleader, Ade says that his group's arrangements are worked out in a communal process that includes both the other musicians and the audience. "I first of all write the lyrics," he says. "And then I will find the music to it, and then I'll send it to the band. I can play it on guitar, or I can hum it—because mostly in African music not every one of us goes to music school, so you can hum it [he demonstrates by singing a short flight of notes], and that way you can tell the other musicians the lines so they can do it.

"Then at the rehearsal we may decide to change the music for that particular lyrics, and we do it together, like we're in the laboratory where we can find how to fix good music. I do eighty percent, but occasionally the band may decide to work and find another music, and if I prefer theirs, I'll fix it. And then we can go and play it when we have a show, and we see the reaction of the people. Like a trial. Occasionally, when I play a nightclub, I play those new songs and the reaction of the people is 'Wow!'"

Ade plays electric guitar and sings the lead vocals, supported by four backing singers. The lyrics are in Yoruba, and the singers' words are echoed and countered by comments from the talking drums. "In the olden days, they used the talking drums to communicate during the tribal and internal wars," Ade explains. "And still today, if you go to any *oba*'s palace—the king's palace—the moment any stranger is sighted, the drummers will sound and inform the king that he's having a stranger, either they are many or few, either they are white people, they are children, so whether to get ready or relax.

"In the band, they can communicate with me. Sometimes, when I'm on and into the groove, maybe the manager is waving to me that the time is up. Then the talking drummer will sound my name and I'll pay attention to him, and he can say a proverb, like 'The moon is about to come out brightly, so eventually let's go and sleep.' So I will know that he's telling me we have to go."

The talking drummers also have set phrases to play in each song. "In between the bridges, I'll tell them to use one of the proverbs," Ade explains. "I will tell them, 'The song goes this way: Now we must hold our hands together in order to dance and we have to go on the right and left steps.' I can tell him to say, 'Check your shoes and lace them very well.' Many people listen to what he says among the lyrics. They judge how good the talking drummers are by the proverbs, the messages in between the singing. They'll say, 'That's nice, you're right. You're a good drummer.' Most of the Yoruba people, they easily know what the talking drum says. And when they appreciate what he says, they give him money—even more than me occasionally."

If the talking drums hark back to the ancient past, the pedal steel provides a modern edge. "It is very unusual," Ade says. "But the sound is very common because we have an instrument called *goje*, and we use metal to brush the string so it gives you that kind of a sound. We had this local guitar, but it was only four strings or six strings, not ten strings, and no pedals. Then when we came to America we saw the pedal steel and we realized that it was what Don Williams and Jim Reeves, Willie Nelson were using. We love that music in our country and we introduced the pedal steel into our music."

When asked if he got any other influence from listening to country music records, Ade demurs: "No, no. I follow my own line. Because in Nigeria we have so many musics that you have to find your own line, or else you just find yourself in another people's music."

He adds that one also has to keep evolving: "You have to go according to the times. You wouldn't like to sit down, because you'd been playing the same songs that you played for twenty years ago. No, no, no. You have to keep strong and you refine it, you introduce new songs, new dimensions."

In the end, though, Ade says that musical innovation is less important to him than the solid dance beat and the message of the songs: "What interests me is to see people moving around with each other, without argument, without fights, without having problems with each other. If you see two people dancing together, maybe friends, maybe husband and wife, having a good time, I'll be singing a song of love. I will sing about fiction—I like pretending—and I'll say, 'We're aiming for a goal, and the goal is love. Let's get it together without no argument, because if we argue, the love will go far, more than where we can go to catch it. So don't let us argue, don't let us pretend, but let us love each other. Because when we've got the love, we're going to return back with love.'"

Madagascar

Tarika Sammy

In 1992, an album called *A World Out of Time* swept the music of Madagascar onto the international stage. Like Ry Cooder's later *Buena Vista Social Club*—though on a far smaller scale—it was a project spearheaded by Western musicians who had traveled to a foreign place, searched out some of the finest local players, and created a showcase for the local tradition that was also a cross-cultural jam session. In this case, the Westerners were the guitarist Henry Kaiser

and the multi-instrumentalist David Lindley, and the Malagasy artists ranged from septuagenarian village musicians to young rockers,
instrumental virtuosos, and singer-songwriters. The most versatile of
these players was Samoela "Sammy" Andriamalalaharijaona, leader of
a group called Tarika Sammy (Sammy's Band).

"Me and Tiana, my cousin, we began playing music when we were
very little," Sammy says.* "I remember playing the accordion when I
was eight. I sang with that in the traditional style, and afterward I
learned to play the flute, to play classical and also a bit of jazz. And
Tiana played piano and organ; he was even a church organist. In '78 I
started a sort of little group, and then in '82 I started Tarika Sammy.
The two girls who sing, Claudia and Hanitra—Tiana and I met them
at shows. I saw Claudia playing guitar, and she was still imitating the
voices of Emmylou Harris and Joan Baez; she liked folk songs and
country music. And Tiana saw Hanitra in a choir, because she sang
classical music. So we got together and formed our group."

Tarika Sammy was a departure in Malagasy music, an attempt by
young, urban musicians to revive and popularize the island's folk traditions. "At the moment, traditional music in Madagascar is on the
way to disappearing," Sammy explains. "On the radio we hear only
foreign music; it is not like in Africa, in Senegal for example, where
they always play their own style, their music. We hear the latest hits
from Europe and America—Celine Dion, Michael Jackson—and
even if people don't know the language, they sing it. It's really bizarre,
and they don't know their own music.

"So Tiana and I decided to do the traditional music, although we
were young, because we liked it very much. Everyone in our family
plays music: our fathers, our mothers, our grandparents. And I had
heard stories of our great-grandfather, who was a true musician, who
played the *valiha*, and traditional music. So we decided to do what our
grandfather had done."

It was no easy process. Madagascar is a unique environment, an
island lying 250 miles off the East Coast of Africa. It was originally
settled in the seventh century by Indonesian farmers, who over the
years mixed with Arab traders, Africans, and later French colonists.

---

* This interview was conducted in French.

Mountains and jungle discouraged travel within the island, and Sammy says that there are eighteen different tribal groups, each with its own musical instruments. And some of the instruments are like nothing else in the world—they often look like what Salvador Dali might have constructed if he had been a luthier. The *valiha*, for example, is a tubular stalk of bamboo with strings running lengthwise all around it. (Sammy says that traditionally these strings were peeled from the inside of the bamboo tube, and later made by unwinding bicycle brake cables and the copper wire coils from electrical motors, though he uses regular guitar or piano strings.) The *marovany* is a flat wooden box with zitherlike arrangements of strings on both of its broad sides. The *kabosy* is like a baritone ukulele, except that the frets are irregular, some only extending under two strings. The *lokanga bara* is a three-string fiddle. The *jejy voatavo* has a wooden neck and a gourd resonator, and Sammy's is his own invention—he has changed the shape of the neck, added frets and put an extra set of strings on the side, giving himself two surfaces that he plays simultaneously.

"I don't like to publicize myself," Sammy says, "but I think I am the first young person in Madagascar—me, and Tiana—who have assembled all the music of Madagascar and tried to play all the instruments. Because in Madagascar, there are groups that play only valiha, or kabosy. But we play almost all the instruments, including some that are disappearing. We do research, we try to show people that there are still musicians and instruments who exist."

Sammy has also learned how to make the various instruments, continuing a tradition in which musicians were expected to double as luthiers. However, although he considers it his mission to preserve the old ways, he is by no means a hardcore purist. He continues to play accordion and harmonica, and often adds an electric bass to give punch to the dance rhythms. A bit like the folk-rock bands Fairport Convention or Steeleye Span in Britain, he is trying to create a fusion that will make ancient sounds accessible to young, urban listeners.

"In Madagascar, we have to play some jazz, some rock, some variety music," he says. "It is always based on traditional music, but to provide some ambiance for the young people we use drums, piano, bass, and that way I can introduce the traditional music bit by bit. You have to do that, or people won't come to see you. So I will introduce a bit of valiha when I play variety music, to give it another style, and it surprises people."

Tarika Sammy was first heard outside Madagasgar in 1985, when two English producers included the band on an anthology of Malagasy music on the Globestyle record label, and achieved wider renown with the Kaiser-Lindley project. What happened next is a complicated and contentious story. A short version is that Sammy and Tiana teamed up with a woman named Hanitra (no relation to the Hanitra in their original band) and her sister in a new Tarika Sammy that was specifically aimed at the foreign market. Hanitra was a gorgeous, dynamic front woman who had been working as a translator and was married to Ian Anderson, an English musician, producer, and editor of the influential *Folk Roots* magazine.* With Anderson's help, they put together a fun, upbeat album backed by an English rhythm section, and blew away audiences with concerts that blended Sammy's intricate acoustic arrangements with Hanitra's energy and charisma.

For a moment, this Tarika Sammy seemed poised to be a major crossover act, but by its second album Hanitra and Sammy were no longer seeing eye to eye. She and Anderson were using the group's earnings to upgrade the instruments and equipment, while Sammy felt that he was being turned into an underpaid backup player in his own band. Matters reached a head when Sammy quit the group, taking Tiana with him, and Hanitra and Anderson got a court order forbidding him from using the name Tarika Sammy in Europe or America for a year, during which they formed a new group called simply Tarika. The result was that neither Hanitra's new band nor the original Tarika Sammy, which resurfaced in 1996, fulfilled the promise of their early successes.

When I speak with Sammy about these events, he sounds both angry and diplomatic. He says he has been robbed and exploited, but does not criticize Hanitra's work, remarking only that it seems to him less like Malagasy music than like a new fusion style similar to that of Belgium's Zap Mama. Meanwhile, he says that he is still trying to balance his two careers, playing a more traditional sound for the international market while creating innovative fusions for the audience at

---

* This is not the Ian Anderson who fronts the British rock band Jethro Tull.

home. The latter approach is apparently a somewhat uncomfortable subject, since when I ask if his fusion recordings would be released abroad, he discourages me from even trying to hear them.

"That isn't for foreigners, only for the Malagasy," he says firmly. "Because we are too influenced by modern music, so I only do this music in Madagascar. I play what they like and introduce the traditional music bit by bit, and I think in the end people will come to like the traditional music. Our work is to persuade people, to make them aware. And it is beginning—people at home are also coming to like this music."

As for foreign audiences, they are easy. "People are very happy with what we are doing," Sammy says. "Because the other groups, they can play this style or that style, but we play almost all the music of Madagascar. So our concerts are not monotonous; we have all the flavors, and everyone can find something that they like."

Cape Verde

The Mendes Brothers

The Mendes Brothers are unlike any of the other African musicians in this book, in that their family has a long history in the United States. Their home islands of Cape Verde provided crews for the American whaling industry in the nineteenth century, and Cape Verdeans have been traveling steadily back and forth from the coasts of New England ever since, to the point that many families can trace four or five generations that have lived on both sides of the Atlantic.

"We've had relatives in the U.S. since the early nineteen hundreds," João Mendes says. "Our grandfather on our father's side came here in 1908, and he was here around eleven years. He had a farm in California, and he went back to Cape Verde with something like twelve thousand dollars between him and his brother, which in 1920 is like a huge amount of money. People were making five cents a week."

The brothers are sitting in their recording studio, in the basement of Ramiro's home in Brockton, Massachusetts. João lived here, too, for many years, and his new place is still in the neighborhood. At first glance, the two do not seem much alike. Ramiro, the older brother, is solidly built, bearded, bald, and serious. João is slim and vibrant, the hip front man. They finish each other's sentences like brothers, though, and they have maintained a seamless working relationship since they arrived in the United States as teenagers.

"We came in the blizzard of 1978," João remembers. "On January 14. It was a nightmare. America was nothing like what we thought it was, believe me."

"Very strange," Ramiro chimes in.

"Being from a Third World country, you think about it differently, with all the stories that you get," João continues. "The houses were weird. That was the first thing that struck me. I expected more like the Prudential Center, all glass and flying buttresses. Certainly no houses made of wood. We see brick houses and rock houses in Cape Verde, and the luxury houses are two stories high with lots of plants and trees around them. So I was disappointed about that. Then, the language was upside-down. You spend the next three to five years learning that. And of course, the customs, the culture, that pops up later, after five, seven years."

Immediate disappointments aside, the brothers landed on their feet. Within four months they had formed a band, with older brother Otilio on bass, Ramiro on lead guitar, João on vocals and rhythm guitar, and twelve-year-old Henrique on drums.

In Cape Verde, Ramiro had played in an acoustic, folkloric group. "It was one violin, one guitar, *cavaqinho* [a small guitar, like a uku-lele], which is the same instrument the Brazilians play, and sometimes if we could afford it we'd hire a guy who played twelve-string," he recalls. "We played all type of functions: dances, weddings, anything from funerals on."

In the States, the brothers opted for a more modern approach, picking up the electric Angolan pop style that swept Cape Verde in the 1970s. "Ninety percent of our repertory was Angolan music," João says. "We played very little from Cape Verde; it just didn't talk to us as well. Angolan music is very direct, it's music to move you, and it has a lot of soul."

Within two years, the group had grown to ten people, with key-boards and a horn section. Many of the new players were Haitian, and the band developed its own Cape Verdean–Angolan–Haitian blend, showcased on its first album, 1982's *Un Novo Método* (A New Method). João says that the international approach came naturally to them: "Cape Verde has always served as a crossroads. It was one of the first slave ports in West Africa, and from there the Portuguese sold slaves to the English and transferred them to their colony in Brazil and to the West Indies. Cape Verde was in the middle of all this and always looked outside for different cultural things, and that is still true. It has a very open ear towards foreign music, and everything that comes in gets transformed and mingled and mashed."

In recent decades, Cape Verdean dance beats have been popular throughout Lusophone (Portuguese-speaking) Africa, and the brothers have been leaders in the field, as musicians, composers, and record producers. However, though most of their sales are abroad, they continue to live in Brockton and to produce records in their home studio. As they explain, it is easy to ship a track abroad, and there are advantages to being based in America.

"The United States is a heavy country," Ramiro says, shaking his head. "If you want a brand new guitar, you just go to the store and pick it up. If you're in Africa and you want a brand new guitar, you dream it."

Still, to launch an African career from this side of the Atlantic was not a normal choice. "You don't have any other band that goes from here to play in Angola and Mozambique," says João, laughing. "We're the only crazy guys who do these things."

In a sense, the choice was thrust upon them. The Mendes Brothers' musical blend was popular in the large Cape Verdean community of Boston's South Shore region, and they found work playing at weddings and dances, but after a few years they were getting tired of balancing gigs with day jobs and school. They decided that if they were going to continue in music, they had to get serious about it. So, in 1986, Ramiro entered Berklee College of Music and began working as a songwriter and producer. Soon he was producing recordings by Lusophone stars like Cesaria Évora, queen of Cape Verde's stately *morna* music, and the Angolan singer Waldemar Bastos.

João meanwhile finished a degree in business administration, and in 1993 the brothers started their own label, MB Records, working out of their new basement studio. That summer, they released the second Mendes Brothers disc, *Palonkon*, with João on vocals and Ramiro multitracking virtually all the instruments.

Unsupported by live shows, the disc attracted little attention in New England, but it did astonishingly well overseas. "People from here would go to Cape Verde and they would be amazed," Ramiro says. "They would tell us, 'Jesus, I can't believe it. People asked if we know you guys!' In Angola, it was incredible. Over there, if you're a Cape Verdean with American citizenship, your passport is not called an American passport—it's called a 'Mendes Brothers passport.'"

In the 1990s, Cape Verdean music was sweeping much of Africa, but the other bands played the islands' high-energy *coladera* style. The Mendes Brothers had a more Angolan sound, which might logically have been a handicap, but instead their music caught on in, of all places, Angola. "I think it's the way people received the Beatles here," João says. "The music the Beatles played was essentially African American, but America had problems swallowing a lot of its own music. When the Beatles came from England playing American music it was like, 'Wow!' So us playing Angolan music is an honor for them, and it's an honor for us to be accepted amongst them."

The brothers were greeted as heroes when they went to Angola in 1994, and they returned the following year on a tour that also included Mozambique and South Africa. Meanwhile, they were expanding their musical lexicon, creating new fusions rooted in the folkways of their home island, Fogo. As João explains, "The problem that most of the Cape Verdean groups face is that our pop music in many ways runs similar to West Caribbean music. The *zouk* bands have already played this sort of tak-tak-tak-tak rhythm, and anything that resembles that is very difficult to distinguish. Our answer is to dig into other areas of Cape Verdean music, like *bandera* and *tchoru*, commercialize them and make them popular. I mean, Cape Verde has a tremendous amount of different varieties of music and rhythms that have not yet been explored."

Bandera is the street rhythm of a festival of saints that is particularly strong on Fogo, but the brothers say it has never been used in a pop setting. "When our CD came out, all the old people that know this style of music, they're crazy about it, but the young crowd don't know what it is," Ramiro says. "Even the musicians say, 'What kind of music is this?' They don't even know if it's Cape Verdean."

As for tchoru, the Mendeses say that few Cape Verdeans even think of it as music. "When we have a funeral, there is a certain way that people wail," João explains. "That is called tchoru; you go deep into this trancelike feeling, where you don't care if somebody's looking at you, you don't care who's there. It's just you and that person who's special to you that's gone.

"So we have put that to music. It's a little bit set back, because if you really go deep into this you're gonna wind up crying yourself. But it's real tchoru. We use the lyrics that people use when they lose someone closest to them. Actually, sometimes I feel ashamed of doing this. We go to funerals ourselves, we cry ourselves."

"And write melodies while people are crying," Ramiro adds, wryly.

"But it's so musical and so sad," João says. "And no one has done this before. This is our morna. It's our slow music."

The brothers also feel that it should be particularly accessible to American listeners. "The bandera, tchoru, they're very close to African American rhythms," João says. "If you go far back into the African American expressions and you go that same length back into Cape Verdean expressions, they'll meet somewhere. It sort of all comes out of the same web. This music is very bluesy, and it's a lot of call-and-response."

The American audience has always been in the back of the brothers' minds. They were encouraged by the startling success of Évora's recordings and concerts, a particular surprise to Cape Verdeans since she had been coming to America to play for immigrant audiences for many years. "Cesaria's success has proven to a lot of people that this music can sell," João says. "It just depends how it's done. You know, the labels here, they have looked at world music with kind of a scared look. They still don't think it's gonna work, just like when rap first came aboard."

While their experiments have not yet captured the ears of mainstream American listeners, the brothers remain acutely conscious of the rewards such a crossover might bring. "No matter how much success you make with Cape Verdean music, it's limited," João says. "It's not music that comes on ASCAP [the American Society of Composers, Authors, and Publishers], where you get royalties till the end of your life. This music is now, it's cash. So we're trying to go into another market and to establish a long career. And we have no big thing about being artists, about being on the stage. If people want to see us perform, we'll go ahead and do that. But we both feel comfortable about producing and writing, being behind a successful artist. It's equal satisfaction."

Sitting in the tiny studio from which they have sent dozens of records around the world, the brothers seem happy and confident. There are still plenty of hurdles ahead, but they are comfortable with their choices. After all, it was ambitious dreams that sent them abroad in the first place.

"Sometimes when Ramiro and I travel around I'm reminded of our grandparents," João says. "I feel like we're sort of doing what they did. In those days, most Cape Verdeans worked in a cranberry bog, but these two brothers ran their own dairy farm. They were always outside of the current. With us, just about every Cape Verdean we know is working in a factory, and we're doing this music. So, we're always on a tangent somewhere, trying to do something a little bit different."

2

THE CARIBBEAN

As a matter of music, if not geography, it is logical to go directly from Africa to the Caribbean. Though the congeries of islands curving from Florida to Venezuela is named for the Carib Indians who met Christopher Columbus at his landfall in Hispaniola, the Indian populations on most of the islands were decimated in the following centuries and largely replaced by a mass importation of Africans, brought to work as slaves on the colonial plantations. As a basis for comparison, the music historian Ned Sublette estimates that Cuba alone received half again as many Africans as the entire United States. And while North American slave owners actively separated Africans who had come from the same region to prevent ethnic alliances, and forbade drums and traditional religious ceremonies, on many of the islands—as in much of coastal South America—African cultures remained more cohesive, and many traditional styles survived largely intact.

As a result, Caribbean music is deeply, obviously African. But unlike the musics of Africa proper, it is also the product of societies that have been ruled for centuries by Europeans, and where people from all over Western Africa were crammed together. This history, dreadful as it is, led to inter-African and Afro-European interchanges that produced some of the greatest music in the world. It also profoundly affected the course of music back in Africa, since in the later nineteenth century thousands of ex-slaves returned to West Africa and in the twentieth century Caribbean recordings of Trinidadian calypso, Cuban *son*, Jamaican reggae, and Antillean *zouk* set off revolutions in African popular music.

Meanwhile, Caribbean music has also been affected by the towering presence of the United States. American minstrel shows toured the islands in the nineteenth century, Prohibition sent a generation of jazz bands and their fans down to party with tropical abandon, and radio and records from the Gulf Coast states made country singers and doo-wop groups a model for many island musicians. And this was always a two-way street. For much of its history, New Orleans had far more contact with Port au Prince and Havana than it did with the inland United States, and when jazz traveled up the Mississippi River it brought with it Caribbean rhythms, instrumental approaches, and singing styles. West Indian immigrants were active in black communities throughout the East Coast, and helped to fuel the calypso crazes of the 1940s ("Rum and Coca Cola") and '50s (Harry Belafonte), while tourists brought back romantic records from island vacations and urban socialites began the *beguine* and formed conga lines. Caribbean dance crazes, from mambo to boogaloo to salsa and merengue, have been a staple of American life since the Second World War, while Jamaican reggae has become so popular that I don't even think of it as part of the world music category, but rather as a mainstream genre like rock or hip-hop.

That list of styles is a reminder that, as with Africa or Europe, the Caribbean has produced a broad variety of sounds, played by people who speak different languages and who may have little in common except membership in an arbitrary geographical grouping. However, due to their history, the islands do not have the same kind of centuries-old, relatively hermetic, rural societies that one can still find in Europe or Africa. Especially if one focuses on pop styles, which are what are played in one way or another by all the groups in this chapter, there is an overlapping Caribbean sound—you can dance salsa to Haitian *compas* or Trinidadian calypso, and though it will not be what the locals are dancing, they will recognize it as a familiar and acceptable variation.

One big difference between this chapter and the one on Africa is that, with the exception of the Cubans, all the artists featured here live in the United States, or at least are based here much of the time. That is in part because, like the Cape Verdean Mendes Brothers, they find it easier to work in American cities. Studios are handy and instruments easy to find, there is more money to be made playing for immigrant communities here than for the folks back home, and in any case it is easy to fly to the islands, so if they get a good offer they can be in Puerto Rico or Haiti in a few hours. Such artists also have an obvious advantage over island-based groups when it comes to getting mainland gigs, and thus have been visible to a broader audience, and were around for me to meet and interview.

Haiti

Tabou Combo

Though the term *Latin music* is used overwhelmingly for Spanish-language styles, with an occasional bow to the Brazilians, French is a Latin language, too, and Haitian communities in Boston, Miami, and New York have created one of America's most active tropical dance scenes. While salsa and merengue bands struggle against the competition of techno dance clubs and a young generation that prefers hip-hop and reggaeton, Haitians continue to support more old-fashioned, horn-driven groups like the System Band, and pack nightclubs for guitarists who mix *soukous*-flavored leads with relaxed island rhythms.

It is odd that these groups have attracted so little attention from non-Haitians, since their music is lilting, sweet, and wonderfully danceable, but there has been virtually no crossover. The only Haitian performers (excepting the Fugees) that have attracted many Anglophone listeners are the vocalist Emeline Michel, whose band mixes players from three continents, and the roots-oriented Boukman Eksperyans. Meanwhile, groups like Tabou Combo and M'zik M'zik play huge dance shows at which one hardly ever sees a white face.

At times, Tabou Combo has tried to bridge this gap. For example, the band's *360°* CD opens with a greeting in English: "Welcome to the musical world of Tabou Combo, a world of diversity and musical pleasure. From the island of Haiti to the streets of New York City. Some of you may choose to relax and enjoy; others may want to set the roof on fire. But whatever it requires you to do, you're gonna have a hell of a good time!"

Then comes a horn-heavy blast of what sounds very much like salsa, though with Kreyòl (Haitian Creole) lyrics, and the rest of the disc mixes tropical dance beats with excursions into soul and rap—not surprising for a group that has been based in the New York area for more than three decades. The blend typifies Tabou Combo's savvy appeal. While proud to be the defining band in modern compas music, the twelve-piece combo does not want to remain a secret of the Haitian community. Along with regular appearances in the United States and around the Caribbean, it has toured Japan and Europe, and claims to have sold millions of records outside the Americas.

"We've always been influenced by all different kinds of music," says singer Yves Joseph. "Because our goal is to be international. We've always been criticized by the purists of compas music, saying that Tabou Combo is like more of a rock-compas band, and this is exactly what we want. To put us into the international map."

Tabou Combo has been at the forefront of Haitian music for four decades. "We started in 1968, 1967," Joseph says. "At that time there was some sort of musical revolution going on, with the Beatles and the Rolling Stones, and all the youth in Haiti were really influenced by that kind of music. Before, there were a lot of big bands like the Duke Ellington and the Count Basie band, and then [in the 1960s] everybody picked up a guitar.

"When we started, the name was Los Incognitos, because we wanted to give it a name that didn't sound too Haitian; we wanted to be different. Los Incognitos is a Spanish name which means 'The Unknowns.' We weren't the only band in Haiti; there were several bands of that sort, from all over, every neighborhood. Then we wanted to participate in a band contest and we couldn't participate under that name because it didn't sound Haitian, so we called it Tabou, to be more in a roots sense."

The band's sound evolved along with its name. "We started out playing bossa nova, we started playing James Brown, we played Frank Sinatra when we started," Joseph says. "And then we found our identity and started playing basic compas music. When you start, you're always looking for some avenue, some way to go to find your identity. So you pick up every little bit of everything to fit into your repertoire, and then we started creating our own songs—and they were compas, because compas is our music, so nobody can play it better than we do."

Joseph traces the roots of compas to the merengue style coming in from the Dominican Republic (which shares the island of Hispaniola with Haiti), explaining that it started around 1955 as a slower variation of the Spanish-language form. By the time Tabou Combo got together, compas bands were adding rock influences, and Joseph feels that a lot of his group's appeal came from the same youthful energy that fueled the rock revolution. "We were a pretty happy bunch of kids, coming from high school," he recalls. "And we always sang our heart out and we were nonpolitical and singing very simple music for people to dance and sing and scream. Our melodies were very simple and the chords were very simple. It's like the Beatles. The songs are very simple and everyone can sing, and we were at the forefront of the youth movement at that point. Our music really related to the people of that generation."

Joseph says that from the beginning they were picking up all sorts of outside influences, from merengue to Brazilian music, rock, and pop styles from America, Britain, and France. Then, in the early 1970s, the band members emigrated to the United States—though not for musical reasons. In fact, Joseph explains that they did not even expect to continue playing: "In Haiti at that time, it would have been almost inconceivable to say that you're gonna be a professional musician. Every parent wants you to be a lawyer or doctor or politician, and music really didn't have its place. So when things started to become serious and we started playing for money, our parents chose to send us to the United States and Canada to continue our studies, and in 1970 the band broke up."

Their parents' logic seemed sensible enough, but when the band members arrived in New York they found a Haitian community starved for music from home. Soon Tabou Combo was back together, playing on weekends and blending its music with new pop stylings. "If you pick up a Tabou Combo record from 1974, '75 you're gonna listen to a lot of James Brown," Joseph says. "Because we were influenced very much by the James Brown era. To tell the truth, we always follow, like, a parallel track with the American music, whatever we listen to on the radio. For example, we didn't have horns at first. Horns came around Earth, Wind and Fire and the Commodores era."

The group was still working exclusively within the local Haitian community, but then, in 1975, they started hearing surprising news from friends in Europe. "We were in New York, playing every Saturday at different clubs and church basements, that kind of stuff,"

Joseph says. "And some Haitians in Europe, they start sending us letters saying, 'Hey, guys I'm hearing you all over the radio—I mean, white people's radio! What's going on?' We didn't even know."

The song on the radio was called "New York City," sung in a mix of English, Kreyòl, and Spanish, and it went to number one in Paris before becoming something of a pan-European hit. Since then, Tabou Combo has considered itself an international band. And along with their success in the United States and Europe, they have also been influential closer to home.

"We have a very strong base of friends in the French Caribbean islands, like Martinique and Guadeloupe, and French Guiana," Joseph says. "I think you can say *zouk* music [the pop style of Martinique and Guadeloupe] is basically the son of compas music, and especially from Tabou Combo. Because all the musicians that fathered the zouk music were listening to Tabou Combo when they were a little bit younger."

The international attention has allowed the combo to stretch out musically. Much as Duke Ellington did, they have established two separate shows: a straight-ahead dance show for the Caribbean audience and a concert act for the Europeans and Japanese. "The music we play at the concert we don't play at the dances," Joseph says. "For dances we play slow tunes, moderato, and what we do onstage is pretty different. You don't want to do a big show because a lot of people come and pay their money because they want to dance. But when we're playing at a concert, we put the show out, we have dancers, a light show, choreographies and stuff. Really, we always wanted our music to be more concert-type, and now we travel all over the world and we only play concerts in these places. So I guess we realized our dream."

This is not to say that they are feeling complacent, or contemplating slowing down anytime in the near future. "Sure, sometimes you feel like, 'How long am I gonna do these things?'" Joseph says. "But it's really hard to turn your back away from success. And it's not hard for us to keep the energy, because we've always been playing; therefore it's like a training. We play fifty weeks out of fifty-two, without stopping, and we love what we do. When you go onstage and you have a crowd in front of you, it's very hard not to follow, not to move the crowd, not to give it your best."

Emeline Michel. Photograph © Jack Vartoogian/FrontRowPhotos.

Emeline Michel

While bands like Tabou Combo are the top draws in Haitian communities, non-Haitians are more likely to be familiar with the roots-oriented Boukman Eksperyans or the hip-hop of Wyclef Jean and the Fugees. Since the 1990s, the main ambassador of Haitian music on the "world" scene has been Emeline Michel, a singer who over the years has touched on everything from traditional street and ceremonial music to mainstream pop and French *chanson*. In the late 1990s, after two years in Montreal and four in Paris, Michel moved to the New York City area, drawn by an invitation from Sony Records to become their new crossover star. It was an exceptional opportunity, and in a 1998 interview she talked of becoming the Haitian equivalent of Celine Dion or Gloria Estefan, carrying on dual careers in Haitian music and English-language pop.

Looking back to that time, Michel has to laugh: "It was a total letdown," she says. "Because it's not like it's a legitimate dream for any foreigner—you want to make it big and it falls in your lap like that. It was like, 'Oh, how amazing!' But I don't think [Sony] knew what to do with me. They saw I had an interesting voice, a couple of interesting gears in terms of the dancing and the drumming, but how do you put all of that into a hip-hop world? Because that's what they were doing at that time—but with a fat accent like mine it just came out strange and everybody kind of left me on the counter, because they don't know what to do. So at a point I really was fed up, and I said, 'Let me go back to Emeline, which is what I know best.'"

That meant, first of all, going back to Haiti: "I went for something like six months, mostly staying in the countryside of Jacmel, which is very, very beautiful, one of the parts that most keeps the beauty of Haiti, a little contrast of hills, very poor, but people are going out as they want instead of being inside the house like in Port-au-Prince. I rented a house near the water and I started writing—writing everything I was truly feeling, about my country, about my situation, about love, about life."

The result was *Cordes et Ame* (Strings and Soul), which Michel produced without record company support, using a studio in Port-au-Prince and local musicians. "That was my baby, my heart-and-soul baby," she says. Rather than using her usual accompanists, she brought in street guitarists, or *twoubadous*, the Haitian equivalent of the West African griots: "It's a singer-songwriter that goes with his guitar and his voice to different towns, singing and giving praise to whoever, and getting paid for just being a singer-songwriter, in the street," she explains. "When you get to the airport in Port-au-Prince, you will find a couple of twoubadous waiting to kind of give you an homage, and there was one that was in the hotel at Jacmel. When I brought them to the studio in Port-au-Prince, they were enjoying it, because they never have ever, ever in their life sung in front of a mike." To add to the local flavor, she also used a *manumba*, a large relative of the African mbira that is played throughout the Caribbean, and which Michel describes as "a kind of shoeshiner's case where they put pieces of metal that make the bass."

For Michel, the album was both a homecoming and a departure. On the one hand, the unpolished, acoustic arrangements were a return to her roots: "That's the way I was vocally born," she says. "I had people coming over with two guitars and sitting under the mango tree where my mom had a house in Caridad, and we'd sing for hours, just for the pleasure of putting words together and putting stories together."

On the other hand, Michel's singing career was made largely outside both the Haitian traditional and popular mainstreams. "I came very late to the traditional music of my country," she says. "Because I came from the church and that background. At twelve years old I was the soloist of my church in Haiti."

In the United States, the step from singing in church to working as a professional is not particularly unusual, but Michel says that in her childhood such a thing was almost unheard of. "Your parents wash your brain, telling you that it's not a career being a musician, and especially being a woman, hanging out late with men, and blah-blah. You know? And really, the male situation, with them always handling everything, it hasn't really changed. Even now in New York, when you are recording, if you notice, there's not that many females being a bass player or anything, and that gives you an idea of how the market is controlled by men."

Despite the challenges, she says that she always knew what she wanted to do. "When I was in school, when the mathematics was going on, I would be just dreaming about singing. I would be writing songs in my geography class, and they would call my parents, and that would not change anything. I just had it into me, and I believed that even if it's very difficult as a career, I could never picture myself doing anything else."

In her late teens, Michel was recognized by a well-connected producer and began to give performances. "I had to leave church because I didn't get along with that whole community," she says. "I wanted to bring some new stuff, so I changed from singing for God to talking about like the fact that in Haiti they're cutting the trees and we're losing our country, and a lot of love songs too."

Though most Haitian singers make their way up through club dates, her sponsor decided to develop her as a concert artist. "I never wanted to be categorized as a singer who performed in the nightclubs," she says. "I frankly avoided it, and luckily the manager I had at that time shared the same vision. So I sang in the big theaters and outdoor stadiums. Then I had the chance to be signed by Sony in France and Japan, and the distribution was well-done and for a while I traveled the world, because I was the first young Haitian female doing only music. I only sang in Haiti once a month, but I sang also for the Haitian community in Miami, New York, Montreal, or in France."

Soon she was also reaching fans outside that community, and was forced to confront the stereotypes and complexities of Haiti's history. She explains that the title song of her first American release, *Ban'm Pasé*, is a plea for foreigners to take a different view of her homeland. "Haitians for a long time were not that proud in the eye of the international scene," she says. "Because other nations have been accusing us for many years of being a small, poor country and carrying so many problems, not only drug dealers, not only AIDS. So this song, it's kind of expressing this rage—that on top of what's going on, we have to carry all those loads."

Michel insists on celebrating the strengths of Haitian culture, not just lamenting the problems: "I don't want to play on the fact that Haiti is a country that has historically suffered a lot," she says. "Some people do that, so that people will pay attention to them because they think they have something serious to say. The programs on Haiti that I've seen on television, all they talk about is what's going on politically, and I find that it's not very fair to the artistic part. We always cover up whatever else Haiti has to offer or to share internationally, and I think there's so many subjects that you could talk about, just being sincere and being an artist, without coming back to the same thing that's been selling. I find it very inspirational to be writing in my country, and I don't only see the problems. I also see—Oh my God!—the strengths that most of the time we end up not seeing because the front page has only the headaches to deal with."

This is not to say that Michel is glossing over the hard realities that Haitians face. "I also need to address certain things," she says. "Because certain experiences jump at you. Like racism and the way Haitians are treated—there was a big boat landed in the shore in Miami, and you see Haitians swarming out of that boat like they finally reached the promised land; they are desperate to reach a place where they can work and give their best, and they incarcerated them and they were not granted bail or any asylum at all. And the other hand, I'm looking at the Cubans, and it felt so wrong. So certain things I can't be quiet about, and on *Cordes et Ame* I expressed what is strongest in terms of the culture, the drumming, so many wonderful things about Haiti—but at the same time the subject was a little coarse."

Michel says that she was a bit nervous about the anger she was expressing, as well as the album's stripped-down musical approach, but she felt she had no choice. "I don't think there's any other way to talk to people than being yourself, and that's what I was going through. It is scary, because sometimes I thought people would not relate, but lately I think that when you talk with your heart, people respond with the same strong feeling, and that's really the core of communication. Before, I said, 'This is so rootsy, you are going too far, too deep,' but it is true that for some reason that is the best way to connect with people."

These days, Michel tours with a band that captures both her roots and her broader tastes. It includes Haitians, Americans, and a Congolese guitarist, and her music builds on all her experiences, from her youth to her international journeys. She returns to Haiti regularly, and plays at events for New York's Haitian community as well as doing international concert tours. "Those gigs are so different," she says, laughing again. "Sometimes when I am touring I do a show where everybody is so reverential that we are like, 'Do they like us?' They are so polite that I have to go out in the audience and say, 'Are you enjoying this?'

"And at the Haitian shows I sometimes have to do the inverse—at the very beginning of the show I have to say, 'I will let everybody know when it's time to come and mess up the stage.' Because people really want to interact, they want to jump on their seat at the first note, and sometimes I go for a whole entire song not even singing a word, because they will know it by heart and they would be wanting to come in front of the stage and sing it from the very beginning to the end. Or someone will want to get the drum from Marcus [the conga drummer] and start drumming. So it sometimes creates a chaos—but it is very elevating, and makes you feel that you're doing that job for a good reason."

Trinidad

The Mighty Sparrow

Today, when people think of the English-speaking Caribbean, the first music that tends to come to mind is reggae, but thirty years before Bob Marley and his friends started harmonizing on American doo-wop ballads, the island of Trinidad had spawned a style that circled the globe. Calypso, with its danceable beat and intricate, socially conscious lyrics, was a key influence in West African pop music, and songs like "Rum and Coca-Cola"—albeit usually in censored and sugar-coated versions—were covered by singers in the United States, Europe, Africa, and even parts of Asia. Reggae pushed calypso out of the limelight in the 1960s, but in Trinidad and its adjoining islands the calypsonians held on, adding electric instruments and a heavier dance beat for a sound that was dubbed soul-calypso, or soca.

Soca leapt briefly onto the international scene in the 1980s when a singer named Arrow made "Hot! Hot! Hot!" into a major dance-club hit, but both it and the older forms of calypso have tended to be overlooked in the world music boom. However, if one keeps an eye on the posters in the Caribbean markets that dot most large American cities, one will see advertisements for "Hot! Hot! Hot!" shows featuring an array of colorfully named headliners. Of them all, the grand old man is "The Calypso King of the World," the Mighty Sparrow. Born Slinger Francisco in Grenada, Sparrow grew up in Trinidad, the capital of calypso. Each year, along with Rio de Janeiro and New Orleans, Trinidad holds a wild and world-famous carnival, and the musical "battles" in the calypso tents are one of its highlights. Sparrow burst onto that scene in 1956, at the age of 21, when his song "Jean and Dinah" led to him being crowned that year's Calypso King.

He has dominated the field ever since, recording at least an album a year and winning the Calypso King crown so often that in the early 1970s he decided to stop competing for the title, a decision he stuck to for almost twenty years. "The competition is something that I really like," he says. "But I like a very good, stiff competition, and there was a time when hardly any of the guys could really beat me, and it didn't make sense antagonizing some of your fans and the people who really wanted to see a new champion. So it was good politics for me to give the youngsters a break. And then, in 1992, when the fans think that a new champion has emerged strong enough to give Mighty Sparrow stiff competition, here I come back on the scene and beat everybody."

Despite his decades of success, Sparrow remembers what it is like to be a young singer fighting to be heard. He grew up during calypso's golden age, and spent his early years in the shadow of legendary stars like the Growling Tiger, Lord Melody, Attila the Hun, Lord Invader, and Lord Kitchener. "I started by falling in love with the music, and went into the tents, as we call it, which is the calypso arena at the time," he recalls. "I tried to get a break, to show the established performers at the time that I was good. And when I got my break I made an impression and after that it became more a part of me." He laughs as he recalls those days: "I was the young fella then. I'm the old man now."

Sparrow says that singing always came naturally to him: "It's like the American kids today into rap and break dancing. Nobody goes to learn that anyplace; it's just all around you; it's part of your culture and you're all wrapped up in it. After a while, because of everybody being different, you would have a style of your own. I just sang as I felt, and it turned out to be a little bit different from what the others were doing."

Sparrow's generation built on the work of earlier calypsonians, introducing new rhythms and performance styles. "We were all experimenting," he recalls. "You would hear all sorts of different calypso, calypso augmented with different beats. Kitchener had the bebop calypso, I had the cha-cha-chá calypso, "Maria." Lord Shorty made an experiment that was the first successful one, and everybody realized that these experiments can really work."

Along with the musical innovations, Sparrow says that he pioneered a new kind of presentation. "The others would stand still and point fingers at the audience to try to make a point," he says. "Like an accusing finger, they would point the finger to say something good or something bad. I would say the same things, but with the mike in my hand and dancing pretty much like James Brown, without pointing. I would try to entertain the people and perform for them."

In later years, the emphasis on dancing helped Sparrow make a smooth transition to soca. Calypso had been like rap, a style driven by verbal skills, the ability to improvise verses on demand and to capture a crowd with intricate rhymes and biting humor—though it had a much stronger political component, and was often censored not for obscenity but for its satires of the colonial government. Soca is all about getting down and partying, and old calypso fans tend to disparage it as hopelessly lightweight.

Sparrow understands the criticisms, but also insists on the need to move with the times: "It all depends on what you're looking for," he explains. "The people nowadays are not so much into giving their undivided attention to the calypsonian and listening to advice and editorial observations. In the old days they did. They expected certain things and they demanded certain things, as to how observant you are, how concerned you are about your community and the society as a whole. But nowadays they get all that information from the newspapers and the magazines, the television, the satellites.

"There are so many young people in the business who are very energetic, and they don't really want to give that undivided attention, to learn and open their eyes and heed what's happening. They're more into party. Young people have an abundance of energy and just will not sit still. So the kind of music that they seem to go for is the soca, which is a simpler version, a version packaged primarily for the young people and those who want to be distracted and don't miss anything."

Nonetheless, Sparrow feels that it is possible to adapt without abandoning calypso's core values. The new style is fine, he says, "but there are some of us who consider ourselves purists, who would like to continue to give them messages in a soca form, so that they get the best of both worlds. They get to enjoy themselves in a party mood, and they get something serious. Because I believe people are more intelligent today, and I can't be singing to them like little babies and repeating everything like on Sesame Street: 'one, two, three, four; one, two, three, four.'

"I'm not trying to criticize that, because a lot of the young people look forward to that; that's what they want. But I draw the line. I think that I have to live with myself, so I continue to sing about what's happening in society: the crime situation, the lack of infrastructure in different communities, and the behavior pattern of politicians and bigwigs and small people alike."

He adds that it is this urge to comment on the world around him that keeps his skills fresh, despite the passage of time: "It's not ever easy to write, and it's getting a little more difficult each year. But there are so many things happening, and we calypsonians try to act as a mirror, to reflect what is happening in the society. So as long as there is turbulence in the society we will have material."

Dominican Republic

María Díaz

While the English and French Caribbean have produced plenty of fine music, it is the sound of the Spanish-speaking islands that has most often captured the attention of mainland audiences. Latin music has been the fastest-growing sector of the American record business since the 1990s, and although much of that boom is fueled by Mexican styles, it is the "tropical" island rhythms that have crossed over, with thousands of Anglos taking salsa and merengue lessons and buying records by Ricky Martin and Marc Anthony. As with most broad-based pop styles, though, the biggest stars rarely make the most innovative, quirky, or rootsy music. Salsa giants like Celia Cruz and Willie Colón have been replaced by a host of pretty young men and women singing over what tends to sound like the same studio band. So it is worth remembering that the mainstream hitmakers are only the tip of a vast iceberg, and below the surface of the Latin boom some very exciting music is being played in the smaller dance clubs of the urban East Coast, for what remains an overwhelmingly immigrant audience.

By the late 1990s, that audience had generally voted salsa out and Dominican music in. In part this represented a demographic shift— the great wave of Puerto Rican immigrants had arrived earlier, and their kids were listening to hip-hop rather than Spanish music— but it was also the infectious power of merengue, which captured even the Puerto Rican market. Not only was it fast, but merengue's straight-ahead rhythmic pulse fitted well with techno beats, creating mutations like merengue house and catching the ears of young dancers who thought of salsa as their parents' music. *Bachata* also took off as merengue's slower, more romantic counterpart. And then there was the ultimate Dominican roots music: *merengue típica*, or as it is colloquially known, *perico ripiao* (ripped parrot) music.

Like bachata, merengue típica was once considered both disreputable and countrified, music that might have been good enough for drunken parties under thatched roofs but would never get an audience in Boston or New York As the merengue and salsa mainstreams became steadily more mass-produced and unoriginal, though, the rawer musics have found a growing audience. So far, they have remained very much an immigrant thing, but at least in the case of merengue típica, this seems a bit surprising. With its quick accordion lines dancing over irresistible rhythms, it is one of the most cheerful and high-energy sounds around.

María Díaz is a notable player on New York's merengue típica scene, the first young woman to follow the lead of the great Fefita la Grande. "When I began, she was the only woman playing," Díaz explains.[*] "I didn't know her either when I began, but when I started doing shows in '79, '81, they brought me to meet her. She was the first, and then me. Before, this instrument was completely a man's thing. When people saw us playing they thought it was unbelievable. Nowadays, there are many women who play, because it is good business, but in that time, no."

Díaz is from Nagua, in the heart of merengue's rural homeland. Her father was an accordionist, and she started playing the instrument at age eight. "It was just born in me," she says. "No one said, 'Come here, I want you to learn to play,' the way they do today. Not even my father ever said that he wanted me to learn. The adults didn't even pay attention to me. I just picked up the accordion every day. I would do it after my brother went out, because I had a brother who was also a musician; he was older and he already had a band together, and he didn't want me to play the instrument because there was only one accordion in the house. But when he went out, I would take the accordion and go off and practice.

---

[*] This interview was conducted in Spanish.

"I just picked it up as a child's thing, as my game. I started playing, and I put together a group with a little brother and a little cousin who played the drum and the *güiro*, and the people began to notice us. I became an attraction, and it has gone on growing from there, because with the passage of time one learns more and more."

While merengue típica sounds old-fashioned compared to the horn- or synthesizer-driven styles that dominate the radio, Díaz explains that it, too, has changed with the times: "The new generation does not know how to dance the old merengue, because as time passes things change. Now it is played in many places where it was not played before, so it is still merengue típica, but compared to the sound of the old days it is very different. We have added new and modern things, to be more original and more danceable." Today, bands typically include saxophone, electric bass, and maybe a drum kit, but Díaz says that traditionally there were just three musicians: the accordionist and two percussion players, one with a home-made drum called the *tambora* and the other on the güiro, which could be either a ribbed wooden gourd or, more commonly, a metal object like a large cheese grater that the player scrapes with a stick.

"In my father's time, they used to play out in the country, in places with dirt floors, or even outdoors, and the people would just dance there," Díaz says. "They used to have parties that went from six to six; they would start at six in the evening, and at five or six in the morning they would still be playing, straight through. It was not like now, when they post a schedule for the show. But I was a little girl in those days, and I didn't go out. I just know about that from my father."

Díaz began playing professionally in 1979, and made her first trip to the United States three years later, touring as a supporting act with the legendary Ciego de Nagua (the Blind Man from Nagua). She found a warm welcome in the Dominican community in New York City, and spent the next six years there, marrying and starting a family. She returned to the Dominican Republic to form a band in 1988, had a big hit called "Regalito" (Little Gift), and has been touring back and forth ever since.

Ironically, while she is based in the United States and packs dance halls with Ecuadoran, Puerto Rican, and Salvadoran fans as well as Dominicans, Díaz's only experience of playing for non-Spanish-speakers was back in the Dominican Republic. "Over there, in Puerto Plata, which is a tourist area, they have brought me to do shows on the beach or in the hotels," she says. "And I have played for tourists from all over the world. But here we always play for Latinos; that is the public that knows this music."

Anytime the Anglos want to seek her out, though, Díaz is ready. "This is very nice music," she says. "It has kept changing, adding things to please the young generation, but without losing the traditional sound. When you hear it well-played, you start to move in your seat, wherever you may be. Especially we Dominicans, we have this in our blood, but it is something everyone can enjoy."

Fulanito

Like any huge immigrant center, New York is a place where old country traditions fight to survive amid the bustle and temptations of the modern world. Life was hard back home, which is why people came, but it is hard in the big city as well. So a lot of people cling to their raw, back-country culture with particular passion, as a last link with

Fulanito (from left to right): Winston Rosa, Rafael "Dose" Vargas, Elvin Ovalles, Jose "Pickles" Fuentes, and Marino Paredes. Photograph © Jack Vartoogian/FrontRowPhotos.

a life they have left behind. Meanwhile, their children thrill to the rawness of the city streets, making for difficult clashes. Occasionally, though, raw meets raw and forms a team that is the best of both worlds. Take Fulanito, who shot to the top of the Latin charts in the late 1990s with a fusion of perico ripiao and rap.

Fulanito has one of the most unlikely line-ups in contemporary pop: five young rappers fronting a band led by a sixty-year-old accordionist. The group is the brainchild of Rafael Vargas (a.k.a. Dose), the son of Dominican immigrants, whose English-language outfit, 2 in a Room, had an international hit with "Wiggle It" in the early 1990s. "We grew up in Washington Heights, and it's pretty much like a little Dominican Republic in New York," Vargas says. "Our main thing was like hip-hop and house music, but there were these other groups doing the merengue hip-hop thing, and we thought, 'Wow, we should tap into that, because we speak Spanish and we dig that kind of music.' So we decided to experiment.

"The other groups, like Proyecto Uno, Sandy y Papo and Ilegales, they were doing it with more of a big-band merengue. But I was like, let's try and go even farther back, to the thing that started the whole thing off. And that was the accordion, what they used to play up there in the mountains. People really dig that—when you play perico ripiao people just go bananas—but it was more of an underground thing. It's the typical folk music of the Dominican Republic, and no one [on the pop scene] was touching that stuff with a ten-foot pole. But my father was telling me, like, 'You should try and rap over that, be different,' and I was like, 'Yeah, let's try that.'"

Vargas's producer and songwriting partner, Winston Rosa, is the son of a traditional accordion player, Arsenio de la Rosa. "He's a pretty famous guy in the Dominican Republic, so we were like, 'Wow, if we're gonna try a Latin thing, let's try and do something with your father,'" Vargas recalls. "So that's when we went into the studio and we recorded 'Guallando.'"

De la Rosa takes up the story, speaking in Spanish: "It took me by surprise when they called me to play rap. But my son said, 'Papi, we want to do something new, we would like you to come to the studio.' So they told me more or less what they wanted, and I immediately played them something and they said, 'That was what we were looking for.'"

De la Rosa is a master of the two-row button accordion, the same instrument used by older Tex-Mex and Colombian players. (The rows represent separate diatonic scales, as if each were a single harmonica, and instruments range from one- to three-row models.) He started playing music as a child, following a family tradition: "My grandfather was a musician of the 1880s and '90s, to 1910; he was around 106 when he died and he still played when he was very old. Then my father also became a musician, and he is a lovely composer. So when I was six I picked up the accordion, and immediately I could play it. When I was eight, I could play more than my father. Then when I was almost twelve, they took me to Santiago, and Trujillo [Rafael Leonidas Trujillo Molinas, the country's dictatorial leader] celebrated a festival there on March 30, and I played for him. His brother had a radio station, La Voz Dominicana, and he wanted me to go there and play, but my mother said no, I was too young. But the next year I went back, and when I played on the radio, they gave a prize for the best artist who appeared, and I won twelve times."

De la Rosa came to the United States in 1963, and though he sometimes took other kinds of jobs, he never stopped performing. His Estrellas Dominicanas became a popular band on the New York Dominican circuit, and he still plays at dances throughout the city's five boroughs.

Meanwhile, his kids and their friends were growing up and getting into the hip-hop and house scene. Vargas married de la Rosa's daughter, and after disbanding 2 in a Room, formed the 740 Boyz. It was still an English-language group, but all the members were from Dominican families, and they had grown up with both horn-band merengue and perico ripiao. So, after several international gold records and tours of Russia and South Africa, Vargas says that they decided to try something closer to their roots.

"While we were doing [the recording], we were like, 'Well, this is kind of bugged out,'" he recalls. "But the thing is, whenever we work out anything, we try to make it kind of off the wall and different, make it to the best of our ability and then put it out and see what happens. So we didn't know what the hell we were gonna do, we were like, 'Let's just experiment with this, try to put a rap, try to make a nice hook, and make it a party tune.'"

At first, the word on the street was not encouraging. "When I told my friends that we were going into Latin music, they looked at it like we were going backwards, because I already had hits in the U.S. and Europe and they all felt I should keep doing that stuff. But once we recorded the track, we showed it around, and people were buggin' out. Especially when it started buzzing in the clubs and on the radio. Then it was a whole different story, like, 'You guys got something pretty big here.' So we decided 'Let's do a whole album.'"

"Guallando" and its subsequent album, *El Hombre Mas Famoso de la Tierra* (The Most Famous Man on Earth), took the Latin club world by storm. The sound was fresh, hip, and completely different from the mechanical beat of most house fusions. With the group's second album, *El Padrino*, Fulanito also began appearing live with de la Rosa's band rather than just rapping over prerecorded tracks.

De la Rosa says that *El Padrino* gave him more of a chance to stretch out: "Merengue is traditional music, but as far as what we play with Fulanito, it is a little different. It is merengue, but one has to play it differently from the typical Dominican merengue; one has to play a merengue that adapts itself to rap, in rhythm and in melody as well. So on the new disc we do merengue, but with a flavor of Colombia, of Ecuador and Peru. We make what we call a *sancocho*, which means that everything is tied up together. So I play a merengue, but it sounds like a cumbia, and it is also a rap."

Both de la Rosa and Vargas are enthusiastic about the direction their collaborations have taken them. "I like playing with them, because they all love me almost as if I was their father, and they respect me," de la Rosa says. "I am sixty now, but I feel as if I were twenty."

As for Vargas, after performing in the United States, Africa, and Europe, he is thrilled to have a band that is finally taking him to the Dominican Republic, and on into Latin America. "Now I get to go to countries where at least I understand the language," he says. "And I dig the food and all that, so it's cool."

Puerto Rico

El Gran Combo

Of all the major Latin styles, the farthest-reaching in recent years has been salsa; the only problem is that no one can say exactly what salsa is. Cubans tend to argue that it is just a new name for Cuban *son* or *guaguancó*, while other people place its roots in Puerto Rico or insist that it was born as a New York club style. In a way, everyone is right: the name got attached to the music in New York, where immigrant musicians were mixing various Latin styles with jazz, funk, and soul, and distilling them into a spicy sauce—salsa.

When salsa took off in the 1970s, it thus presented a broad range of performers. There were young, street-smart New Yorkers—not all of them Latino—along with musicians who had cut their teeth in island bands and been playing roughly the same rhythms for decades. Among the Puerto Rican contingent, the most respected older group was El Gran Combo de Puerto Rico. Rafael Ithier, El Gran Combo's founder, pianist, and principle arranger, has been playing professionally since the 1940s, and has seen several new waves of musicians get hailed as revolutionaries. Meanwhile, he insists, very little has really changed.

"It was the same music," he says.* "There is more technique now, we have developed new harmonies, we use some different instruments, but the music is pretty much the same, only with different hues."

Ithier was born in San Juan in 1926, and began playing professionally in the mid-1940s. "Pretty much all my family was in music," he says. "Those who didn't sing played guitar; those who didn't play guitar danced. For myself, I am an autodidact. I never studied, practically. I learned a little from my family, and then I taught myself—the little I know."

A chuckle undermines the modesty of that final phrase, but it is hardly needed. Ithier has been a major figure in Latin music for longer than most of the current stars have been alive. He started out in a small group called El Conjunto Hawaiiano (The Hawaiian Band). "We were a group of young guys, restless," he remembers. "I didn't

---

* This interview was conducted in Spanish.

play piano, I played guitar, all of it by ear. And afterward I played a bit of bass, and so I went on, and in '48, '50, my older sister began to study piano, and I got enthusiastic about that."

At that time, he says, the only Puerto Rican bands that had pianos were the big orchestras that performed in the ballrooms and hotels. After he became skilled on the instrument, he began to get work with these groups, and then was hired by Rafael Cortijo, who was forming an ensemble featuring the charismatic singer Ismael Rivera. Cortijo's combo became Puerto Rico's top band, then traveled to New York in 1959 and attracted wide attention with its combination of expert musicianship and dynamic choreography. On its return to Puerto Rico, however, Rivera was arrested on drug charges and soon Ithier concluded that it was time to move on. "The original group lasted six or seven years," he says. "But then it got disorganized, it was undisciplined, and I didn't like that, so I decided to get out. Five or six other musicians decided to leave, too, and they came to my house and suggested that we form a group, and from that was born El Gran Combo."

That was in 1962, and, while most people hearing their music today would call it salsa, Ithier says that is an anachronism. "We called it *música afroantillana, música tropical,* or *música afrocubana,*" he remembers. "Salsa came when Fania [Records] started in the 1970s; that's where that little word became popular."

Still, El Gran Combo's music combined many of the same Caribbean styles that would define later salsa: the traditional *bomba* and *plena* of Puerto Rico, Cuban rhythms, a bit of merengue, and the Latin jazz coming in from New York.

"Salsa was a blend of Latin jazz and *música típica* [traditional music]," Ithier says. "What happened is that the Latin jazz that I first knew was American numbers played with Latin rhythms, like Stan Kenton, Machito playing 'Welcome Train,' some pieces by Tito Puente. But salsa is Latin numbers with concepts from jazz; not exactly jazz, but with a wider knowledge, modern harmonies, different voicings.

"Like the timbales of Tito Puente—before, it was a full drum set, but now the timbales are separate. And the era of the congas, like Chano Pozo, Willie Bobo, Mongo Santamaría. And Eddie Palmieri, who added trombones, and then the synthesizer. This was the era of soul music, the *super soul americano,* and someone wanted to find a literal translation of this word, which we didn't have, to apply it to this new music. So someone had the idea, instead of calling it soul, to call it salsa."

Ithier points out that the New York Latin musicians had received a very different training than he had on the island. They studied at Juilliard or Boston's Berklee College of Music, or played in American big bands and jazz outfits. Ithier admired their work, and had visited New York several times starting in the early 1950s, but he says that he never considered moving there. He couldn't stand the cold winters, for one thing, and the professional scene was less rewarding than he had expected: "I found out that the great metropolis, the big city, was marvelous, with all the enormous things it had to offer, but I also realized that Latin music was not so well remunerated, that the economic side was not so attractive," he says. "It is not that I am so attached to monetary success, but this is how I make my living. And I found that the work in Puerto Rico paid me better than in New York. At least on the Latin scene. Maybe on the American scene it was different, but in the Latin part the remuneration was not so good. So I realized that, for what I was doing, it was not the place to be."

At least in part because it remained based at home, El Gran Combo tended toward a less jazzy, more solidly dance-oriented style than the big mainland bands. "It's not that I'm more Puerto Rican than anybody else," Ithier says. "But I love my island very much. So we stayed there, and because of that our way of thinking is more Latino, we have a much more *típico* [traditional, or rootsy] sound than the bands in New York. Though we have that influence, we are not as *mestizado* [culturally blended]."

Working on a scene where music has always been inextricably linked with dancing, El Gran Combo had no reason to develop sophisticated concert pieces. Instead, it put together one of the hottest stage shows in the Caribbean. "You must understand that we are from an era when television was beginning in Puerto Rico," Ithier points out. "For television, you have to do certain things in addition to playing well. Sound is one thing, and image another. So we presented ourselves with a singer or dancer in front, and thus was born the choreography of El Gran Combo de Puerto Rico. Then many other orchestras appeared doing the same thing, but one can say that this practically started with us."

El Gran Combo remained Puerto Rico's most popular band well into the 1980s, and though it has since been challenged by younger generations of sexy stars, it continues to play its hot, rootsy version of what is now called "tropical" music. As time went on, Ithier commissioned some pieces from modern arrangers, but the backbone of his show is still the classic hits. "We include some of the new styles, so people will understand that we are still alive, but not too much," he says. "What people want most are the traditional themes. We can't detach ourselves from those, because those are our roots, and it's what the people want to hear. It's what we created and what we do best, so we do this to please ourselves and to be our best in front of the public. Maybe from a harmonic point of view it is a bit different, we have improved in certain ways, we have used some little arrangements from the new boys, but we are still the same Gran Combo. We have evolved a little, but we haven't changed."

And, after some sixty years in music, Ithier has no plans to retire. "Sure I get tired," he says, laughing. "How could I not? But I enjoy it. And El Gran Combo is like a family. We have many years together, and as I am the oldest and the director, the boys depend on me. In the second place, El Gran Combo is, as it were, a national patrimony, a symbol of Puerto Rico. So that is an additional responsibility: We have to try to maintain our image, being a symbol of the island that we love, and one must respect that."

Yomo Toro

People often talk about the rural roots of popular music, linking rock stars to Mississippi Delta guitarists and African rappers to the ancient griots. In the same way, New York *salseros* will sometimes talk about their music's roots in the *jíbaro* bands that used to play string instruments in the countryside of Puerto Rico. Yomo Toro is a unique link between these disparate worlds. He was one of New York's Fania All-Stars of the 1970s, and still appears regularly with reunion groups from that period, startling audiences by rolling on the floor and kicking his feet in the air as he plays dauntingly fast solos, but his roots are in the traditional acoustic groups of the 1920s.

Toro is a short, spherical man, and bounces around his living room like a Superball. His conversation is punctuated with laughter and his eyes sparkle as he races from one corner to another, playing a cut from his new album, tapping out rhythms on his desk, or miming lead solos. Only his graying mustache betrays the more than half century he has been a professional musician, working with everyone from Harry Belafonte, Willie Colón, and Eydie Gorme to David Byrne, Linda Ronstadt, and Paul Simon, as well as in dozens of television commercials and appearances on *Sesame Street*.

Toro is the king of the *cuatro,* a ten-string Puerto Rican cousin of the guitar. Since the word *cuatro* means four, the number of strings is a bit puzzling, but he explains that it is a matter of evolution: "When they started making the cuatros, they used just four simple strings," he says. "Then they added strings to make four pairs. And then lately they added another pair of strings to produce more chords, deeper chords."

He adds that each country in Latin America has its variation of the instrument: "In Cuba they have the *tres*. In Mexico there is the *quinta jarocho*. Then in Venezuela they have another cuatro, but it is a different thing, with four single strings, and they use nylon strings. And Puerto Rico builds the cuatro with ten strings, and they are metal."

Toro is clearly interested in a wide range of styles, and his virtuoso performances mix old and new influences, and rhythms from all over Latin America. "I play any kind of music," he says. "Salsa, merengue, music from Central America, South America, and the United States. I please everybody, and that is why I am still working in music. But I have to keep my roots, I cannot get rid of that. So what I do is, I put my roots together with the modem music and make a combination."

Toro was born in 1933, in the small coastal village of Guánico, and he says that music was a natural part of his life: "All my uncles, they used to work in the sugar company, and then the weekends they get together and they form a group called Los Gallos, the Roosters. But you know, they play for fun, they don't charge money or nothing. And when I was six years old I start following my uncles when they'd play there in the barrio."

Shortly, he decided he wanted to try it for himself: "My father had a cuatro on a nail there, on top of the bed. He didn't want anybody to touch it, but when he'd go to work, then I'd climb the bed and I start, dun, dun, dun, dun, but I didn't move the cuatro from there. I remember that I don't use the guitar picks, I use the teeth of the combs. I was one year straight, climbing this bed till I learned a little bit. Then one day he came home too soon. All of a sudden, I looked back and he was standing there. He had his eyes very big and I said, 'Oh my God. He gonna kill me.' So boom, I fell down on the bed.

"He told me, 'You climb there again and do what you was doing before.' I was very scared, so I tried to put on a show and play very good. When I looked at my father, he was crying; I saw the tears on his face. Then he went to the yard and started cutting a tree. I said, 'What are you doing?' And he tell me, 'I'm going to build a cuatro for you.'"

It is a touching story, but Toro cannot resist giving it a humorous coda: "Four weeks I was waiting for this cuatro. Everyday I was bothering my father, but he told me, 'Keep practicing in my cuatro, keep there.' And then he made me a cuatro, but he was no artisan, and he did it his own way. When he finished, the cuatro looked like a fry pan, to fry potatoes. It was not tuned; it sound flat, ugly. But it had a little sound, and I was still learning there."

Soon Toro had developed a local reputation, and at age twelve a producer brought him to San Juan to play lead guitar and cuatro for a popular quartet, Los Cuatro Ases (the Four Aces): "There was a man there, Mister Tato Ardín, and he owned the Mardi Records, and he had the toppest groups on the island. He was looking for a guitar player, a melody player, what they call *requinto*, and they told him about me: 'There's a little town there in southwest Puerto Rico, there's a kid there who plays.' So he went to my town and they look for me and I went there and he told me, 'Play the cuatro.' And I start playing the cuatro. 'Play the guitar.' And I start playing the guitar. He opened his case and took out a paper and he said, 'Sign here, you have a ten-year contract.' I was just a kid, but I was playing very good."

Los Cuatro Ases were a string and vocal group on the model of the Cuban Trío Matamoros or the Mexican Trío Los Panchos. "It was all acoustic guitars," Toro says. "We played four boys together, and when we make the recording there was no mixing, just one microphone for everybody. When I have to play a guitar solo, I come very close to the microphone, and then I step back again, because that was the balancing."

Toro came to New York in 1952 and soon established himself as a studio and concert stalwart, playing everything from Latin dance music to the electric guitar parts on Spanish covers of rock 'n' roll hits. "When I arrived to New York, then there was a kid named Miguel Juventud, he was about ten years old. You remember Frankie Lymon, his times? Well, in those same times this kid used to sing very high notes, so I used to make versions of this music of Frankie Lymon in Spanish. That's when I started playing the funky guitars and the electronic guitar from here."

Today, Toro's playing still moves easily from jazzy rhythm licks to lightning flamenco runs and the lilting strains of Cuban *danzón*. "I play anything," he says. "Every music. Because if you play every music, everybody calls for you. If I played just the Puerto Rican music, just the Puerto Ricans gonna call for me. But like at the World Trade Center, they don't want just a Spanish band, a salsa band. So they call Yomo Toro. Because I please all the people— Chinese, Japanese, everybody. This is the idea that I'm still working in music."

Toro adds that in any case he always liked to listen to a variety of styles: "When I was a kid they had those radios named short-wave radios. I used to hear music from here [the United States], the country music, and my mind pick up from there. Then I used to hear a lot of music from Spain, and my mind pick up from there. I used to hear music from all the countries, and then I put it in my mind and when I play I remember that." He points out that this breadth of taste comes naturally to Puerto Ricans: "Nobody is strictly Puerto Rican from Puerto Rico; our bloods belong to different countries of the world. And the music, too—we pick it up from the other countries and then we play our way, with our instruments. We take music from the whole world and we make it part of our folklore."

Toro adds that, having been in the business so long, he can recognize the sources of new styles, and thus find ways to bring old and new together. "When you don't have too much experience in music, then you got problems," he says. "But I am playing long years already. So I hear a song and I say, 'It is here.' Because I used to hear a lot of this music before, in the old-fashioned way. It's the same music, but they put it in the new-fashioned way. It's modern, but if you hear the bottom of the idea it's gonna be the same music always. Never change. What change is the combination of instruments and things like that. But everything is a derivation, a copy from old music, from the roots. Cause you hear the rap, the rap is like rock or like the other kind of music. The only thing is they are using a different way. They use one beat—pah, pah, pah, pah—and to that beat you can put whatever you want to put. You can put any instrument you want, but the thing is this downbeat there. It's the same old music in a modern way."

Whatever Toro plays, that beat is always crisp and clear, making feet tap and people want to dance. "Everything starts with the rhythm," he says. "If there is no rhythm, music is empty. And then, you add the instruments to the rhythm and you have the whole thing. If you just listen to the music and you do not dance, there is something missing and I don't feel comfortable. But if I play the music to hear it and to dance it, too, in my mind the project is complete."

Except the project is never complete, because there is always more music to be played: "I'm very happy to be alive, thanks to God, and to be playing around," Toro says, smiling broadly. "I feel good, and I feel happy and I feel young. Cause I don't drink and I don't smoke. And this is one thing that kids know about me: I am a very, very serious person, and when I finish playing the music I come straight to my home. I am not a crazy guy. So that is another reason that everybody calls me. Because if I have a dirty name, they don't call me never, but if I have a very clean name they say 'Yomo Toro is the man.'

"I'm in the books, the university books, the school books, all over. I play for old people, young people, and when I finish playing everybody feels okay. And I don't know when it's gonna finish; I think it's gonna finish when I die. As a matter of fact, I made a composition that says, 'When I die, don't bury my clothes, because when I come back I want to use them again.'"

Rubén Blades. Photograph © Jack Vartoogian/FrontRowPhotos.

New York

Rubén Blades

Rubén Blades came to the attention of the New York salsa world in 1975, as vocalist on Willie Colón's groundbreaking album, *El Bueno, el Feo, y el Malo* (The Good, the Bad, and the Ugly). If Yomo Toro (who also appeared on that album) was the most traditionally rooted artist in the Fania Records stable, Blades was the label's proletarian poet, revolutionizing what had been good-time dance music by writing complex, gritty fables of life in the big city. It was protest music with a beat, the smartest, most rhythmically inspired sound of what the Anglo world remembers as an era of disco and punk rock. In 1978, Blades and Colón created their masterpiece, *Siembra*, which became the best-selling album of salsa's golden age and included "Pedro Navaja," Blades's epic reimagining of "Mack the Knife."

Blades has covered a lot of ground since then, and yet, much remains the same. The angry young man has become an angry older man, still making music that addresses the injustice and ugliness around him: "No one chooses his family or his race when he is born," he writes, in a song titled "Vida" (Life), from his *Tiempos* album. "Nor to be rich, poor, good, bad, brave or cowardly." And yet, "Between baptism and burial each person makes a road, and, with his decisions, a destiny."

Blades has made many surprising decisions in his life, and his complex, literary songs have earned him the label of "the thinking person's salsero." Far from being flattered by such designations, he reacts to this label with irritation: "First of all, I was never really a salsa musician. I used Afro-Cuban percussion, but my feeling was always that I was attempting to write or describe situations within a city or within a society, and addressing issues that were of interest to people who danced or didn't dance. A lot of people write for the feet, but my music, you can dance if you want, but that's not my whole direction. I'm not gonna give you stupid lyrics because I need to babble some idiocy while you move.

"I always felt a tremendous need to document realities and communicate, and because I moved within the dance circuit and the songs had a very strong rhythm to them, people defined me within the salsa boundaries. Not knowing what else to say, they said, 'Oh, this is the more educated salsero, the more intelligent one'—as if we were some subspecies they were studying, and some of us could manage the trick to press the blue button and get water faster than the other ones."

Since Blades chooses not to be classed as a salsero, it might seem logical to consider him as part of Latin America's politically oriented singer-songwriter movement, the *nueva canción* (new song), but that suggestion leaves him equally unhappy: "The thing there is that there is a very strong ideological base, or at least there's a suspicion that the nueva canción guys are more interested in questioning [Augusto] Pinochet than questioning Fidel [Castro]. So, I never liked that either, because of the basic dishonesty of criticizing just right-wing dictators. I think you have to criticize all forms of dictatorship.

"Also, I was trying to reach the largest possible group of people, looking at them all as my peers, as human beings. I wasn't trying to reach the educated, university-trained professional who would be able to decipher my imagery. I was trying to create something that would resolve my own need to present things in a literate way—in a poetic way, if I may—but without alienating the audience."

In his life, Blades has charted a course that fits his independent stance. He was born in Panama City in 1948, of Colombian and Cuban parents (a West Indian grandfather supplied the family name, which he pronounces the English way, though he has no objection to Spanish-speakers saying *Bla-dace*). His early tastes ran to rock and Frank Sinatra, and he became politicized as part of the student movement of the 1960s. Along with his musical career, which includes three Grammys, he has earned law degrees from the University of Panama and Harvard University; acted in films, television, and on Broadway; and, in 1994, finished third out of seven candidates for the Panamanian presidency.

Gabriel García Márquez called Blades "the world's most popular unknown," and it is true that, despite collaborations with everyone from Ray Barretto and Tito Puente to Elvis Costello, Lou Reed, and Paul Simon, he has remained something of a cult figure. Even the much-vaunted Latin boom, which made Ricky Martin a household name, left his reputation virtually unchanged. This does not seem to trouble him in the least. While he speaks respectfully of Martin and of Marc Anthony, both of whom have named him as an important influence, he is openly furious at the whole concept of crossover.

"I refuse to even acknowledge that term," he says. "Because *crossover* depends intrinsically on your acceptance that there is a chasm there. And I refuse to accept that. I think music is one common ground, and that means that some guy in Budapest can play rock 'n' roll, and some fourteen-year-old in China can play salsa, or a Japanese guy can play Irish music.

"The whole crossover thing has an economic and a racist connotation, but the racism is not colored, it's cultural racism. And I will not accept that we are divided. I mean, right now as I speak to you I'm listening to an Irish band called Solas. Does that mean that they're crossing over to the Latin market? That they're not gonna eat any more potatoes, they're gonna have some rice and beans now, and maybe the girl will grow a mustache so when she does the *Riverdance* thing the mustache goes up and down? Come on. That's bullshit. You listen to whatever you're gonna listen to."

As for the fact that other singers are getting a lot more press and record sales, a man who cites Bertolt Brecht as a major influence can hardly be expected to worry about the latest fashions. Though the undertone of anger in his speech makes it hard to describe him as happy or satisfied, he is clearly proud of his accomplishments, and has come to terms with the destiny he has made:

"I'm not on the cover of *Rolling Stone* or *People en Español*—or in English or Apache—I'm not that kind of celebrity. But I'm doing my films, and I try to produce music with intelligence, and that has kept me alive. Because the audiences are smarter than the idiots that sell the records. Basically, that's what keeps guys like Tom Waits alive, and Bob Dylan, for that matter, and myself. Not because people say, 'Oh, he's cute,' or 'Oh, he's got a nice voice,' or 'Oh, he went out with so and so,' or 'He sold X amount of million records.'

"I don't think that what I'm doing is the only thing that should be done, because I think everybody's got their own taste and I respect music in general. But by the same token, I do resent being measured by the sort of mediocre standards that are reserved for what is mass-produced and passes for talent today in every field. I believe that people respect me not only because I did well, but because of where I have been, what I have done, what are my positions. I don't think about sales. If people don't want to buy my records I couldn't care less, because I think this is something that needs to be done. We're presenting different positions for people to listen to, so that future generations will have something else to sample than all the crap that's out there."

Cuba

Eliades Ochoa and Compay Segundo

In terms of the world music boom, one Caribbean country stands alone: the success of the Buena Vista Social Club's album, film, tours, and offshoots has made Cuban music a craze unto itself. Before Buena

Eliades Ochoa (front left) and Compay Segundo (front right) with Ibrahim Ferrer and the Buena Vista Social Club. Photograph © Jack Vartoogian/FrontRowPhotos.

Vista, Cuban artists had been largely absent from the stateside scene, due to American government restrictions that prevented them from coming to the country and their recordings from being imported. Cuban styles remained a notable presence, played by Puerto Ricans, Central and South Americans, and immigrant stars like Celia Cruz who came to the United States after the Cuban Revolution, but most Americans tended to think of artists like Cruz and Gloria Estefan as Latin or salsa musicians, not distinguishing them from non-Cuban peers like Eddie Palmieri and Ricky Martin.

There was no such confusion about the wave of performers that arrived with the Buena Vista project. The record appeared at a perfect time in the world music boom, providing a mix of exoticism and familiarity, and a gentle, old-fashioned sound that attracted the Sinatra fans along with the folks who were listening to Afropop. Which is not to say that its success was simply a matter of luck and fashion. Cuba has had a particularly strong musical tradition for at least a century, exporting styles like *danzón* and *bolero* throughout Latin America. As Cuban players regularly stress in their interviews, the government of Fidel Castro also did a lot to promote and preserve the island's culture—and their comments are not simply a matter of currying favor with the politicians back home. There is no other country in Latin America, and very few anywhere in the world, that has put as much funding and energy behind its musical heritage. The *casas de la trova* (sort of traditionally-oriented open-mike venues) have provided a forum for traditional players, and young musicians have gotten formal conservatory training that has made them famously versatile and virtuosic. This has been a somewhat mixed blessing—conservatories are not necessarily the best incubators of popular music, and the Cuban system has undoubtedly discouraged some innovative players even as it has helped others—but the vigorous variety of the Cuban scene is testimony to its virtues.

Much of the hardcore world music crowd viewed the Buena Vista phenomenon with suspicion, in part because it erased roughly forty years of evolution, passing over two generations of brilliant musicians in favor of a nostalgic sound that recalled Havana's days as a pre-revolutionary tourist paradise. The elderly stars in their white suits, swaying gently as they sang along with the rhythms of the bolero, the mambo, or the cha-cha-chá, conjured up a romantic and unthreatening image of rum cocktails drunk in the shade of palm fronds, rippled by a soft Caribbean breeze.

Be that as it may, the music was beautiful and, for many of the players, the international success was not only well deserved but long overdue. As with any genre or region, some Cuban musicians are better than others, but the standard is extraordinarily high, and the blend of expertise and entertainment is singularly appealing to both serious music addicts and casual listeners. If Buena Vista had some shortcomings, it more than balanced them by providing a platform for unique masters like the pianist Rubén González and the irrepressible Compay Segundo.

Though the abridged version of the Social Club that went on tour was a big band recreating the sound of the Havana hotel orchestras of the 1940s, the album's catchy lead track was from a very different tradition. Featuring Compay and Eliades Ochoa, it demonstrated the power of the small, string-driven groups of Oriente, or Eastern Cuba, the heartland of Cuban *son* [literally, "sound," son is best known as a key ingredient in modern salsa]. Separated from the rest of the island by an almost impassable mountain range, Oriente developed its own culture, more countrified than the cosmopolitan music of Havana. In a sense, it bears the same relationship to the orchestral style that blues does to jazz, and Ochoa at times makes that connection explicit. He has recorded with the blues harmonica player Charlie Musselwhite, and when he appeared at the House of Blues in Cambridge, Massachusetts, he at one point reached out into the sea of hands in front of the stage, grabbed somebody's bottle of beer, and played a guitar solo using it as a slide. The loud, smoky bar was clearly a pleasant change for him after a tour full of formal concert performances, and seemed to take him back to the days of his youth in Santiago.

At the time of the Buena Vista sessions, Ochoa was fifty-three, which made him one of the album's youngest featured performers. He had also been one of the most consistently successful. "With the Cuarteto Patria, I had already traveled through the United States, through America, the Caribbean, and Europe," he says.[*] "I was less well-known than I am now, but I traveled the world. I was not in the situation of other artists, who were forgotten or unknown."

Indeed, it was Ochoa who originally revived Compay's career in the 1980s, bringing him back from Havana to Oriente's capital, Santiago de Cuba, and then to the Smithsonian Folklife Festival in Washington, D.C. Ochoa clearly regards Compay as something of a father figure—like the older man, he plays a self-modified cross between a guitar and the Cuban *tres*—and he has devoted his career to celebrating the traditional styles of Oriente. "Santiago de Cuba is the cradle of Cuban music," Ochoa says. "It is where son was born, and also *bolero, guaguancó*, the *rumba*—all these things are *santiaguera*."

Asked why he thinks Santiago has been so musically productive, Ochoa laughs. "You would have to find scientists to answer that," he says. "Ask them whether it has anything to do with the earthquakes, because Santiago de Cuba shakes every once in a while. And the sun is hotter than in the capital. And the rum is hotter than in the capital. And the *mulatas* move their bodies more than in the capital. But

---

[*] These interviews were conducted in Spanish.

one would have to hunt up a scientist to discover whether the son has anything to do with all these things."

Ochoa started playing music as a child: "I was born in a musical family and have it in my blood," he says. "My father played tres, and my mother as well. My sister has her own group, and all my siblings played guitar." Though he was born in the countryside, his family moved to Santiago when he was still a child, and by age ten he was performing for tips in the city's streets and the bustling brothels of the red light district.

The revolution closed the brothels, but provided new support for traditional music, and in 1963 Ochoa was given his own radio show. His biggest break, though, came in 1978, when he was chosen to take over the Cuarteto Patria, one of the most respected groups in the region. The Cuarteto had been formed in 1939, and he gave it a new, young energy while retaining the classic sound.

Ochoa's specialty has always been the string-driven style of east Cuban masters like the Trío Matamoros, but he brings a special flavor to the music. "Style is born in a person," he says. "Sometimes one does not even know how he comes to create a his own special stamp, his style, but there it is." He also welcomes the chance to broaden the tradition, as with his collaboration with Musselwhite: "He wrote to me in Cuba," Ochoa explains. "Because we were both playing at a festival in Norway, and he wanted to see if we could do something together. I listened to the discs he sent, and when we met we got together, we rehearsed a lot, and I showed him how to play some Cuban music on harmonica. I like to try this sort of thing very much, because it enriches both cultures."

Ochoa is leaving the door open for future collaborations, but meanwhile he is enjoying the greater exposure he has received since Buena Vista. "It is a lot of traveling," he says. "But that is the way to prepare the future. Buena Vista Social Club changed things a lot, for me and for many Cuban *soneros*. The concerts have multiplied, and when the concerts multiply, life changes. And for this I have to thank Ry Cooder for his idea. He put me together with various glories of Cuban music and, despite my being younger than them, they realized I had the ability. And that gave me great satisfaction."

It might seem strange to think of a new career opening up in one's mid-fifties, but the particularities of the Buena Vista project make Ochoa feel like a young man. After all, his main collaborator on the album was a man more than thirty years his senior, who was showing no sign of slowing down.

"Retire?" At age ninety, Compay Segundo seems hardly to understand the question. "No, no. In Cuba, when I walk past a school, a child shouts, 'Look! Compay!' And they all begin to sing: *'De Alto Cedro voy para Marcane, luego a Cueto voy para . . .'* [the opening lines of his trademark song, "Chan Chan"]. And the teacher is yelling, 'Children! Children!' So I cannot retire. I am in the hands of the children."

Compay is sitting in a rooftop hotel room in New York, holding court as reporters, music-business figures, and his Buena Vista bandmates wander around outside. Elegant as always in his trademark white suit and hat, the inevitable cigar in hand, he speaks in slow and refined Spanish. Beside him sits a young, female translator, whom he flirts with throughout the interview. The previous evening, he stole the show at the full Social Club's sole United States appearance, dancing along to the rhythms as he sang with majestic grace and played glittering solos on the *armónica*, a modified guitar of his own invention.

So one has to ask, how does he do it? "Easy," he says. "I started playing music very early, in my childhood. I learned well, and I also learned classical music, because I played clarinet. I always liked to deepen my knowledge of music, learn its origin and everything. When I began, I played Brazilian music, Spanish *pasodobles*, French music, and I enjoyed it all."

Yes, but the real question is, how does he keep up this pace at age ninety? "I never overdid it," he says, the gleam in his eye belying the sober lecture. "Don't overdo things. I did not eat much. Just normal. Women, just normal. Not too much, or one gets bored."

"*Anda!* Go on!" the translator breaks in, laughing. "Nobody believes that, not even you."

Compay nods solemnly. "If they serve you a chicken, just eat a little piece. Because if you eat the whole chicken, the next day when they serve you chicken you won't want it."

"Don't point at me," the translator says.

The oldest and most charismatic of the Buena Vista stars, Compay was also the one best equipped to take advantage of the album's success. Unlike many of his younger bandmates, he was not in retirement when Ry Cooder came to Cuba. He was traveling annually to Spain, writing new songs and collaborating with flamenco artists. With the boost the album provided, he added three clarinet players to his basic rhythm section, but he has continued to chart his own path, touring as a soloist and treating audiences to long, enthralling concerts. Watching him thrill crowds of young admirers, it is astonishing to recall that he has been performing since the 1920s.

Compay was born Máximo Francisco Repilado Muñoz, in Cuba's eastern capital. "I was born in Santiago," he recalls. "On the beach of Siboney, by El Caney, where the fruits are like flowers, full of aromas and saturated with honey." (The quotation is from "Frutas del Caney," a song on his *Lo Mejor de la Vida* album.)

He received his professional name, which means roughly "Second Buddy," in the 1940s, as half of the popular duo Los Compadres (Lorenzo Hierrezuelo sang first voice, and hence was Compay Primo). They were radio stars and recorded roughly a record per month, as well as doing side projects like the jingle Compay wrote for the Paper Mate pen company. For much of this time, Compay was also working as a clarinetist, playing for twelve years with the legendary Miguel Matamoros.

Things slowed down in the late 1950s, and Compay spent two decades as a tobacconist. He returned to music only in 1989, when he was invited to the United States to perform with Eliades Ochoa's Cuarteto Patria at the Smithsonian's annual folklife festival. Reinvigorated by the international attention, he put together a quartet of his own, and soon was touring Europe. The success of this new career surprised some of his friends back home, but he seemed to take it almost for granted: "My music is not common," he points out. "It is very special, and people enjoy it; they even cry when they hear me."

In Cuba there was less acclaim, but until Buena Vista pushed his touring into high gear he ran a weekly casa de la trova in Havana, keeping the spirit of Santiago alive in the capital. With his international success, he has been forced to spend less time at home, but when he is there he is treated as a legend. "I cannot walk in Havana," he says. "Because everybody wants me to come into their house. They say, 'Come in, so my children can see you.' And as soon as I leave one house they want to bring me into another, and I can never get to my own. So I've gotten myself a little car. Now I wave hello and rrrrrrr, wave hello and rrrrrrrr, and that's it."

And what are his plans for the future? "What now? To live life. I am starting again at ninety. I plan to get to 115, like my grandmother. And when I get to 115, I plan to ask for an extension, to live some more."[*]

Los Van Van

While the world thrilled to the sounds of the Buena Vista revivalists, a lot of Cubans and Latin music fans looked on in bemusement. Why was everybody so excited about that old stuff? Didn't they know that Cuba was still a hotbed of innovation, and that a lot had happened since 1950? As the craze caught fire, though, even the more modern players found that it was bringing them a new, broader fan base, and no group was better prepared to take advantage of this than Los Van Van.

Los Van Van has been hailed as "the world's greatest salsa band," and though Juan Formell, the group's leader and bassist, is not happy with this designation, he no longer sees much point in arguing. "People always call our music salsa, all over the world," he says, sounding tired.[†] "It's a problem of distribution and a thousand other things, and by now we understand how it happened. But really, what they categorize as salsa is not what we play. Salsa has a lot of Cuban influence, but the salsa groups are more standardized, they follow more or less the same lines, the same tunes and sound. The Cuban style—Los Van Van—is more open; we use more polyrhythms."

Currently a fifteen-piece orchestra, Los Van Van has been the most popular dance band in Cuba since the early 1970s. When they developed their trademark sound, Formell named it *songo*, but now he groups it among other new Cuban styles as *timba Cubana*. Whatever name one uses, it is superbly energetic and rhythmically complex, the

---

* Compay Segundo died in 2003, at the age of ninety-five.
† This interview was conducted in Spanish.

sort of music that gets Cubans out on the dance floor. And it is truly different from salsa; as any Latin club owner can attest, a lot of salsa dancers are hopelessly confused by the intricate timba rhythms.

It is not simply the rhythms that set Los Van Van apart. Formell says that one of his primary inspirations was the arrival of the first Beatles records in Cuba: "For me, personally, their approach was very influential, the way they broke with the old structures. I didn't adapt their music directly, but at the beginning my orchestra had guitar, and the guitarist tried to get something of the rock 'n' roll sound. Since we are Cuban, it didn't come out the same way, but we were influenced by the guitar and by the timbres of that music."

Formell already had a solid grounding in older Cuban pop styles, since his father worked as a pianist with bands that played the Havana *son* of the 1940s and '50s. He says he started out as a guitarist, but switched to bass at his father's urging, because it could provide more regular work: "He told me that bass players always eat. Whoever is eating—quartets, duos, or orchestras—the bass always goes along."

Formell learned the rudiments from his father, and then studied with some of Cuba's top bassists. Soon he was working in show bands, theater orchestras, and small combos, eventually getting a job with Orquesta Revé, one of the main groups playing *charanga* music. Charanga evolved in the early twentieth century as roughly the Cuban equivalent of American ragtime, but its combination of bright violin and flute with catchy dance rhythms showed remarkable staying power and had a modified revival at mid-century, led by groups like the Orquesta Aragón. With Orquesta Revé, Formell began writing arrangements that added a new rhythmic and chordal complexity to the classic style, and then broke off in 1969 to form his own group. He named it Los Van Van (roughly, "The Go-Gos") after a government slogan for the 1970 sugar cane harvest.

"At that time, the whole form of the Cuban orchestra was changing, with the arrival of electric instruments," he says. "The way of singing changed, the harmonies, and we changed the way of playing the violin and piano. It was more rhythmic. I had a different conception of the music, and when we started, there was a lot of controversy. The public loved the freshness of our sound, but the more conservative people were opposed to us—to break with tradition is always very hard. But after a while they realized that we were crazy, that we were going to do whatever we wanted, so now they don't worry about us."

Formell's approach continued to evolve as he tried out different rhythms, harmonies, and instrumentation. He brought in electric keyboards and synthesizers, but the most distinctive addition was a line of three trombones to balance the three violins and flute as the group's principle instrumental voices. "We had the violins and flutes in the upper register, the rest of the orchestra in the lower register, and so we were looking for something in the middle register," he explains. "So we brought in the trombones, and that filled out the whole sonority of the group."

Adding touches of jazz, rock, funk, and whatever else came along, Los Van Van has stayed in the forefront of Cuban music and spawned a raft of imitators around the world. Considering this, it is odd to find Formell downplaying the band's musical impact: "I think our main influence has been not so much in the music itself as in the way we work," he says. "The part we played was of the vanguard, the innovators, of having more freedom in composition, more experimentation and openness in the sound."

In recent years, Los Van Van has seen further changes as older members retire and are replaced by young musicians. Formell says this is as it should be: "The young musicians are very good, and they have had a big influence on me and on the group. Because throughout the lifetime of Van Van, I have been influenced by all of my musicians, and I have always had musicians who helped very much in forming the group's development and that has shaped my own concept of the music."

La Charanga Habanera and Gema 4

One of the many unfortunate results of the United States government's ban on trade with Cuba is that American fans have been unable to keep up with recent developments in the island's music. It is very hard to import Cuban recordings, and without a record it is impossible to build up an audience that could support a tour. Meanwhile, getting visas for a hot young Havana dance band has always been harder than for a classic son master—and that was before the post-9/11 crackdown cut off even the limited degree of musical interchange that existed.

That is why Americans have missed out on groups like Charanga Habanera, who by the 1990s were supplanting Los Van Van on the dance band scene, and quirky outfits like Gema 4 (Gema Cuatro), a female a cappella quartet from Havana's little-known classical music world.

The links between classical and popular music are stronger in Cuba than anywhere else on earth. Due to government support and control of the arts, the postrevolutionary generations of professional musicians have almost all received formal training. As a result, it is common to interview a dance-band star like Isaac Delgado and find that he studied classical cello or—turnabout is fair play—to talk to a conservatory student and find that he or she is looking forward to playing timba or jazz, or even forming a punk or rap group.

As Gema 4's Odette Tellería explains it, "Here, one studies classical music as a way to enter the profession; one studies music as if it were medicine. But after you graduate, you don't have to play symphonies; there are very few who go on to do that. Everyone thinks of classical music as a technical base to be able to do something more experimental. Of course, we have groups that are purely classical, but I think that the Cuban musicians are more curious than that, and they always try to invent something new. And almost all of them go into Cuban popular music, which is very strong. Even in the symphonic groups, the groups that are *classical* classical, they play a lot of repertory that could be called popular Cuban classical. And then, almost all the salseros, vocalists, jazz musicians, are classically trained."*

David Calzado, the leader of Charanga Habanera, is a perfect example. His group is known as a high-powered dance band with acrobatic stage routines and music that takes Los Van Van's approach in new, funkier directions, but where Los Van Van's founders were rock musicians before returning to Cuban styles, his training was as a classical violinist. "I have played a great deal of Bach, Mozart, Liszt, Chopin," he says. "And for me, that is a wonderful music. I always dreamed of being a concert artist, but here in Cuba the market for classical music is very limited. People don't go to symphonic concerts.

---

* These interviews were conducted in Spanish.

So I realized that to take that career path would be very difficult, very demanding—I like complicated things, but I thought it would be impossible. So I decided to lean toward popular music. But I have always had an itch to be able to play Mozart in a beautiful hall with a good symphony orchestra behind me."

Instead, Calzado got a job playing violin with a charanga orchestra at one of Havana's most famous nightspots, the Cabaret Tropicana, where he was spotted by a French impresario in search of a dance band for the Sporting Club of Monte Carlo. "It was miraculous," Calzado recalls. "He decided that he wanted an orchestra like this, and he wanted me in it. So I formed La Charanga Habanera to play only in the summer in Monte Carlo. For four years, we were doing that, playing only traditional Cuban music, and then in '92 we began to play contemporary music and we became an official orchestra [that is, recognized by the government] and began to play in Cuba."

In any other country, that breadth of experience—classical training, several years playing an older pop style, then transformation into an innovative contemporary group—would be considered highly unusual. In Cuba, where young musicians remain very much aware of older styles, it is fairly common. "I think it is a cyclic phenomenon," Tellería says. "Recently, people have been listening to a lot of salsa, to a lot of pop music, Cuban pop and rock. So people have returned to the tradition, first of all to revive those genres, because they were getting bored with always hearing the same things. So they had to go out and find their own music, the traditional culture, and reclaim it with a more modern sound. I think it was a good thing to do, because there is a lot of music that was forgotten and that is very good music. So almost all the groups of the new generation are doing this."

Gema 4, for example, was formed by four women who had been singing classical choral music, and then decided to explore what could be done as an a cappella quartet within the Cuban tradition. "In Cuba we have a lot of quartets, but always accompanied either by a small group, by a guitar, or by a piano," Tellería explains. "But we started a cappella, really as a practical decision, because at that moment we didn't know how to put together an orchestra, with musicians. So we decided to try to sing without accompaniment, and we have stayed that way.

"We began to work on the music we call *filin* [from the English 'feeling'], which was a Cuban variant of bolero that was developed in the fifties, with a foundation in jazz. In the epoch of the thirties, forties, fifties, Cuba was eager to hear quartets, but afterward they disappeared. I think it was a question of fashion—the soloists came in, and the orchestras—but there were still plenty of people who liked the style and they received us very well. Not only in Cuba, all over the world. Really, we have made our career more in Europe than in Cuba, because at the beginning we signed with a European company, and the promotion really came to Cuba as a boomerang."

In the 1990s, Gema 4 recorded with Ibrahim Ferrer on a solo album Ry Cooder produced to follow *Buena Vista Social Club*, and Tellería was hoping to work more in the United States and with American musicians. "Basically, we have the same musical roots," she explains. "For many years it was very natural for Cuban musicians to play in the United States and, vice versa, Americans in Cuba. That is a period we have lost, and it would be very interesting to reclaim it. And I think all the musicians in the world are interested in the North American market, because it is very prolific. It is where you can really prove yourself as a talent, because there are so many people who are practically doing the same thing you are, so it gives you the chance to see whether what you are doing is really valuable or not."

Like many Cuban musicians, Tellería and Calzado have been impressed and inspired by the success of the Buena Vista project. Charanga Habanera has always maintained its repertoire of classic charanga, and Calzado assumes that foreigners will find that music more familiar than its more modern club style. Still, he has his eye on the innovations of hip-hop, and stresses that his group is not a nostalgia act. "It is not just the music," he says. "The orchestra has a very special style when it comes to dressing, which broke with all the parameters which the salseros had established of suits, bow-ties. We dress more disorderly, which is completely intentional, breaking with the style of the salseros. And on stage we have a very strong show, in that the singers will suddenly be playing percussion, the percussionists dance, it's a very violent show, with the fourteen players all dancing, no one escapes from it."

And he adds that, much as he loves the older styles, Cuba is not a country where you can stand still: "The traditional music is lovely, it has a lot of feeling, a lot of heart, but naturally the compositions and arrangements from the old days have evolved with the technique that Cuban musicians enjoy today. They have elaborated on that work, and the music has taken a new road, keeping in mind the idiosyncrasies of the country, which have varied—they are not the idiosyncrasies of the fifties, forties, sixties, but idiosyncrasies of this time. We have other customs, other concepts, and that has affected the contemporary music very much. It is stronger, more aggressive, hotter. And you have to understand that Cubans are a very dancing people—so we have to keep changing our music in response to the popular movement of every person living in this country."

3

LATIN AMERICA

Considering how much music has come into the United States from the Caribbean, it seems odd how little has come from the rest of Central and South America. With the obvious exception of Mexico, most of the countries of Latin America have sent few musicians north, and even the Mexicans have tended to work only within immigrant communities. Brazil has certainly made an impression over the years, and since the 1960s there have been Andean groups from Peru and Bolivia playing for Anglo audiences, if only on sidewalks and in subway stations, but the vast range of Latin American music has remained surprisingly absent from the world music scene.

There have been a handful of exceptions: Mercedes Sosa has filled large halls with mixed audiences of Argentines and Anglos, and tango has cropped up as a popular style for dancers—though rarely with live music. Peru's Susana Baca has also reached an audience through her association with David Byrne, but as the "voice of Black Peru," she has tended to appeal to fans of Brazilian and Cuban styles, rather than as part of any broader interest in South American music.

As a result, this chapter is much smaller than I would like. I would have loved to include *cumbia, vallenato, gaita, mariachi, huayno,* and all sorts of folkloric styles that I have heard only on records. The musics of Central and South America are at least as varied as the populations that have produced them. There were hundreds of different Native American cultures, and each has interacted with a different mix of newcomers over the last five centuries. Where broad areas of Bolivia, Guatemala, and Peru remained almost purely indigenous, Brazil and the countries around the Caribbean basin received a huge population of Africans, while Argentina and Chile welcomed waves of European settlers, not only from Spain but from the British Isles, Germany, and Italy.

One would have expected that the musics of these neighboring cultures would have been among the first imports to come to the United States with the world boom, but for one reason or another, that was not what happened. Outside of immigrant communities, the Latin American musicians who have tended to be most visible up north are rock acts—Aterciopelados, Juanes, Los Jaguares—that fall outside the scope of this book, since they work on the rock scene and have attracted few "world" listeners.

In part, this is due to cultural prejudices. The great wave of Spanish-speaking immigrants in recent years has made a lot of Anglos nervous, and also led to stereotypes—few people would put it so bluntly, but I can imagine them thinking, "What's romantic about listening to the music of dishwashers and gardeners?" In some cases, there are also problems with the music itself: *norteño*, *cumbia*, *gaita*, and *vallenato* all are driven by accordions, and to many Americans accordions remain painfully reminiscent of Lawrence Welk.

Another factor is that the world boom has to a great degree been driven by European producers. The Europeans have been far more active in traveling, recording, and importing music, and for them the Americas are a long way away, while Africa and Western Asia are far more accessible—historically, if not in the age of modern transportation. And there may be prejudices at work there as well: Europe has been importing so much pop music from America, for so many years, that it is hardly surprising if they now tend to look elsewhere for new sounds.

In any case, and for whatever reasons, Latin American music has never had an impact commensurate with its variety and value. Brazil is the one great exception, and in a sense it proves the rule, since Brazilian songwriters like Gilberto Gil and Caetano Veloso are as much heirs to the bossa nova boom of the 1960s as part of the new world scene.

All of which said, a number of fine Latin American performers have entered the world mix. As with the Africans, the Latin Americans here include both pop and folkloric performers, though in this chapter the big stars certainly dominate. This is partly due to the Latin American immigrant communities, which have continued to provide a core audience for most of these artists in the United States, but it also has something to do with the music. Most of the major Latin American pop styles blend African and European flavors, which makes them sound at least somewhat familiar, so that tango and bossa nova could mix comfortably with jazz and other Afro-American music. And, if immigration patterns mean anything at all, there will be a lot more of this music heard in the United States very soon.

Argentina

Mercedes Sosa

The word *legend* gets thrown around a lot, but in Mercedes Sosa's case it is deserved. She is a superb singer, at home in styles ranging from traditional Andean genres to European art music, but her reputation rests on more than her musical gifts. She was a living symbol of resistance during the decades of dictatorship in her native Argentina and its neighboring countries, and one of the founding artists of the *nueva canción* (new song) movement. That movement's finest songwriters, from Chile's Violeta Parra to Cuba's Silvio Rodríguez, owe much of their international reputation to Sosa's stirring recordings of their songs. A small, stout woman with markedly Indian features, she commands such respect that during one concert Joan Baez knelt and kissed her feet, and she has frequently been called the Voice of Latin America.

Sosa finds such encomiums a bit ridiculous. "It's impossible to be the voice of a continent," she says firmly.* "Just think about it: from Argentina to Venezuela is six hours by plane. It is an easy thing for reporters to say, but I know perfectly well it is not reality. I have a great deal of feeling for my continent, great respect and great sadness that some things still have not improved. I have sung for Nicaragua, for El Salvador; I sing in Costa Rica for the students and for the people, and they know that I am an artist who feels for every place in Latin America. But to be the representative of the continent is too difficult."

It is also too confining for an artist whose recordings range from her familiar acoustic-guitar-based folk style to encompass everything from tangos to Greek music, French cabaret, an homage to Enrico Caruso in Italian, and a Spanish translation of Sting's "Fragile." "I think people are the same everywhere," she explains. "They eat

---

* This interview was conducted in Spanish.

different foods, they have different climates, but they suffer and laugh just the same. That is a tremendous thing. So I feel love for human beings—not only those in Latin America."

Sosa's internationalism was to some extent forced upon her. In the late 1970s she was banned from performing in her home country, and for several years she lived in artistic exile. She returned in 1982, shortly before the fall of the Argentine dictatorship, received a hero's welcome, and today is regarded as a sort of living national treasure. Though this degree of respect clearly pleases her, she refuses to exaggerate its importance. "When I have a concert, my face shows up a lot in the press," she says. "The rest of the time I stay in my house and have a good time with my friends or I go see my mother in Tucumán. I can enjoy both things, and I am very protected by the journalists and by the people. I get a lot of prizes. So it's all good for me now in my country."

The reference to Tucumán is a reminder that, much as she has traveled, Sosa retains a strong sense of her roots. Stories about her often give undo weight to this, painting her as a simple Indian girl from the rural north and ignoring the breadth of her interests, but in a country that is so dominated by its capital, her northern identification continues to be very important to her. For example, while she has occasionally recorded tangos, she says that she does not expect to do so again. "The tango belongs to Buenos Aires," she says. "Though all the country has absorbed it and loves it—sometimes I think they love it more in the interior than in Buenos Aires—and I sang it because I want to include all the music of my country. But it was hard for me to pronounce the R of the tango singers, because for a northerner it is almost like saying the R of the French; it is terribly difficult for us. So I made this my goal, as another test for myself."

The idea that she must keep constantly pushing herself is a recurrent theme in Sosa's conversation: "I like to try to do different things, to test myself as an artist," she says. "And sometimes it is very hard work. For example, I recorded 'Pavanne for a Dead Child,' by Ravel, and that was not easy for me; it took a lot of study."

Listening to some of the albums recorded since her return, such as 1995's *Gestos de Amor*, one might be tempted to think that its lush, pop flavor reflects not only the wish to try new styles, but also the more secure and relaxed situation in which Sosa finds herself today. However, she adamantly denies that she has mellowed, or shifted her essential focus. "That is just one record," she says. "And in concert, you are not going to hear these things. I will only be singing two songs from my new album, and the rest will be 'Gracias a la Vida'; 'Todo Cambia'; two songs by Atahualpa Yupanqui [the father of Argentine nueva canción]; a very wide mix."

Indeed, Sosa says that she has mixed feelings about her newer material. She is pleased to be working with a wide range of musicians and continuing to expand her repertoire, but feels that the lyrics sometimes fall short. Of the songs on *Gestos*, for example, she says, "The words are not so fully developed. But I am a singer and I must sing songs, and these were what there was. There will be others that will be better, with more literary force, a stronger poetic conception."

She adds that it is not just a matter of needing new material. She feels that her popularity brings with it an obligation to showcase the work of less familiar musicians and writers. "We artists, we frequently have the duty, when composers are good, to give them a hand to get into certain venues," she says. In the case of the Ravel performance, for example, a friend wanted to present the piece and needed her help to get backing and attract an audience. "I don't do these things for money," she says, "because I make nothing, not even five centavos. But I do it as part of my trajectory as an artist."

Likewise, Sosa maintains her commitment to broader social issues, and dismisses any suggestion that her recent musical experiments might reflect a shift away from the fierce political material for which she is best known. "No, no, no, no," she says, clearly upset at the idea. "I remember the pain of my people, and I don't in any way want you to think I have changed my way of thinking. Not at all. I think the same about human rights, about the social injustice which some human beings face simply because they were born in marginal areas. I have the same feeling for world peace, and the same suspicions as to why there is no peace. As the songs says, 'I do not change my love, no matter how far away I find myself.'"

Sandra Luna

Say the word *tango*, and people inevitably picture dancers, gliding graceful and dangerous as bullfighters across a polished wooden floor. The music is recalled only as accompaniment, the accordionlike tones of the *bandoneón* weaving the rhythm to which the dancers move. So it is a bit surprising to hear Sandra Luna, one of the most respected modern tango singers, say that she has never sung for dancing: "I never sang in *milongas* [tango dances] except maybe for a festival or to help raise money for a school. Aesthetically, that is not what I do, because the people go to milongas to dance, not to listen. I'm a woman who has been very lucky, and God has protected me—I am a strong believer in God, and that he has helped me to get ahead and keep my beliefs—so I have always sung in the *tanguerías*, places where people come to listen to tango. Not to dance, just to listen."*

If such comments suggest a delicate, self-absorbed artist, Luna's performances instantly dispel any such notion. The title song of her first international release, "Tango Varón" (Masculine Tango), is fearsomely sung, and in performance she acts out every word, striding the stage and locking the audience in a gaze of fierce intensity.

"I studied theater for a long time," Luna says. "And I also studied opera, because along with being a singer of the *pueblo* [the people, or the town], I tried to study and prepare myself like any lyric singer. So now the critics say I have the deep essence of tango, but I have my own style. What matters most to me is the interpretation: when I sing a song I have to find a way with my gestures, with pianissimo, with fortissimo, so that you will understand what the poet who wrote it was trying to say. For me, a song must have meaning, and tell a story that is real."

According to Luna, this focus on story and meaning has been at the core of tango since the first singers appeared. Indeed, she explains that before the tangos were sung, they existed as a sort of popular chant: "It was like a football cheer, rhythmic, like, '*Sandra Luna / Viene caminando / Viene caminando / Viene por acá.*'" Her phrasing has

---

* This interview was conducted in Spanish.

the steady beat of a jump-rope rhyme: "Sandra Luna / She comes walking / She comes walking / She comes here."

"They were just short verses," she continues. "The first tangos said things like, '*El presidente / Augmentó la carne / No le da de comer a los pobres / Ta-ra-ra-ra-ra.*' [The president / Raised the price of meat / The poor cannot have it to eat. . . .] It was always a music of protest, with words that talked about what was going on. Then Carlos Gardel and other authors and composers gave it another form, and the *tango canción* [tango song] was born, which is not the *tango arabalero* [street or barrio tango], but a more elaborate style, with structure and poetry, and music suited to that poetry."

Modern listeners may think of tango as elegant, but in its early days it was very much the sound of the lower classes of Buenos Aires, and of the bars and whorehouses that made the city's port a legend throughout the world. As with flamenco, fado, or jazz, the music's reputation changed over the years, first with the international success of the singing idol Gardel, and later through the work of composers and musicians like Astor Piazzolla. Still, when Luna first fell in love with tango, she recalls that her parents were anything but happy.

"My family is Spanish," she says. "Some Gallegos and others from Andalucía—my real name is Montoya, very Gypsy—and they were quite proper and respectable. So we did not often hear tango in my house. But my mother had a cousin who was more Bohemian, and he liked to sing tangos and go out to the neighborhood clubs. He would wake me up on Sundays by singing tangos through the window. He wasn't a singer, he was just a neighborhood guy, but he was a very important person to me, and through him I came to love the music he loved.

"But really, I think that this was always part of me. I was born with the tango, like with a hand or a foot. A friend of mine who is a poet, he says that when I was born God was dividing people up into different careers and he said to me, 'You will sing tango.' And really I don't have another explanation."

Luna certainly found her calling very young. Born in 1966, she was performing in public by the time she was seven years old: "At midday, or in the afternoon, when I would go out someplace to eat with my parents, I would ask if I could sing. Because I have a spirit—I felt like

I was a grown-up, I didn't feel like a child. So I would ask, 'Señor, can I sing?'

"They would say, 'Yes, okay. So are you going to sing a children's song?'

"'No, no. Tango.'

"'Tango?!'

"Not only was I very young, I was very small, smaller than most children. I was seven, but I looked five. So they thought it was very charming, and they would give me the microphone and say, 'Okay, sing.' And I would sing, but I sang like a grown person, not like a child. And what's more, I sang tangos with a base and a structure that was complete; I understood what the songs were about."

Soon Luna developed a local reputation: "The other singers heard me and they adopted me and encouraged me, because they knew that my parents didn't want me to sing. In those days, to be a woman and sing tangos was terrible, because it was a completely masculine ambiance—today it is more equal, but at that time it was still very much frowned upon—so my parents resisted. But people kept applying pressure; they would come to my house and say, 'Tonight she has to come out and sing in such-and-such a place.'

"'No, no, she has school in the morning.'

"'No, she has to go.'

"So finally these people convinced my parents that they couldn't stop this thing that had been in me since birth. It was like a duty that I had to fulfill. So they scolded me for a while, and then they said, 'Oh, all right.' But they made a pact with me; they said, 'You can sing, but you have to do well in school.'"

As she remembers those years, Luna's voice fills with an odd mix of pride and tenderness: "I worked very hard, because I knew that this was what I wanted to do, so I did everything possible to make it happen. I slept very little, because I had school, and also I went to the conservatory, I studied guitar and piano and singing. So I was working all the time. I didn't play like a child—for me, play was to go and sing somewhere. I tried to do everything well so that they would let me go and sing. And I was very serious about it. People would say, 'If you want to hire her, you have to talk with her father,' and I would say

Sandra Luna. Photograph by Leendert Mulder.

for them to talk to me directly. Or I would say, 'It's no problem, my father will bring me'—so then my father was committed.

"He would accompany me, because my mother couldn't go out to nightclubs; that wasn't good. And I would see everything that was going on, the Bohemian atmosphere, the people drinking, and my father would point out all the things I shouldn't do. He would say, 'If you want to keep your voice, if you want to be a great artist, if you want to be a fine singer, you mustn't drink alcohol or take drugs.' Ever since I was very little, I knew about alcohol and drugs, and I saw the damage they did to people, so I never took or tried drugs, because of the scare it gave me."

Soon Luna was appearing on the radio and with the orchestras of famous bandleaders like Héctor Varela and Mariano Mores. With Mores, she toured all over Argentina, and on to Chile, Uruguay and Brazil. At eighteen, she traveled with her own group to Japan, and in the 1990s she came to the United States, and then lived for eight years in Spain. She was relatively successful—in Tokyo, she says that she filled a 3,500 seat theater every night for a week—but made few recordings, and she describes her career as a constant battle. "There are very few singers who can make a career in tango," she explains. "Because a people's music does not have any power. It is the same story with blues, or even jazz. There is no production, no one who promotes you. You sing one night, and maybe you are lucky enough to be seen by somebody who hires you for something better, and after that you see somebody else who hires you, but there are no real producers.

"In Argentina, they do not appreciate what they have. We talk about the 'Gardel effect,' because he was not so successful here; he had to go to Paris and make films in the United States, and then he came back famous. Argentina is a country of immigrants, and they are always looking for the approval of their parents, the Europeans, as if they were the adults and we were little children. So if they don't approve of you abroad, it is very difficult to get recognized here. To succeed, you have to be very hardheaded and have very firm ideas about what you are doing."

Luna adds that tango has also suffered from political repression. "In its lyrics, it always talks about what is happening, the events of life. And governments are never happy with this kind of music. So on the one hand they hold 'festivals of tango'—in quotation marks—but on the other they do nothing to support this music, because it would be a way of working against themselves. For example, in the 1980s we had a military dictatorship in Argentina, and there was a list of tangos that one couldn't sing, that were banned. So the artists, we have to do everything *al pulmón*—by force—we put our whole lives into it. It is like a peaceful war.

"I am proud of this, but it is not easy. Like I remember when I was fourteen or fifteen years old, companies like Odeon contacted me, and they offered me a chance to record, but the contracts they proposed were terrible: they wanted to change my way of singing, choose the songs, you couldn't sing that people were poor; you had to just sing about love—things like that were in the clauses of the contracts. They try to change you into another person, in order to make you popular and famous. For me, as for most of us who sing tango, we do this because we love what we are doing, so we are not going to accept that, even if it means that we remain less popular. But it is not easy."

Despite such tribulations, Luna sounds relatively happy with the way her life has gone. She performs every Thursday at a well-known club in Buenos Aires, appears in provincial theaters on the weekends, and with *Tango Varón* has begun to reach a broader international audience. She has also developed a distinctive musical approach, forming a quartet anchored by her cellist husband, Daniel Pucci, along with piano, bandoneón, and guitar. She adds, a bit wistfully, that the quartet has changed a good deal over the years: "With musicians, it is like a love affair: you think you have found the great love of your life, and then you find it was not the love you believed it to be. But I always have a quartet."

And she continues to learn and evolve. "I am always trying to add more," she says. "There are songs on *Tango Varón* about which many people say, 'That's not tango.' And it's not the tango of the thirties. But tango keeps developing. To me, tango has the same value as any of the world's great music, and I always wanted it to be treated with honor, as something that is important for the soul, like a vitamin. I want it to have all the resources possible, in music, in presentation, in interpretation, so that the person who is seated there can understand and can come to love this music. Because the music is saying something, is giving something, and it nourishes the spirit."

Peru

Susana Baca

In 1995, David Byrne's Luaka Bop record label issued an album called *The Soul of Black Peru*, which introduced American listeners to the wave of musicians leading a revival of Afro-Peruvian culture. This has been largely a grassroots, folkloric movement, and among its leaders is the singer who opened Byrne's record, Susana Baca. Baca's warm, lilting voice, backed by an acoustic guitar and percussion ensemble, provided a perfect introduction to the style, and she followed with solo albums and several American tours, becoming the voice of an Afro-Peruvian population that had been all but ignored for centuries.

Baca says that she started singing as a child: "Music always had a very great attraction for me. I would go to the park as a little girl and dance to the bands. The music was in my home, in my father who played guitar, all of that. Then I started to think of singing professionally after working a little as a teacher. I felt an urgent need to sing, and so I dedicated myself to singing and to remembering the songs of my grandparents."*

Like most of her fellow artists in the Afro-Peruvian revival, Baca is trying both to preserve the tradition and to carry it forward. As she explains, "If we take a song like 'Zamba Malató' [an upbeat dance on her first album, *Susana Baca*], it's a traditional song that has been sung for generations and generations, but now we play it in a different way. We have taken what we know and put it together with contemporary trends."

Told that most Americans know Peruvian music only as Andean folklore, and are not even aware that the country has a black population, Baca laughs. "It is the same in Europe," she says. "When they announced my presentation, 'Susana Baca: Music of Peru,' and when I went out on stage and people saw that I was black and that the musicians I play with are black, after the concerts there were always

---

* This interview was conducted in Spanish.

Susana Baca. Photograph © Jack Vartoogian/FrontRowPhotos.

questions. People were curious about where we came from, how, what is happening with blacks in Peru, and we always ended up giving a lecture about all of that."

As in the rest of the Americas, Peru's black population arrived as slaves. "Their music was the only way for them to keep their culture alive," Baca says. "Denaturalized, taken from their home, from their culture, they kept it through music, through song, through the rhythms and the few instruments that they managed to reproduce in this new place.

"The blacks were brought to Peru to work in the mines, but they couldn't endure the height, the thin air, so they had to be brought down to the coast to work in the plantations of sugar cane and cotton. So, because of this, there were black centers of population all along the coast. But now they have been disappearing, as a color. The culture persists, but the color has disappeared because people mix a lot—which is a very good thing."

The music blended along with the people. "Now we have a *mestizo* music," Baca says. "There are songs where the beat is African, the melody is Andean, and the words are Spanish. These three cultures come together in present-day Peruvian music. It is a sweet music, very melodious. The softness comes from the Andean influence, but you can still sense the Afro-Peruvian rhythms. Above all, in the *landó*, a slow dance. It is not possible to be completely sure, but it seems that even the word *landó* comes from *lundu*, which is an Angolan dance."

In the late 1960s, with the rise of international black pride movements, Afro-Peruvians joined in rediscovering and repopularizing their disappearing traditions. Some developed styles that fused the local music with other Afro-Latin forms, creating a modern dance pop, while others, like Baca, stayed closer to the old styles. "I think that this music has a particular accent, which is the way I try to sing it," she says. "Now that it has become a bit fashionable, there is a motivation to sing this music, and it is being commercialized. So people try to do this music, and sometimes it doesn't come out so well. My way of singing it is what I have, and of course I recognize that there are other artists in Peru who sing and perform this music in a very traditional form, and this is very beautiful."

She adds that although their work is now known throughout Peru, it remains largely a minority taste: "It is thought of as folk music. It is not the music that people go out everywhere and dance to. It is played at home, in *penas* [the Latin equivalent of folk clubs], and there are some musicians who sing it in concerts. There is an interest among the public to hear this music, but the record companies still have not taken much notice."

Because of this ambivalent reception, Baca is doubly pleased by the warmth with which she has been received in Europe and North America. "People are very interested, and they have many questions, and this is very gratifying, because in our country there has not been enough attention given to the manifestations of Afro-Peruvian culture. It makes me very happy, because I remember the old singers and composers, some of whom are dead, who were only recognized by very few people."

Now Baca finds herself acting as an international ambassador for Afro-Peruvian culture, and she is doing her best to rise to the task. "It is very difficult," she says. "On the one hand, it is a great weight, a great responsibility. I have to remember everything I have read and sought out and investigated, to be able to tell people. And also, I would be so glad to be able to record the older artists on video, so they could be seen in their homes, playing, making music. But on the other hand, I feel very chosen, and very proud."

Brazil

Gilberto Gil

As the continent's only Portuguese-speaking country, Brazil has always stood apart from the rest of Latin America, but that hardly begins to explain the country's musical impact. Since the days of *choro*, the Brazilian equivalent of ragtime or Cuban *danzón*, Brazil has produced uniquely intricate, delicate music that is driven by complex polyrhythms but is most striking for its lilting sweetness, along with a self-conscious intellectualism that is unmatched by that of any other major pop scene. Brazilian artists have broken out to the North American market at least twice, first in the 1940s with Carmen Miranda and again in the 1960s when jazz musicians discovered the bossa nova. As with Cuban music, though, the Brazilian pop world has continued to evolve in directions that the outside world has heard only in random snippets, and often many years after the styles appeared.

These days, the best-known Brazilian musicians are the singer-poets Gilberto Gil and Caetano Veloso, who in the late 1960s helped spearhead the movement known as *tropicalia*, a subgenre of MPB, or *música popular brasileira* [Brazilian popular music]. While Veloso has become ubiquitous on the international scene, appearing in movies and writing articles for the *New York Times*, Gil has chosen to devote more of his attention to the situation at home, serving in both local and national government posts, as well as maintaining his musical career.

The *tropicalistas* were part of a worldwide explosion of youth counterculture, exemplified by English rock bands like the Beatles and Rolling Stones and the American folk-poetic fusions of Bob Dylan. However, while young musicians in other countries tended to imitate these British and American models, tropicalia was inherently and persistently Brazilian.

"That's been our destiny since the very beginning," Gil says. "When the Portuguese came [to Brazil], the first thing that the Indians did was to eat a bishop. And so it became congenial for Brazilian culture: We eat things that come from outside, we process, we digest it. We really digest it thoroughly, so it goes in the blood and it nourishes a body, an organism by itself that goes its own way, with its own shape, its own character."

Gil has been one of the most voracious of the tropicalistas. His music starts with the blend of African and European elements that are at the heart of Brazilian traditional music, and adds influences from around the world. "That was the whole idea," he says. "To be able to pay attention to whatever was coming from outside, but at the same time giving a lot of attention to what had been our tradition, our own ingredients. From the first tropicalista album we had already this kind of balance between what is autochthonous and what is from outside."

That being the case, Gil is one of many Brazilian artists who consider the world music boom very old news. Already in the 1920s, the poet Oswald de Andrade was advocating "cultural cannibalism," with Gil's analogy about the Indians and the bishop as his defining metaphor. By a fortunate coincidence, the bishop's name was Sardinha, Portuguese for "sardine," and Andrade wrote that "Brazil began the day the Indians ate Bishop Sardine."

"Since the very beginning we are a mixed society," Gil says. "And differently from the United States, which historically should have been living the same kind of situation. But the States became hegemonic; they became an empire, so they forgot the other side of the thing, to let things from outside come in. They'd rather go places and impose things. Brazil, for many reasons, has never become a strong, very powerful nation. We've never been warriors, and we've never been leading [in] economic profits, and what's left for us is to take things that come from outside, so this became a profit here."

That Gil should analyze his music in geopolitical terms is hardly surprising. His English, which is clear and precise, was learned while in exile in Britain. The military dictatorship that ruled Brazil in the late 1960s was scared by tropicalia, so both Gil and his friend Veloso were first jailed, and then deported to Europe. Typically, Gil turned the exile to his advantage, jamming with English bands like Pink Floyd and reshaping his musical image.

"I was excited about becoming a bandleader, in the very pop sense of the term," he says. "Before, I was just a songwriter and a singer, mostly performing solo. Sometimes having a band, but a band that would be like an orchestra, you know—behind me, but not really driven by a bandleader. I became interested in this thing of driving a band, like the Rolling Stones, Beatles, the Moody Blues, or Canned Heat. This wasn't happening before in Brazil. This is modern, this is pop."

Returning home in 1972, Gil put together his first real band, but in truth it was less a departure than simply one more step in a gradual evolution. Gil was born in the northern interior, and his earliest music was the style known as *forró*: "At the age of five, six, I used to listen to Luís Gonzaga, who was processing folk, natural, peasant music from the north into pop music," he recalls. "This music is rhythmically African, but with a lot of Iberian elements, like accordion playing and folk elements from Portugal."

Gil began playing accordion and singing in Gonzaga's style, and then at seventeen heard João Gilberto on the radio, bought a guitar, and turned to bossa nova. That in turn led him to jazz and the contemporary singer-songwriter styles of France and Italy. With tropicalia, he expanded further, writing songs with titles like "Chuck Berry Fields Forever," and in the 1970s he discovered reggae, going on tour with Jimmy Cliff and recording with the Wailers.

Gil says that the decisive event in his later life came in 1977, when he was invited to play at a pan-African festival in Nigeria. There he met Fela Kuti and King Sunny Ade, as well as Stevie Wonder, and rediscovered the power of his own African roots. When he got home, he joined a Carnaval samba group and submerged himself in Afro-Brazilian traditions. "That was a turning point," he says. "As a musician, definitely, the rhythms and the highlife music and juju music, all the blending processes that were happening. Caribbean music was becoming very influential in Africa, and I could see some processes concerning the black diaspora. So it was a big impact on my music, and also in my personal, general, spiritual situation.

"I was not that much engaged in performing that consciousness before. Sure, I had a little consciousness about that, but I was not a militant. Now I am. When I came back, I recorded an album that was specifically about that, *Refavela*, and I started to follow the political movements here, the black movements, and I've been ever since."

In the late 1980s, Gil decided that he had responsibilities that could not be fulfilled just by playing music. He involved himself in cultural affairs, then served for several years on Salvador's city council, and later was appointed as Brazil's minister of culture. In between, he occasionally has found time to write new songs, record albums, and go on tour, but he refuses to say what he will be doing in the future.

"Changing is the only way of living," he points out. "Change is the only constant in nature, and paradoxically, it is the only established, remaining, staying thing. And I'm a natural-law-obeying soul."

Caetano Veloso

In the last decade or so, Caetano Veloso has become a one-name star—Caetano, alongside Dylan, Elvis, and Madonna—and yet, he is quite unlike other pop musicians. Not even Dylan has managed to be

Caetano Veloso. Photograph © Jack Vartoogian/FrontRowPhotos.

so internationally accepted as a poet and intellectual, someone who is respected as a writer, commentator, and cultural critic, as comfortable talking about films or literature as about music. When he records albums in Spanish or English, they seem less like attempts to broaden his audience than like personal explorations, on a par with his album-length homage to Federico Fellini and Giulietta Masina. When I spoke with him in 1997, he was on his first American tour, and typically, rather than providing a "greatest hits" show, he was perplexing halls full of longtime Brazilian fans with a selection of songs drawn almost entirely from a recent Spanish-language release, *Fina Estampa*.

On the telephone, Veloso sounds much as he does on record: relaxed and intelligent, but making no overt attempt to please. Though he is unfailingly polite, he has no time for foolishness: handed a sycophantic conversation starter like, "How have you managed to remain at the forefront of Brazilian music for thirty years, and always kept developing and appealing to a young pop audience?" he simply says "I don't know" and waits for another question.

Veloso grew up in a small town in the northern province of Bahia, singing samba and bossa nova and writing songs and poetry. In his teens, he moved to Bahia's bustling port city of Salvador, the center of black Brazilian culture and home to João Gilberto, the bossa nova singer and guitarist who is Veloso's greatest musical hero. In 1965 Veloso followed his sister, the singer Maria Bethania, to Rio de Janeiro, and with a group of transplanted Bahians that included Gal Costa and Gilberto Gil they became the pioneers of tropicalismo. Not that Veloso can provide a clear explanation of what *tropicalismo* means: "It is very difficult, because nothing exactly does it. Everything could do it, but never exactly."

Pressed to expand a little on that comment, he says the word was simply a name that the press and public gave to what they were doing: "This movement had to do with a pop view of things, in the sense of Pop art, but attached to music. It had to do with the neo-rock 'n' roll that the British presented then, which made American rubbish sound like precious things. Rock 'n' roll in the fifties was considered rubbish, and the English in the sixties were so inventive that they brought some sort of respectability to the tradition.

"Tropicalismo in Brazil was somehow parallel to this. What we did was we included neo-rock 'n' roll from England in our interests, but not only that, also Brazilian rubbish—sentimental, commercial songs and bad taste, Brazilian and non-Brazilian, Latin and South American styles like tangos and boleros and things from Cuba."

Tropicalismo became the voice of the emerging Brazilian counterculture, young artists, hippies, and rock 'n' roll fans. While few of the songs were overtly political, the movement's outlook was clearly in opposition to mainstream bourgeois culture and the social order being imposed by Brazil's military rulers, so like Gil, Veloso was thrown in jail and later sent into exile.

"Tropicalismo created a scandal," Veloso recalls. "Because it sounded commercial, but it was too pretentious poetically, but at the same time it was against protest songs because it was not like a linear, protest song. It was anarchical and violent in the lyrics, and it could use electric guitars and quote the Beatles or Jimi Hendrix, and at the same time part of an Argentinean tango and an old sentimental Brazilian song. It put together styles that were strangers to each other to create a comment on the cultural panorama and try to turn the Brazilian soul inside out."

Like Gil, Veloso traces the philosophy of tropicalismo to Oswaldo de Andrade's "Cannibalist Manifesto." He fell in love with the idea that Brazilian culture is a digested mass of influences from abroad, and also with Andrade's surrealist blend of serious artistic intent and anarchic humor. "There is a poem by a modernist Brazilian poet," he says. "It's very short. The title is 'Amor,' and the poem is 'Humor.' It's just that [one word]. So amor/humor, love/humor. That was the approach that we had to those sentimental, naive, commercial songs."

Veloso's music has always provided an odd mix of innovation and nostalgia, and he stresses the genuine affection he and Gil had for earlier Brazilian styles. They admired the Beatles and Rolling Stones, but remained very much "two sons of bossa nova." Indeed, though his music sounded revolutionary to Brazilian ears, to a North American listener much of it seems well within the gently melodic Brazilian mainstream.

Veloso laughs at this observation, but agrees: "It's sweet and hazy, the sound of the Portuguese in Brazil, and the melodic tradition also sounds caressing. So when we are saying horrible things, if you don't understand us, you don't think horrible things are being said. In the sixties, we did some aggressive sounds, but we were never really able to sing aggressively. Gil is better than me, but even he is not very good at it. Even the rock 'n' roll groups. And I'll tell you I'm proud of that, because French singers, Italian, Spanish, who modernize their music by trying to sing like white English who imitate black Americans—they sound horrible to me. I hate that, and I'm very proud that Brazilians never do it."

Though his voice exemplifies the lilting beauty of the Brazilian tradition, Veloso has never been simply a sweet bossa nova singer. His work has been consistently daring, both lyrically and melodically. He has sung alone with his acoustic guitar, with rock bands, with street percussion groups, and with full orchestras. He has recorded in English both during his years in exile and more recently, and *Fina Estampa* concentrated on Spanish-language pop songs remembered from his youth, blended with everything from Carmen Miranda to classic tropicalismo, as well as an angry song about Haiti in what can only be called Brazilian rap. He says the Spanish project was something he had contemplated for years, in part from a desire to reach a larger audience in the Spanish-speaking world, but primarily to acknowledge a part of his own musical education.

"In Brazil, there is a tradition of recording sometimes the same material that we record in Portuguese in Spanish, to try something in the Spanish market. Robert Carlos has done that for years, he sings everything in Portuguese and then immediately he sings everything in Spanish on top of it to release in Mexico, Argentina, Peru, Chile, etcetera. Even Maria Bethania and Chico Buarque and Djavan, many artists have done that, because it's a way to try and be present in the rest of Latin America. Because Brazil, although it occupies most of the territory of South America and it's continental in its bigness, it is kind of apart from the whole of the Americas. We feel like an island, like a giant island here.

"But I didn't want to record my songs translated into Spanish for two reasons: First, I don't think they sound necessarily interesting that way, and also people in the Spanish-speaking countries who are interested in my music, they like it sung in Portuguese. They find that the charm of it comes from the Portuguese language. They are a small minority, but they exist and I prefer to deepen my dialog with them and enlarge a little bit the number of these people, then try to reach a larger audience in a more superficial way.

"So instead I said, 'Well, I'll do something else: I'll record the deepest-felt Spanish American songs that I have in my personal history.' Because when I was a very young boy I heard lots of Spanish American songs, because that was a normal thing for my generation in Brazil. So these songs belong to our formation, they belong to me. And I wanted to record them as mine, as something that made part of my life and of my culture."

Veloso expected *Fina Estampa* to do better than his previous work in Spanish-speaking countries, but was bemused when it also became the biggest-selling album he had ever had in Brazil. He is quick to point out, though, that none of his albums has been outstanding in terms of sales. His influence, like Dylan's, is far out of proportion to his chart success, and he suspects that the album's surprising popularity was due to the fact that the old Spanish songs were less weird and threatening than much of his original work—which, he admits, adds yet another layer of irony.

"There's a hint of humor to the whole thing, although it's deeply felt," he says. "Because it's the traditional Spanish American material filtered through bossa nova and tropicalismo. So you have the impressionistic harmonies and the not-macho approach to the songs that's entirely bossa nova, and you have a hint of the tropicalist humor. Not too much, because in the amor/humor equation amor is stronger—it has to be stronger, and the kind of laugh that you give at yourself is a very special kind."

In any case, it was just one project, and did not herald any further explorations of the Spanish repertoire. "Always, the impulse is to find what is regenerating and revitalizing to the creation and production of popular music in Brazil," Veloso says. "And to keep on being demanding, because popular music in Brazil has always showed such strength. It has produced such a genius as João Gilberto and such a great composer as Antonio Carlos Jobim. And if it did so, we cannot be satisfied with less. We must be risky. We have to be courageous and even heroic, because popular music in Brazil demands it. That's the impulse we had from the beginning that led us to tropicalismo, and that keeps leading us now."

Olodum

Rio de Janeiro is Brazil's biggest city and foremost cultural center, but time and again Bahia has proved to be the country's musical heartland. To a great degree, this is because of the northern state's large Afro-Brazilian population—think of Bahia as Mississippi or Louisiana, and its principal city, Salvador, as Memphis or New Orleans. João Gilberto traveled from Bahia to Rio to pioneer the bossa nova sound, and the tropicalistas made the same journey ten years later. In the 1980s and '90s, Bahians once again invaded the south with a wave of rootsy, African-influenced styles.

The most widely heard musicians in this wave were the drummers of Olodum, a group that lent its polyrhythmic underpinning to a range of international pop stars from Caetano Veloso to Paul Simon and Michael Jackson. From the beginning, Olodum has always been more than just a hot rhythm section. At full force, it includes some two hundred members, or, if you want to count all the costumed marchers, something like four thousand. And it is not even a typical Afro-Brazilian Carnaval organization, though it started out that way back in 1979.

"The idea was to give opportunity to the neighborhood of Pelourinho," says Esmeraldo (Billy) Arquimimo, one of the group's multiple directors. "Pelourinho is the oldest neighborhood of historic central Salvador, but until that time there was no group, no nothing to represent that neighborhood in Carnaval. The idea was to create an Afrobloc, to keep the African tradition in Bahia. At the time, we were losing many things because of the racism that we faced—things like our dance, food, religion—so we decided to preserve the African culture. That's why the name is Olodum. Olodum is an African name, in Yoruba, and it means God of the Gods."

The version of Olodum that goes on tour is a stripped-down outfit of about twenty musicians, and mixes Carnaval drumming and dance with electric guitars, keyboards, and brass. Ask Arquimimo if the play-

the restaurants and all I sang was pure stories. I was doing that when I was very small, eight years old, with a girl, as a duet. A man played guitar and we sang."

Hernández was born in the small Sinaloan village of Rosa Morada, in the foothills of the western mountain range that is the heartland of the drug world. While still a teenager, he formed a band with two of his younger brothers, a cousin, and a family friend. In 1968, they came to the United States to play at a festival, and as they were crossing the border a customs agent impressed with their courage at traveling alone called them "little tigers." The name stuck, and they became Los Tigres del Norte, "The Tigers of the North." Settling in San Jose, California, they caught the ear of an Englishman named Art Walker, who had started a Mexican record label there, and began making albums.

At first they had only modest, local success, but on a trip to Los Angeles Hernández and Walker happened to hear a mariachi singer named Joe Flores singing a corrido about a female smuggler who kills her lover after a cross-border run. Flores's recording had not reached beyond Los Angeles, but when the Tigres did their version, "Contrabando y Traición" (Smuggling and Betrayal) became an international smash, inspiring two sequels and several movies and making them into the hottest act on the norteño scene.

"When I came out with that story, I couldn't believe the impact was so strong," Hernández says. "The majority of stories are about a male character, a person X, but none had a woman who was so unusual, a woman who had the bravery to kill somebody, to say to him, 'You know what? For me it's money first, and then you second.' That totally changed the history of the corrido. I imagine that if you could analyze the stories and the corridos, you would find that Benjamín Argumedo [the hero of a classic corrido of the Mexican Revolution] was in love, but he always won—and here it was the opposite: she beat him, she killed him, and she kept the money."

But it was more than just the song. "There are two kinds of situations that come up," Hernández explains. "There are songs that make an artist and there are songs that are made by the artist. 'Contrabando y Traición' is such a strong theme that it could make you, or make anybody. It was strong enough that it put Joe Flores on the map for a while, but he didn't put anything into it, for the song. It is the same with 'La Banda del Carro Rojo' [The Red Car Gang, which was the Tigre's next single and an even bigger hit]. The earlier interpreters had done those songs for money, but I do them because I feel the story, the character.

"Since I was a child I wanted to be an actor, and I take on the role that the character needs to be, and I think that is the great difference. When you record a theme, you have to imagine your own film, what you want to say to the people, with something of your own feelings wrapped up in it, so that it will get through to the public. You don't sing it because you need to earn a peso, or because you have to say, 'Fine, I'll sell twenty records,' but simply so that they hear your feeling, they hear your style, which is what matters."

The Tigres were more than just a hit band. They became symbols of working class success and immigrant pride, and the movies made from their songs led a new wave of Mexican film, featuring tough border characters in a sort of modern western. "Before, the directors and producers didn't want norteño music because norteño musicians were not on that level," Hernández recalls. "They wanted María Grever, Agustín Lara [the mainstream pop composers in Mexico City]; at that time Javier Solis was active, José Alfredo Jiménez, all kinds of soloists, and norteño music didn't appear." Thirty years later, there have been literally thousands of films and videos made with corridos as their driving force. Most of them are cheap action movies, but the Tigres also used both music and film to explore issues of racism and illegal immigration, and to celebrate Mexican pride on both sides of the border.

Indeed, at times the Tigres have sought to distance themselves from ballads of smugglers and gunfighters. Hernández traces the origin of this shift to the 1980s: "I began to get letters from the governors of Chihuahua, of Sinaloa, saying that they didn't want me to sing those songs there, in the stadiums where I went to work, that when people asked for them I should clam up. But if that's why the people come to see me—can you imagine? It's for those songs that they pay to come in and see me, and then if I didn't sing them . . . So that's when I thought ¡*Ay caray*! I need to change. I can't keep singing these things, because tomorrow or the next day they'll finish me off. So I recorded religious songs, 'Un Día a la Vez' [One Day at a Time]. I changed the whole scene, for precisely that reason."

In the late 1980s, the Tigres returned to their hard-edged style with an album called *Corridos Prohibidos* [Banned Corridos], which became their biggest seller to date and reestablished them as masters of the form. However, it also reflected their new social consciousness, including the story of a crusading Tijuana reporter, El Gato Felix (Felix the Cat), who had been assassinated by the drug lords. A few years later, the band recorded "El Circo" [The Circus], a song attacking the corruption of Mexican ex-president Carlos Salinas, and in 1997 they issued a two-disc set, *Jefe de Jefes* [Boss of Bosses], which covered everything from the drug world to the corruption of the political system and the difficulties of immigrant life in the United States.

Along the way, the Tigres evolved from young trendsetters into elder statesmen, but unlike most aging pop stars they continue to have the power to put a record on the top of the charts, and their concerts still draw at least as many teenagers as longtime fans. That they have managed not only to hang on but to grow in stature over four decades is a tribute to Hernández's cool judgment. For example, though he is the group's artistic director, accordionist, and principal singer—as well as the oldest brother in what remains, despite personnel changes, very much a family band—he has been careful not to hog the spotlight. "Each of us has his charisma," he says proudly. "Each has his manner, and I have each sing songs that the people believe—I have one sing funny songs, another sing romantic songs, another children's songs, and I do the stories. Like my brother Hernán, he sings the funny, rowdy songs. Why? Because he is that way. He likes jokes, he's a Bohemian, he likes to have a good time, so he has to sing what he likes. You wouldn't have him sing a corrido, because no one would believe him. So that's how it is."

In the same way, Hernández has cultivated long-lasting relationships with some of Mexico's finest songwriters, and uses each in a different way. "I visit them, spend time with them, try to get everything for them that I can, go with them to their villages, live with them, try to know their lives, what they like, what they don't like," he says. For example, there is Paulino Vargas, once leader of the popular norteño duo Los Broncos de Reynosa, but now better known as the defining composer of the modern corrido style. "Paulino always told me stories," Hernández says. "Because he sang for all those people [the drug lords]; he went personally and sang and saw all that they did. So I said to him, 'I want you to write me corridos that tell of real events, as they are, as you saw them. Put the things you tell me about into the songs, so that the people will believe that what you are saying is really true." Vargas's hits with the Tigres have run the gamut from "La Banda del Carro Rojo" to a biting critique of the presidency of Vicente Fox, and he remains a fixture of their writing team, along with younger composers like Teodoro Bello, who with the Tigres' backing has become the biggest-selling songwriter in Mexican history.

As they approach their fortieth year together, the Tigres have become almost respectable, numbering novelists and college deans among their fans and supporters. These days they prefer to steer clear of drug ballads, but their albums still include tough, well-written corridos of current events, and they are hailed as national troubadours, the "voice of the people." Hernández is pleased by their new stature, but he insists that it is simply the reward for dedicating himself to honesty: "The story of the Tigres del Norte is that the people believe what I sing. It is like how you win a woman: when I tell her that I love her and that she pleases me, she has to believe what I am saying in order to feel affection for me. And that is what a song is like for me. When I come onstage and sing a story, the character is there and everybody is listening and making their own film, in their own way—and mine is that when they are looking at me, they say, 'Yes, what he's singing is true.'"

4

EUROPE

Since the whole concept of world music is essentially Eurocentric, it is a bit tricky to figure out which European styles should be included in the world bag. After all, to a Hungarian, Hungarian music is not "world"; nor is flamenco to a Spaniard. It is easier if one is American, since one can simply say that both the Hungarians and the flamenco players are coming in from abroad, but then why not include Bjork or Elton John? As far as I can see, the only reasonable solution is to appeal to the rules of the marketplace: some musicians get put in the rock bins in record stores (and interviewed by the rock critics when they come through on tour) and others end up in the world bins. And those choices, while somewhat arbitrary at the edges, do have a degree of logic behind them. World music, at least as I understand it, has a sense of place. It may not be traditional, exactly, but it is music that could not have sprung up anywhere else than where it did, and that continues to show a connection to its roots. That is why the South African disco stars, popular as they are throughout central and southern Africa, have never broken out onto the international scene the way King Sunny Ade or Ladysmith Black Mambazo has.

All of these standards and definitions arise at least to some extent from colonialism and cultural imperialism, but that doesn't make them any less real. Even rap, which has shown unprecedented power to remake itself as it travels around the world, remains overwhelmingly an American export with local offshoots rather than having become a truly international form. Every rap fan in the world knows Snoop Dogg, but only the francophones and hipsters are aware of MC Solaar—and Solaar has had much greater global penetration than Akwid or Aisha Kandisha's Jarring Effects. This is not to deny the excitement of regional hip-hop styles, by any means, but only to point out that they have not succeeded in adjusting the balance of power in the international music market. Given this situation, it is natural that most of the Europeans who get filed as world artists are folkloric, perform in distinctive regional styles, or play music that shows the influence of immigrant roots in Africa or Asia.

Definitions aside, a couple of the European interviews touch on a subject that should provoke much more discussion than it has within the world music movement: that the same national or ethnic pride that leads to the preservation and presentation of traditional, regional styles can create serious problems in other contexts. Love of one's own culture can make one resentful of newcomers who are diluting that culture, and pride in one's own ethnicity can easily tip over into disparagement of someone else's. When I was in Hungary in the 1980s, I constantly heard people on the folk scene bemoan the fate of the ethnic Hungarians in Transylvania, who were being driven off their lands and wrenched from their traditional culture by the Romanian government. These relocations were a clear example of what has come to be known as "ethnic cleansing," and rightfully deplored—and yet, as the new spate of ethnic wars broke out in the Balkans I couldn't help wondering how many of the Hungarian musical revivalists would support an invasion and countercleansing of Romanians from the region. In the following interviews, Márta Sebestyén's attempt to distance her music from political nationalism suggests that the issue has indeed been a subject of discussion on the Hungarian scene, while at the other end of Europe, Mísia describes how the Portuguese dictatorship attempted to use *fado* for its own political ends.

As nationalist parties gain strength throughout Europe, this is going to be an increasingly troubling subject for folk and world music fans. We are going to see the aim of "preserving regional traditions" used as a code for anti-immigrant movements, the suppression of Gypsies or other minority groups, and attempts to "cleanse" areas of inhabitants who are designated as foreign though they have lived in a region for hundreds of years.

It is important to remember that such associations of folk revivalism and love of local traditions with ethnic and nationalist politics are by no means automatic or unavoidable. The British folk scene that produced people like Dick Gaughan framed the music as an art and voice of the working class. Far from being blinkered nationalists, British and American folk revivalists have actively encouraged exchange with other traditions, and folk festivals in both countries have in general done their best to present multicultural smorgasbords of traditions from as far afield as possible.

In international terms, though, America's country-and-western scene is probably a more typical example of the traditionalist impulse than is its folk scene. While often apolitical, and occasionally producing an artist committed to some strain of leftist populism, country-and-western music has tended to espouse the values of conservatism, nationalism, and sometimes outright xenophobia. This is not a critique of the music per se—in many periods, the country scene has produced more exciting music than the folk scene—but it is something that those people who love world sounds and sneer at Nashville should keep in mind. World music fans are, by definition, interested in hearing sounds from outside our own cultures, but it is a mistake to assume that the people we are listening to share our values.

In Europe, this issue remains very much alive. When I first traveled through Germany in the 1970s, it was more common to find young Germans playing Irish or American folk styles than anything from the German tradition, since any explicit celebration of the German *volk* was still associated in many people's minds with Nazism. Today, in many regions of what was once considered Eastern Europe, folk ensembles may be cheered as much for their ethnic symbolism as for the quality of their performances, and it is not surprising that many progressive young music fans would rather hear international styles like rock or hip-hop, which unite audiences around the globe.

That said, Europe has the most active international music scene in the world, and much of the greatest music it presents is played by traditionally rooted performers based within its ever-expanding borders. For every artist included in this section, there are dozens more who might have been equally good choices.

Italy

Paolo Conte

It is a sign of the times that Paolo Conte came to the United States as part of the world music boom. When cabaret music was strong, Americans greeted singers like Edith Piaf, Charles Aznavour, and Nana Mouskouri as part of a continuum with Eartha Kitt and Frank Sinatra. Conte is not at all a folk or traditional musician, and though he is Italian, his music gives little if any obvious sign of his origins, owing as much to Jacques Brel or Paul Whiteman as to any Italian style. When he nonetheless managed to capture a sector of the world audience, it was because—regardless of what genre one places him in—he is one of the most astonishing performers alive. His first Boston show was unlike anything in my previous experience, and what was most striking was not the music but the inexplicable way he took control of the audience.

As I wrote in a review of that show, "Conte does not exactly front this band, at least not in the normal sense. It is more as if he is starring in his own, private movie, and the band is playing the background music. He sits and chats with his listeners in the offhand, casual manner of a guy late at night in an empty bar, repeating old stories to the bartender. The music sets the scene." It was such a low-key and intimate performance that it should have gotten lost in a large hall, but somehow Conte made everyone feel as if he were singing directly to them, and the concert ended with the only genuine encore I have seen in twenty years as a music critic—not just the formulaic return after a rousing false ending, but a heartfelt refusal of the audience to let him escape after that first encore, even after the house lights had come up, and then, after he finally came back and repeated one song, an attempt to bring him back yet again, until he was forced to come out and pull his finger across his neck in a signal for us to cut it out. I still don't know what it was that made us all stay there, applauding. None of us could claim that Conte had done anything astonishing— except, in his gruff, understated way, to have given one of the greatest performances we had ever seen.

Conte's music is an odd mix: to American ears, it has the sultry, saloon ambience of early Tom Waits, though Conte is Waits's senior by more than a decade. There is a bit of French *chanson*, some Argentine tango, some Neapolitan pop, and frequent traces of show tunes and jazz. His seven-piece band on that tour consisted of his piano, three or four horns, a jazz rhythm section, and a bandoneón, plus the occasional kazoo solo.

Then there are his lyrics, fraught with names of exotic places like Minneapolis, Mocambo, and Timbuktu, and phrases of French and off-kilter English: "Good luck, my babe, it's wonderful, it's wonderful, I dream of you . . ." Mostly, though, Conte sings in his native Italian, songs of romance that translate as something like, "Her pungent odor beckoned him / Like an old-fashioned grocery / Its doors flung open / To the spring outside"; or odes to the spirit of Woody Herman or Ernest Hemingway.

"I like the old style of composing," Conte says.* "The old Cuban style, the old American style, the old French style, from the teens and twenties, and a bit of the thirties. For me, the strongest spirit of the twentieth century was at the beginning: the new ideas, the artistic revolutions. The twenties were the strongest—not just in music, but in painting, in all the arts."

And yet, Conte's appeal is not nostalgia: "I do not play the old music in a philological way," he says. "I write with that spirit, but it is still something being written today. But I think it is good, at the end of the century, to keep alive something of the force that was there at the beginning. And maybe, for the young people, a bit of swing does no harm—it is something new for them, maybe."

Swing was the music of Conte's own youth. He started out in music as a jazz vibraphonist, inspired by Lionel Hampton and Milt Jackson. In his hometown, the north Italian wine-growing center of Asti, there were too few places to play jazz, so he turned his efforts to composing, meanwhile earning his living as a lawyer. "I quit because I lived in a small town and it was difficult to travel, to go play," he recalls. "So I quit playing jazz and began, bit by bit, at home, on the family piano, to compose songs.

---

* This interview was conducted in French.

"That is how I began this adventure. As a writer, without thinking of singing myself. I wrote songs, and I had good success, with the best Italian artists of the time [the mid to late 1960s]. Then, afterwards, someone from the RCA record company forced me to put out the recordings I had made to demonstrate my songs to these other artists."

Conte says that at first he resisted: "I had no desire to be a singer, because I just liked to write for others. But he said, 'There is something authentic about your way of singing.'

"I said, 'No, I'm not a singer. I don't have the voice of a singer or the technique.'

"But he insisted, saying, 'No, it is good for the public to hear this material in an authentic way.'"

When Conte's first album came out, in 1974, the public instantly agreed, and it was followed by many more. Conte still finds this a bit astonishing. "It always surprises me," he says, laughing. "Because I never adopted any strategy. I always composed, sang, arranged, worked according to my own taste."

Of course, it is exactly this obliviousness to contemporary trends that gives his music its uniqueness. The blend of styles, and the difficult romanticism of Conte's work come through even if one does not understand his lyrics. The lyrics, though, are quite wonderful, as is demonstrated by the translations on his first American release, *The Best of Paolo Conte*.

"I very much liked the classic French chanson," Conte says. "The French song showed us a certain technique, how to work in three minutes—because a good song should last three or four minutes at most—to take advantage of this bit of time to present a little play.

"I like the idea of telling a story, rather than making a declaration. And to give the idea of a little story in a song, one must work with poetry. This is more typical of North Italians than South Italians. The Italian most familiar to outsiders is the southerner, who is more accustomed to making declarations. I am from the north, and we are used to telling stories. For me, each song is like a little film."

Take "Hemingway," for example, an understated piece whose laconic minimalism neatly fits its subject: "I wanted to write of a ghost in the night. So I began by thinking of a scene that was a bit mysterious, a nighttime scene, and within that a special place, Harry's Bar, where one could talk a bit with the bartender and make a ghost come to life, the ghost of Hemingway. It is a song with very few words, just some exotic words which make the character come to life, with his love of Africa and exoticism. And then the music, as if he was listening to a record in the background."

Likewise, Conte says that the moments when he lapses into English are reminders of American musicals: "I like to write a bit with things like in the movies, and also the Italian language is not too rhythmic, so I add a few words which give a bit of swing. And, understanding the rest, the Italians take those moments when I say a few little words of English as a moment of joy."

Conte has made only a few visits to the United States, but with his musical background it is natural that he should have a particular affection for the country. "When I have played in America, the public was very hospitable," he says. "And when I am there I feel the presence of the great ghosts of the past, the great masters. It is something magical that was always part of my memories, and of my dreams."

Portugal

Mísia

Mísia was the first of the new wave of young fado singers to make it to the United States, blazing a trail that was shortly followed by Cristina Branco, Mariza, and Dulce Pontes. In New England, at least, she arrived with a ready-made audience, since there is a strong Portuguese immigrant population and, especially along the coast, it is easy to find restaurants that feature fado singers on weekends. Even today, when the world boom has brought the music thousands of new admirers, a typical fado concert in Boston will draw an audience that is half Portuguese.

Mísia was born to a Portuguese father and a Catalan mother, and raised in the northern Portuguese city of Porto, but she says that it was only after moving to Barcelona at age twenty that she devoted herself to fado. "By going so far away from home, I began to feel more of the nostalgia and yearning, and more desire to sing fado," she recalls.* "If

---

* This interview was conducted in Spanish.

Mísia. Photograph © Jack Vartoogian/FrontRowPhotos.

I had stayed in Portugal, I would probably not have felt it in the same way, and I might never have become a fado singer."

Fado typically speaks of heartache and loneliness, and was brought to the world stage in the 1950s through the magnificent voice and presence of Amália Rodrigues. The music's roots are far older, though, reaching back to the turn of the twentieth century, when its meltingly melodic fusion of African and European strains was the sound of the Lisbon bars and brothels. Rodrigues helped elevate fado's reputation, but Mísia explains that the music fell out of favor again for political reasons.

"Fado went through a difficult period after the Revolution of the Carnations [in 1974], because it was considered a song of the Right," she says. "There were anarchist fados at the beginning of the century, but no one remembered that. People only remembered the fados of the time of the dictatorship, and those tended to say, 'We are a little country, very poor, very clean, and very happy to be this way.' So people said that there were three fatal F's—Fátima [the church], fado, and football—that had kept the people's eyes shut."

Mísia returned to Portugal in 1990, settling in Lisbon, and, after some early recordings that established her as a vibrant young voice, set out to create a contemporary fado. However, while other modernizers have blended the classic style with modern instrumentation, African percussion, or poppier melodies, she decided to keep her sound thoroughly traditional and acoustic: "I say, jokingly, that I don't use home appliances in my fados," she says, laughing. "I like electronic music, but in other things, not in this type of music.

"The music of traditional fado is made up of roughly one hundred pieces, for which each singer can choose whatever lyric he or she wants, so you can hear the same music with different poems. And I use this traditional music on my albums. But the words and the way of writing is very contemporary. For me, it is more subversive—in the good sense of the word—to make the fado contemporary through the poem, which is the nucleus, the interior, the content, than to use a synthesizer or a drum, which is the form, the exterior."

Although in retrospect it seems profoundly logical, Mísia's idea surprised both aficionados and outsiders: rather than turning to experienced songwriters, she solicited lyrics from Portugal's most esteemed novelists and poets. "I went to people like [the 1997 Nobel Prize winner in literature] José Saramago—he did not have the Nobel at that time, but I would have gone just the same if he had—and asked them to write fados for me," she says. "All of the living writers I used were people who had never written for music. To me, it seemed a fascinating idea that people with other artistic languages could communicate through fado, have a dialogue with fado."

At first, she says, many of the people she has approached have been hesitant: "The first reaction is of prudence, because fado—like flamenco, like tango, like blues—is a world closed in itself; it is like a ghetto, it is a genre with its own laws and its special codes. So at first they are very surprised and they do not know if they can do it."

In the end, though, she says that there is plenty of common ground between fado and the more academically hallowed literary forms: "One can write fados about anything, because fado comes from the Latin word *fatum*, which means fate, destiny, life. There are all kinds of fados; fados that say very innocent things—'I entered a tavern and you were sitting there, there were curtains and a glass of wine'—and there are others that speak of the great sentiments of the human spirit, of life, of death. And these are the type I like to sing. They speak of the human spirit, with its greatness and its misery. I have also used the work of great poets who are already dead, and I find lovely passages that can be adapted to fado, because they speak of melancholy, of nostalgia, of solitude, of all the themes that fado sings."

Her lyrical innovations helped Mísia to win a new audience for fado at home, and her dark, supple voice and lilting, acoustic arrangements made her an international favorite. She has toured widely in Europe, Asia, and South America, and her albums *Garras dos Sentidos* (which includes the Saramago lyric) and *Paixoes Diagonais* sold beyond all expectations, winning over not only young newcomers but also the old guard of Portuguese fado fans. "At first, my image, which is pretty cosmopolitan and contemporary, was a bit shocking for the purists, the orthodox," she says, referring to her bob-haired, edgily sexy persona and the modernist, arty designs she favors for her CD covers and videos. "In the beginning it was a bit difficult, but now time has passed and they respect me, they understand."

Indeed, with their broad appeal and international travels, young fado stars like Mísia and Mariza have been hailed as successors to Rodrigues's crown. Mísia is flattered by the comparison, but also finds it somewhat disturbing. "We all owe a great debt to Amália," she says. "Because wherever we go, she has been there before and left the fado very well placed, at an insuperable level. But Amália was unique. When she died there were three days of national mourning. Three days that a whole country stopped, for a singer!

"So when I read, 'the second Amália,' or 'the successor to Amália'—which they don't just say about me; every ten years they say it about somebody, and Amália must have laughed a lot about that—it is not that it annoys me, because I know that people mean well by it, that it is their only point of reference. But I think there are no second Amálias, just as there are no second Frank Sinatras or Billie Holidays or Edith Piafs. That was a different time and race of artists, and they had their time and their public, and now we have ours."

George Dalaras. Photograph © Jack Vartoogian/FrontRowPhotos.

Greece

George Dalaras

In musical terms, southern Europe could easily be grouped alongside northern Africa. Until the last hundred years or so, sea traffic was faster than land travel and the only way to carry large shipments of goods, so what we now think of as the cradle of European civilization was not simply Greece and Italy, but all the countries lapped by the Mediterranean—hence the sea's name, which means "middle of the earth." Music is one of the deepest forms of culture, retaining rhythms and tonalities that reach back for millenia, and the traditional music one hears in southern Greece, Italy, or Spain still tends to be much closer to what one can hear on the coasts of Egypt, Lebanon or Algeria than to anything in northern Europe.

Portugal and Greece form the European poles of this Mediterranean continuum, and the journey from fado to *rembetika* is an easy one—though in terms of instrumentation and tonal approach it might have made more sense to group the Greeks alongside the Lebanese or Iraqis. As the oft-hailed founders of European civilization—Europa was born in what is now Lebanon, but a Greek god carried her to Crete—the Greeks would be the first to insist that they belong in this chapter, but it is important to remember that all such groupings are to a great extent arbitrary. When it comes to Greek music, this is particularly true, because it has remained so much in a world of its own. *Zorba the Greek* and *Never on Sunday* gave Americans a taste of Greek styles, but unlike fado or flamenco, rembetika and *laïkó* have never found much of an international audience. In the United States, Greek concerts have the distinction of being pretty much the only European musical events that have remained entirely within immigrant communities. Yiorgos (George) Dalaras and Haris Alexiou fill huge concert halls in American cities, but their shows are rarely even advertised to non-Greeks.

As a result, it is no surprise that Greek music is so widely misunderstood. When your idea of a country's style is based on vague memories of happy peasants dancing in movies, balanced with the schmaltz of Demis Roussos and Yanni, there is little to prepare you for the soulful, roots-oriented sound of George Dalaras.

Dalaras was hailed in his youth as "the Greek Bob Dylan," and more recently has been called "the Greek Bruce Springsteen," but these comparisons are misleading and, if anything, understate his stature. Since the early 1970s, Dalaras has sold over eight million records (a stunning figure when one considers that Greece's population is roughly ten million) and led the revival of interest in a panorama of Greek musics, as well as exploring other Mediterranean and Latin styles. While not a musical purist, he has kept much of the directness of the folk tradition even in his most pop-oriented recordings, and his work might best be compared to that of Latin American *nueva canción* (new song) artists like Mercedes Sosa.

Dalaras's musical roots are in rembetika, the Eastern-inflected music that flourished in the early decades of the twentieth century among the brothels and hashish dens of Greece's crowded port cities. A fusion of Mediterranean styles, rembetika reached its peak in the 1920s, deriving a characteristic Asian tinge from the musicians who arrived with other ethnic Greek refugees from Turkey. "Rembetika is very much like American blues," Dalaras says.[*] "It has striking resemblances, first in the lyrics and then the music. It was a very characteristic, very deep, very flavorful style."

Like blues, tango, or fado, rembetika was often disparaged by respectable people, who considered it not only disreputable but dangerous. "Rembetika and the musicians of rembetika were considered by the conservative society to be something marginal and unacceptable, revolutionary both socially and artistically," Dalaras says. "Especially around the Second World War, the upper and middle classes were trying to see life in pink colors and happiness, and the rembetika was describing the pain, the need for the people to revolt, to change the situation."

Dalaras was born in 1950 in the port city of Piraeus, a legendary rembetika center. His father and uncles were musicians, and he grew up around some of the music's most renowned players and composers. By age twelve he was accompanying his father on guitar in the local

---

[*] This interview was conducted through a translator (Dalaras's wife).

bars. "Music was always the magic thing for me," he says. "I felt this tie coming from within my heart since I was very, very young boy."

By the mid-1960s, rock had hit in Greece, and for a few years Dalaras was caught up in the new sound, forming teen groups that played Animals and Beatles tunes. By the time he recorded his first album in 1969, though, he had shrugged off these influences and was singing laïkó, or mainstream Greek pop music. Then, on his second album, he began to explore his roots, and in 1975 his double album *Rembétiko* became the first official platinum-seller in the Greek market. "It was a shock for the Greek music scene of that period," he says. "The record company was not very confident of what I was doing. But I was very lucky from the beginning to score a big hit and, more than that, to earn the love and the trust of the people and especially the young."

With the fall of the Greek junta in 1974, Dalaras was hailed as a voice of youthful liberation. He can now count three decades as the king of laïkó, with over forty albums to his credit. While they range from orchestral and rock-flavored ventures to a tribute to the composer Mikis Theodorakis and collaborations with Al DiMeola and Paco de Lucía, he says rembetika has remained at the heart of his work. "It's not pure rembetika, but it has this origin," he explains. "Sometimes it is evident and clear, and sometimes it affects the songs from underneath, but at the end of the day rembetika is always present, even in the more contemporary pieces. It's like if we consider contemporary rock, there is still the blues in it. They are somehow connected, and when it is done successfully it has a very interesting result."

The fusion of styles that informs Dalaras's music is represented in the instrumentation of his touring groups. He will typically have three *bouzoukis*, the long-necked, mandolinlike instruments that provide the main drive in rembetika bands, along with guitar, keyboards, bass, drums, accordion, flute, and Eastern imports like the *oud* and *baglama*—the former an Arabic lute, and the latter a sort of miniature bouzouki that is often singled out as the defining instrument of the rembetika sound. His concerts include both electric and acoustic sections, the more recent songs balanced with old favorites for traditionalists and longtime fans.

For himself, Dalaras openly prefers the older styles, and he bemoans the steady Americanization of the world pop scene. "This is a big question for me," he says. "People in all the European countries are imitating the American style of promotion and show business. It is strange, because they are very critical of the American way of life, but it's a hypocrisy, because at the end of the day they try to follow this model.

"This of course happens because the United States takes 'good care'—in quotes—to brainwash people through the different channels of the television, the satellites, and they are unbeatable. People see the huge amounts of money that are spent, and they seem to be captured by the glamour and leave the substance and the real thing behind.

"The terrifying thing for me is that in recent years I see people and civilizations and cultures—rich cultures like the Balkans, for instance, or the Arabs, or the music from Iran, or even the unique school of Indian music—all these people are sacrificing their legendary heritage at the temple of American commercial music.

"It is good that the two important schools of rembetika in Greece and flamenco in Spain still exist, but this is a crucial issue for all of us. People believe that progress means dropping the boundaries between different cultures, but in music this always seems to happen in terms of making it more American. Meanwhile, in politics and other aspects of life, nationalism is rising. It is strange. I strongly believe that through music and art we can have this osmosis between cultures, but it would be better if we had the same thinking in other aspects of our life. Music cannot do this by itself."

Haris Alexiou

If George Dalaras is the king of laïkó, Haris Alexiou is the queen. Like Dalaras, she has a breadth of musical approach, a beautifully modulated voice, and a passionate artistry that should have brought her a far larger audience that she has outside the Greek world. Within that world, she is a giant, and her tours abroad fill large halls with adoring admirers who have laughed and cried to her music for decades.

Though laïkó is usually translated as "Greek popular music," Alexiou's style is deeply rooted in folk traditions. "The first sound that I heard was folk songs," she says, speaking in clear but accented English. "My grandfather was great musician, but my parents, no. But they had lovely voices and my house was full of music. Just like this, we used to sing in our house, not professionally. My mother, her family comes from Asia Minor and my father was from Thebes, and they sang the songs from their regions. I was very lucky to have this base, because the Greek folk songs are very difficult. If somebody can sing folk songs, then after that he can sing also popular songs."

Alexiou began to sing professionally in her teens. "Some friends, they were actors and singers, they asked me to go with them to a nightclub, Arkitektonika," she recalls. "It was a place the young people and the intellectual people used to go. I could not believe that I would be a singer; it was just like play for me. But I went there for one night, and after that I stayed."

Soon the young singer attracted the notice of Athens's thriving popular music world. "I had just started singing in the nightclub and somebody from a record company listened to me and asked me to sign a contract. So, very early, I recorded in a very famous composer's album." This was *Mikra Asia* (Asia Minor) by Apostolos Kaldaras, which also featured Dalaras. Released in 1972, it became the most popular Greek recording of the decade.

"I started by singing three songs on that album," she continues. "And it was a big opportunity for me, because other composers listened and asked me to participate in their albums. Then, after four years, in 1975, I did my first [solo] album and I had my first hit and after that it was very easy to create my career."

Alexiou laughs, as if even after all these years she can't quite believe her luck. As one listens to her recordings, though, it is easy to see why she was so immediately successful. She has ranged across the breadth of Greek music, from traditional acoustic groups to modern electric bands and orchestras, from rembetika to smooth pop compositions, but she always sounds superbly relaxed and at home. Her voice is rich and warm, with a control that allows her to make microtonal shifts recalling the Eastern-influenced music of Asia Minor.

Indeed, to an American, the tonality and melisma of Alexiou's style is reminiscent of Arabic or Middle Eastern music. This is a sensitive subject for many Greeks, since they were the front line of Christian Europe during centuries of battle with Asian and Islamic armies and they remain acutely conscious that Asia Minor, now Turkey, was once considered part of Greece. "For us this is very difficult," Alexiou says, when asked about the Arabic flavor in her singing. "We don't like to say that. I understand that for you it sounds like this. But it's the traditional Greek way. In ourselves there is something Eastern, but we don't call it Arabic, because it's something different for us."

In any case, Alexiou has remained at the forefront of Greek music through her ability to blend many styles and adapt to changing times. After the thrilling period of the 1970s, when the end of the dictatorship and the rembetika and folk revivals brought a new generation of young artists to the fore, she says that laïkó went through a period of stagnation: "Before, we had very famous, very strong composers, and after them we had a long period when the new generation tried to imitate these great composers. So we listened to the same style of music because everybody was trying to do what the old people, the old composers did."

In the 1990s, though, the focus shifted to singer-songwriters. "This is something new for Greek music," Alexiou says. "Before, we always had big stars on one side—Alexiou, Dalaras and this one and this one—and from the other we had the famous composers, and a great singer and a great composer would make an album. Now, the new generation of musicians, they write the songs and they also sing, even if they have an ordinary voice. I love this, because we have a new spirit in the songs now. Before, if you were a writer you had to service a star, to make things for a star, but now you don't have to service a star, you have to write a song. And sometimes this song is very, very good, very important, very beautiful. So we have this kind of authors now."

Alexiou wrote occasional songs before, but in recent years she has recorded entire albums of her own compositions. The result has been a sort of revitalization, giving her work new focus. "It's different—not always better, but sometimes—but it feels different for me, because I have to say my own stories and to express myself," she says. Her new songs deal with romantic subjects, but also with issues of homelessness and poverty: "I am touched from the stories of the people. Of course, I think they're love songs, but even in my love songs there are some messages from this sentiment, from the life, from the solitude, for the lonely people, for the homeless, for different stories."

While she finds the role of singer-songwriter liberating, Alexiou adds that she has found strengths in every period of her career: "What I have done all these years is that I never stay in a particular style of music. Because if something feels inside me, I want to keep it. I don't want to follow one style just because I'm very famous and the people know me like this. I like to always change, to do things that keep me alive."

Despite her zeal to move ahead, Alexiou has also remained true to her early repertory, especially when she is in the United States. "I have to pass throughout my whole career," she says. "Because I don't come here so often, so I have to sing the well-known songs. The Greeks here, they love to hear the favorite songs."

Alexiou adds that while she draws an audience of Greek immigrants wherever she goes, the United States is pretty much the only place where she does not also draw non-Greeks. She would love to see that change, but meanwhile she has little reason for complaint. "Of course, everybody wants to be famous, so I can't say that I'm very happy that other people don't know me. But I'm very happy because I have been singing for so many years, and I can still say that I create more and more, and I'm still feeling important in my music, because I'm alive and I'm still doing new things.

"Sometimes I do get tired, of course. But when the tour is over I will go home and find a very quiet island with no tourists, with some caves, and I will go there to have a month, to be with me. Just me, the God, and the sea."

Turkey

Barbaros Erköse

There are obvious problems to classifying music by region, and nowhere is this clearer than in cultural borderlands like Turkey. For most of its history, this region was part of the same cultural belt as Greece, and Istanbul (then named Constantinople) went on to be the capital of the Roman Empire and the seat of the Orthodox Christian church. The Turks arrived from Central Asia, part of the expansionist wave that included Genghis Khan's Mongolians and Attilla's Huns, adopted the Muslim religion, and for centuries carried on an active cultural exchange with the neighboring Islamic populations of Persia and the Arab world. So where should one classify Turkish music? Is it Asian, Middle Eastern, or European?

To the extent that any geographical division can be made, Barbaros Erköse fits best in the European section, but it is not a simple choice. His family's roots for the last few centuries have been in the Balkans, and later in Greece. Then, after the Treaty of Lausanne in 1923, there was a forced population exchange between Greece and Turkey, much like the partition of India and Pakistan. Many of the greatest rembetika players arrived in Greece with the population that came west, while Erköse's family was among those forced to move east. As a result, Erköse fits musically into the same family as many Greek and Balkan players, though in other ways his branch has been separated by religion and shaky ethnic categories.

As an example of the latter, Erköse's concerts are advertised as "Gypsy Music of Turkey," but he emphasizes that the Gypsy designation is no more illuminating than the national one. His music recalls klezmer with its wailing, dancing clarinet lines, Persian or Arabic flavors as the oud or the *kanun* (a sort of trapezoidal zither) come in, and always the sprightly dance rhythms common to villages in both Greece and Turkey.

That is exactly how Erköse likes it. "I have a friend who is a researcher, a historian, and he says that he himself does not know what his roots are," he says.* "So how can people call me a Gypsy? This is something that is very hard to know. I do not even feel Turkish. I know people from all over the world, and I feel that I am a human; I do not enjoy national descriptions, national adjectives. There is no nation that I do not like. So I am not Gypsy or Romany or Turkish—I am a musician."

Erköse points out that he plays many Greek melodies, though reworked in his own style, as well as elements drawn from all the other sounds he has heard in his life. "This fusion is really beneficial to the music," he says. "You listen to the music of Americans, then you will capture something from it. You listen to the music of the

---

* This interview was conducted through a translator.

Germans and you will capture something from it. A good musician listens to music from everywhere. Everywhere has different music, but the same emotions. When somebody dies in a village in my country, there is a kind of music, a lament that goes with it, but if somebody dies in India there is also a music that is sad for that occasion. So, the music is different, but the emotion is the same."

"Lingo Lingo," the title song of Erköse's only internationally available album, is inspired by another common emotion: "The name is from the sound empty bottles make when they hit each other," he explains. "The song is about this lover finding his loved one, and he also sees empty bottles. A part of the song says, 'Did you drink *raki* without me?' So it's basically observing his loved one in a drunk situation. It is a very familiar tune, probably the whole [Turkish] nation knows this melody."

Erköse comes from a long line of musicians on both sides of his family. Born in the Turkish city of Bursa, he gave his first concert in 1948 at the age of twelve. He got his training by playing for the local theaters, which he describes as more like a circus or vaudeville show than most European or American theater performances, with acrobats and dancers as well as actors. With his two brothers, he formed a trio that became popular on Turkish radio in the 1960s, and then traveled throughout Europe and spent a brief period in the United States.

The clarinet is one of the most popular instruments in the Balkans, and Erköse says that it became common in Turkey around the turn of the twentieth century. He started out learning the styles of the local masters, but soon was absorbing music from all over, especially American jazz. "As a kid I really enjoyed listening to jazz records, the old 78 rpm's," he says. "Especially the Benny Goodman style of jazz, where one was able to break free and improvise. I liked the improvisation in jazz, I was attracted to that because it was different. And I also listened to classical music and picked up things from different individuals that I liked, and I combined all of this to create my own sort of color."

Goodman was Jewish, and it has sometimes been suggested that his playing was affected by the klezmer clarinetists who had come to the United States from the Balkan region. Asked if, along with the foreign jazz flavor, he also heard a hint of home in Goodman's work, Erköse at first seems puzzled by the question, saying he was very young and didn't really think about regions, but then avers that indeed the music had "a familiar smell" to it.

Over the years, Erköse has continued to experiment, performing with Arabic musicians, American jazzmen, and European classical players. In his own music, he remains deeply rooted in the Greek and Turkish tradition, but always with his own touches: "When I play the melody, I am playing the traditional music," he says. "But when I am improvising, that is where I am unique. That is where my music is considered modern, and it is what has influenced other clarinet players in Turkey to imitate me."

The quartet Erköse carries on tour includes his son Tuncay on cello, a traditional percussionist, and a player of the kanun. Erköse explains that the kanun is a somewhat unusual choice—it is more common to use an oud, the fretless ancestor of the European lute, as an accompanying instrument—but he prefers the kanun because of its melodic richness: "The kanun is as rich as a piano. When we play, I just have to motion to that player to go into a solo, and the instrument has that capability to draw the audience in."

Unfamiliar as his music may be to international audiences, Erköse says that listeners always get drawn in: "When I am improvising, I am going somewhere. The music I am playing, it is unique at that moment, I am playing whatever I am feeling, so it is kind of like discovery. And the music is very alive rhythmically, the speed and strength of it get a lot of response. When people are involved in the music, it carries them along, wherever I am playing."

Hungary

Muzsikás and Márta Sebestyén

In the 1980s, the east emerged as Europe's world music frontier, and the most influential group in that emergence was the Hungarian folk ensemble Muzsikás (pronounced "mujhikash"), with its frequent guest vocalist Márta Sebestyén. However, although it opened the door to Eastern Europe, and its fiddles and bagpipes have often

Muzsikas (left to right): Sándor Csoóri, Dániel Hamar, Márta Sebestyén, Péter Éri, Mihály Sipos. Photograph © Jack Vartoogian/FrontRowPhotos.

provoked comparisons to Irish and other Celtic styles, the Hungarian folk revival was unique. Some of the credit must go to Béla Bartók and Zoltán Kodály, who combined their classical composing with intensive explorations of local folklore, with the result that Budapest conservatory students studied roots folk styles with a seriousness that does not exist on any other classical scene. This tendency was reinforced as a means of preserving national identity under the cultural and political hegemony of the Soviet Union. But even before Bartók and the Soviets, that identity was unlike anything else in Europe. The Magyars, or ethnic Hungarians, have a good deal of European blood, but trace their roots to colonists from Asia—even today, one of the most popular boys' names is Atilla.

Along with these factors, the Hungarian folk scene was never just about music. It was driven by a broader interest in folklore and culture, and centered on the *táncház* (dance house, or folk dance club) organizations, where students would gather, many of them dressed in traditional clothing, to learn old village dances. Muzsikás ran the most popular táncház in Budapest for seventeen years, and their performances have the enthusiastic rhythmic power of a great dance band, driven by the bowed, three-string bass and flat-bridged, chordal *kontra* fiddle.

Along with accompanying dancers, the members of Muzsikás explored and revived all sorts of traditional musics, from laments to lullabies, and in the West the group is probably best known for its work with Sebestyén. One of the most acclaimed traditional vocalists on the European folk scene, Sebestyén has the high, lonesome sound of the old rural singers. Indeed, she says it was that distinctive vocal timbre that first attracted her to the music.

"I was about twelve," she remembers. "I won a school folksinging competition and the first prize was a record with original field recordings. I was absolutely shocked by the voice of those peasant ladies, and I realized it was very different from everything else. From that point I was crazy, I was mad for this music."

At that time, she says, the genuine Hungarian folk tradition was almost unknown: "Folk music in the radio and TV was a sweet, entertaining, well . . . rubbish. You could hear so-called Gypsy orchestras playing this sweet stuff that is said to be the Hungarian folklore, but it has nothing to do with the real folklore. Nobody ever heard the real music except the researchers who were collecting this music and working in the archives. Ordinary people had never the opportunity to hear such music."

What particularly impressed her was the music's honesty: "It sounded like heart music, right from the heart. In this age—I call it the Coca-Cola age—when everything is artificial, it's very rare to find such pure things. Now people are realizing that pure cotton and pure this and that is the most important thing, when this world is fading. And this music is as important for me as clear air or water."

Like many folk revivalists around the world, Sebestyén and her musical partners are university-educated city dwellers, many of them with classical training, and they took to the music of the countryside with the zeal of converts. But it was not always an instant or automatic process. Dániel Hamar, Muzsikás's bass player, laughs when he recalls his first encounter with a real folk recording. "I thought it was horrible, unbearable and out of tune," he says. "It shocked me. I was a classical musician and it was so different from the music that I was used to."

As he studied it, though, he began to recognize the music's complexity and internal logic. "My purpose when I got the first recording was to write down what the double bass player is playing," he explains. "It was so difficult for me that I had to listen to it a hundred times. After the twentieth time I got used to the music and after the fiftieth I start to like it and after the hundredth I start to love it. It was the same as for the music of Béla Bartók. When first you hear it, it is so difficult, it's like mad people, but if you listen many times you more and more like it. And that is the secret in this music, that you never get bored of it."

Muzsikás built its audience slowly, gaining converts at weekly dances in a Budapest community center. The fans were young Hungarians rediscovering their ancient traditions, and both players and listeners were soon making trips to the mountains of Transylvania (an area of Romania where isolated Hungarian communities had held onto ancient rural traditions) to hunt up old tunes and discover a heritage their urban parents had abandoned.

"It's a very strange situation," says Sebestyén, who made her first trip to Transylvania at eighteen. "If you want to find the really old and very pure music, you have to go out from today's Hungary. After the First World War, two-thirds of Hungary was given to neighboring countries. Our finest old music remained in those areas, because for the Hungarians living there that was the only way to keep their national identity."

A similar search for cultural roots had been going on in all the industrialized countries, but for Eastern Europeans it had an added appeal. "We were grown up in a dictatorship, where our identity was taken away," Hamar recalls. "The government said that folk is nationalism, and nationalism is equal to fascism, so we had to be international—which in practice meant that we had to serve the Russian nationalism. What we heard on the radio was fakelore, which had nothing to do with the real tradition and was an imitation of the Russian folk ballad style. And when we discovered this music, we felt immediately that it was ours."

In some ways, Hamar says, this discovery went hand in hand with the discovery of rock, blues, and jazz. Each was, in its way, outlaw music: "There was a feeling that 'This is only mine, it's a secret language that only we fifty people know.' With the folk music, if you wanted to learn it you had to fight for it. You had to travel, you had to go to a village, you had to go to another country where they don't like you. So everything was made a mystery, and it was exciting—not only nice and beautiful, but exciting."

The overlap of interest in folk and Western styles briefly tempted Muzsikás to become a sort of Hungarian version of British folk-rock groups like Steeleye Span, but instead they opted to become more purist and traditional. "Many years ago we tried to add something to this music," Hamar says. "We were inspired by blues and jazz, and we thought that if some little common thing connects this, where the feeling is the same, we could make some kind of fusion. So we made new arrangements, using even drums and bass guitar and electric guitar. But then we realized that the music didn't become better—just a little bit more commercial, maybe, a bit easier to understand. But if I trust myself, if I believe that the music I play is good and I don't interest myself too much that it's profitable, I think that slowly it makes an audience."

During the communist period, the Hungarian folk music scene was small, intense, and beset by constant suspicion: "In the past regime, it was a forbidden subject to talk about national identity and being Hungarian," Sebestyén says. "Folk music is a strong weapon in the hand of people, and the communist regime didn't like this at all, so our music was a very oppositional music."

However, it was hard for the government to explain what exactly was threatening about folk dances, and Hamar says that one result was that they could sneak in subtle messages of protest that would not have been allowed if they had been singing modern music. "We were not so dissident that they arrest us or they occupy our flat, but all these secret police were in our concerts, and we were always suspicious because we never knew who is that and what type of report they are writing about us," he recalls. "But there was an interesting trick that we could use. There was only one record company in Hungary, Hungaroton, and they controlled every song, every word. But when we wrote that all the words are traditional folk songs, it went across without control."

To a lot of listeners, the messages came through clearly. For example, there was "Rabnóta" (The Prisoner's Song), a favorite Muzsikás number. Though it was an old folk lyric, Hamar explains, "When we speak about an unwilling guest, everybody knows it means the Russians; when we speak about the free bird and how nice it would be to feel like the free bird feels, then everybody understood that it speaks about the people of Hungary. So the record became very popular also among those people who were not totally into the folk music. Many rock musicians were envious and asked how could we push across these words with the communist record company."

Now that the communist government is gone, Hamar says he feels personally "one hundred percent better." He notes, "I am not controlled. I can freely travel, and feel myself not a second class citizen of the world. You can say what you think. You don't have to be afraid. For me it's the biggest thing that could have happened."

However, the new era has brought its own dangers. Nationalism in the Balkans has taken on a much darker aspect, and folk groups risk becoming rallying points for ethnic purists. Muzsikás has done its best to avoid this, playing not only the music of the ethnic Hungarians, but also Gypsy and Jewish styles, and since the coming of democracy the group has carefully steered clear of politics.

"After the changes, many parties wanted our music, to use it for their ideas," Sebestyén says. "But we said that we want to be neutral, we don't want to serve any party. We just want to play this music and let people know that they should be proud of this heritage."

Even this task has been somewhat complicated by the fall of the Iron Curtain. Where the music was once a rallying point, it now risks being swamped in a flood of Western imports. Also, although the communist state supported cultural affairs as a way of controlling them, at least the support was there. Muzsikás and the other tánchász groups performed in state-subsidized cultural centers and their music was issued on the government's record label, without concern for sales. Today, Hamar says that there is still an audience both at home and abroad for Muzsikás itself, but for younger players the situation is bleak.

"It is not just difficult, it is impossible," he explains. "There is very little hope for beginners to be known or to be famous or to have anything—a record or a club or even a small concert." Still, he says there is no shortage of talent. "There are hundreds and hundreds of young people, they are very diligent to learn this music and they are very good." And, despite the changing times, he feels that the music has lost none of its relevance and power: "All the time, when we listen to the traditional recordings we discover new things. We always try to progress with our knowledge of this music, and as we go deeper and deeper we are discovering that some musicians were not only musicians, they were philosophers. It is not only dance music, but there is a deep philosophy behind it—why they are playing what they are playing.

"An old musician, one of our masters, he lived in a village from childhood to the end of his life, and he said something very interesting to me once. He said, 'Oh, young man, you know that there are only two kinds of music in the world: the good music and the bad music.'

"And I said, 'Oh, but what's the difference?'

"He said, 'It's very big: the bad music lies to you, and the good music tells the truth.'"

Kálmán Balogh

One of the foremost missions of the Hungarian folk revivalists has been to overcome the stereotyped picture of the region's traditions presented by government ensembles and restaurant bands. While older styles languished in rural villages, Gypsy violinists traveled around the world, making their version of Hungarian music a common sound from Budapest to New York. The revivalists regard this as "fakelore," and have struggled to make the world aware of the genuine rural playing styles of both the ethnic Magyars and village Gypsies.

This battle against ersatz folk arrangements makes perfect sense in its context, and has helped to preserve a great deal of fine music that was in danger of dying out with the growth of urbanization and mass media. At the same time, though, the characterization of Gypsy restaurant musicians as fakes includes elements of racism and condescension—one is reminded of the white blues fans of the early 1960s who celebrated seventy-year-old rural guitarists like Son House and Mississippi John Hurt while dismissing Sam Cooke and B.B. King as slick pop stars.

As a result, the arrival of Kálmán Balogh's Gypsy Cimbalom Band on the world music scene offered not only some excellent music, but also an overdue corrective. "In every style it is the same," Balogh agrees. "Like the classical musicians like to say bad things about the Gypsies, but I can say that a lot of Gypsy musicians in the restaurants, they are very, very good players, and some of them can do very difficult classical things. But the people are not open. And the folk musicians, they don't like the Gypsies because we don't play the original folk style."

Balogh has made it his mission to bridge the gap between the folk scene and the restaurant virtuosos. A Gypsy himself, he learned to play cimbalom from his uncle, a restaurant-style musician, before studying classical music at the Liszt Academy and then becoming involved in the tánchaz scene. "The other young Hungarian folk musicians, they were university students," he recalls. "They found out this old village music, nobody played this, and it is very nice and interesting and a good feeling to play it, but they were not Gypsies. This dancehouse movement, only a few Gypsies are in it, me and maybe five others."

The cimbalom itself is not exactly a folk instrument, though, like the piano in the United States, it has been common in some rural areas for over a hundred years. The largest member of the hammer dulcimer family, which exists in various forms throughout Asia, the cimbalom is essentially a piano without a keyboard. The player sits in front of a large wooden frame like a clavichord body, and plays the strings by hitting them with delicate, felt-tipped hammers. "Today, the cimbalom is dying out in the villages," Balogh explains. "Because it is very big and expensive. So when the musicians are dying, there is not a next generation. The old traditional life is changing to the new Western culture, and the young musicians want to play electric guitar."

Once again, a parallel can be made to the American blues scene, where revivalists have tried to preserve the acoustic music of the 1920s or the Chicago sound of the 1950s, while young black musicians in Mississippi and Chicago overwhelmingly turn to more modern and potentially lucrative styles.

"It is a very interesting situation," Balogh says. "The professional Gypsy musicians, especially in the city, for them it is like a step going back if they play this folk music, the village music. For them it looks like they are going back fifty or a hundred years in the past. And for the village musicians, they would like to be city musicians, they want to play all that kind of repertoire, what we can call the new style, like the big names. The Gypsies, they really have no interest in going back in the village and playing the old music."

Balogh himself is something of an exception. His group plays both traditional folk music and something like the restaurant style, as well as a Hungarian variant of the French-Belgian Gypsy jazz style pioneered by Django Reinhardt. He was a member of the tánchaz movement, and has devoted much of his life to mastering the older village traditions, while remaining equally respectful of the city players.

"In Gypsy music, we can see two different styles," he says. "Mostly the Gypsies who play the town style, they are studying also in school. Maybe they are not finishing high, but they learn the basics of the classical techniques. The village musicians, they don't have this possibility, and they play more authentic, older folk music. The ornamentation, the tempo is different, and the harmonies are very different from the city. They can play the same melody, but it is a totally different style."

He adds that even the city musicians play quite differently from non-Gypsies: "One time, I asked my friend, a classical musician who was a violinist, to play the melodies for us, and I would show to her a note, and it was completely different how she played the melody. And I recognized that it is not possible to play the notes if you don't know the style. It is the same as with jazz, I think."

Balogh's own group includes three other Gypsies, trained in the restaurant style, along with a Jewish musician who plays Balkan folk music and an ethnic Hungarian trained in jazz and classical. "When I want to play authentic folk music, normally I play with groups like Muzsikás or Ökrös [another revivalist ensemble]," he says. "But when I want to play something else, I play with my band, and in this band we would also like to find a connection with other music, like jazz or sometimes some classical harmonies.

"My idea is that music is one language, only with different dialects. Of course, there are still people who think we need to stay in our own styles, and it's true that you need to focus on something. But I think it's also possible to study the different things and play many different styles, and do it in the right way. And I think the future is that."

Scotland

Norman Kennedy

If we can say anything about the origins of music, it seems safe to assume that the first instrument was the voice. At least, it was the first instrument capable of capturing all the complexities of music, the subtleties of melody, tonality, and rhythm. One of the saddest results of modern technology has been a massive reduction in the amount of singing people do around their homes and workplaces. By rights, the various folk revivals should have concentrated on singers, as the overwhelming majority of music made in any folk community is sung, and generally without instrumental accompaniment. However, the reality is that unaccompanied singing is routinely pushed into the corners of the professional music world, folk or otherwise. Even if they were raised in traditions based entirely on a cappella performance, when singers take to the stage they almost always team up with instrumentalists. This undoubtedly makes their music more accessible, in the sense that it becomes more homogenized and similar to the pop mainstream, but that is simply another way of saying that it becomes easier to ignore. A single voice demands attention, while a band can be pleasant background noise.

The old singers set their own rhythms, which shifted with their mood, their breathing, or the sense of the stories they were telling, and they had no tempered or chorded instruments forcing them to even out their scales and match defined pitches or harmonies. A great singer, working alone, has a freedom that disappears when she has to fit into a band, or even to tune her voice to an accompanying instrument.

The one place where unaccompanied singing flourished on the folk revival stage was in the British Isles, especially in the 1960s when folk-club managers like Ewan MacColl enforced rules designed to steer people toward their own traditions, forbidding English ballad singers to use guitars or sing American songs. This "folk-nazism" was despised by a lot of young musicians, but it meant that there were a few places where the a cappella tradition was maintained. For a while the English, Irish, Scottish, and Welsh balladeers had a forum, developed fans, and made records, and anyone who has never spent an evening listening to people sing, unamplified and without accompaniment, as if they were just talking to you, has missed one of the greatest and most essential musical experiences on earth.

Norman Kennedy is one of the finest ballad singers alive. He is also a brilliant showman who can keep an audience enthralled without any apparent effort. There's no trick to it; he sits in his chair and tells stories and sings songs, and you feel that you are lucky to be able to spend an evening with such a sharp and entertaining fellow. If more people have not heard of him, that is because he has never dressed up his music with any instrumentation, and because he would rather teach weaving than tour around the clubs and festivals.

Unlike a lot of contemporary Scottish singers, Kennedy came to traditional music not through the folk scene, but just by spending time around old people in his native Aberdeen. "I was raised and born in my grandma's bed," he explains. "She got up and let my ma lie down for a while to have me. But my ma got up right soon cause she was in the middle of washing. It was a big washing, too. They didn't fool around much in those days."

Kennedy says that his family provided his first musical experiences. "They were always singing to me, you see. I had a great aunt, she was one-legged, so she'd just hold me between her leg and her stump, and sing, 'Speed bonny boat, like a bird on the wing.'"

Though he has lived in the United States since the 1970s, Kennedy still speaks with a broad Scotch accent—and despite the current style experts, he insists it is "Scotch," not "Scots." "That's people that don't speak the language [who use the new jargon]," he says. "That's Anglicized people, and I don't have any time for them at all. It's just snobbery, laddie. It's a class system, you see."

Kennedy is old enough to remember when the traditional music and speech patterns were still treated with contempt, often by exactly the sort of people who now celebrate them. "It's the same with 'Celtic,'" he says. "When I was young you never heard anything about Celtic music; folk wouldn't have pissed on it. But now there's money to it and they call it Celtic. It's bloody ridiculous, to tell you the truth."

The prejudice even existed within his own family: he recalls his mother telling him to "Speak richt," and his father scolding him for speaking Gaelic: "He said to me, 'You're gonna get yourself into a bunch of trouble speaking that bloody Arabic'—that's what he called it. I knew people that got beat up in school and were told they were stupid because they were talking that. So it was country folk and poor folk that spoke Gaelic when I was young."

Kennedy was fascinated by the traditional culture, and World War II provided him with a rare opportunity: His family's house was bombed, and they moved across the street from Jeannie Robertson, among the finest Scottish singers of the century. Soon Kennedy was singing with Robertson and picking up her style and repertoire, though with no idea of making music his profession. Even when the folk music boom hit Britain in the 1950s, he recalls thinking that it had nothing to do with him. "Folk songs to me was 'Michael Row the Boat Ashore,'" he says. "We were singing 'old-fashioned' songs. We didn't use the word *folk song*. But I went down there to a folk club, and then I started joining on choruses, and the fella who was running it, he said, 'Hey man, you can sing.'"

"Oh, aye . . ." Kennedy pauses, realizing he has left out an important part of the story. "I was gonna tell ya, I was about seventeen before my own folk knew that I could sing. My mother said to me, 'You ken song verses?'

"And I says, 'Oh, aye.'

"And she says, 'Well, sing 'em.'

"We were all sitting in the kitchen, and I got up and I went to the cupboard where the dishes and the pots were, and I sung there. Because I'd never sung in front of folk."

Kennedy had considered the old songs, with their complex stories of people who lived long ago, a sort of private treasure. He recalls learning the classic "McPherson's Rant" from a street singer named Davey Stewart: "He sang in the Friday Market, in Strickall, an ancient market since the thirteen hundreds in Aberdeen. I'd stand there, and I wouldn't go home for my dinner that day. I'd go home at night for my supper, and my mother would say, 'You've been listening to that bloody old stuff again.' I was twelve at the time, but I knew it was valuable. But I kept it to myself, for fear they would stop me.

"People thought it was weird, you see. You know Alasdair Fraser, the fiddler? We were speaking the other morning and he says, 'Norman, when I was getting me fiddle lessons, I'd take the back alleyway.'

He said, 'If my mates would have seen me, they'd have thrown stones at me.'"

Once he started spending time around the local folk club, Kennedy realized that there were other people who valued the old songs, and though it took some urging, after a while he began performing the ballads that had made up his private world. From Richardson and others he had acquired a style and repertoire that was unique among singers of his generation, and soon the folk fans were sitting up and taking notice.

Kennedy did not always return the compliment. Mention Ewan MacColl, dean of British folk revival singers, and Kennedy's response is typical: "Jimmy Miller was his name. He was an actor, and Mac-Coll was his stage name. He kept some songs alive and he brought it to an audience, but he couldn't speak broad Scotch. The first time I ever met him, it was a concert for the 'ban the bombers.' They came out around, and they'd ask people to sing, but most of the local singers wouldn't do it because they were communists, you see. But they were offering us five pounds—that was a whole week's wages—so I made it across to Jeannie's, and I says, 'See, Jeannie you going to sing?'

"She said, 'How much are they paying us?'

"'Five pounds.'

"She said, 'Do you need the money?'

"I says, 'Christ, yeah.'

"She says, 'We'll do it.'

"So she and I were the only ones that sung. And when I started singing [MacColl] was up at the back—we'd never met—and he walked down and sat right in front of me. Afterwards, I said to one of the fellas, 'What's he sitting in front of me for?'

"He said, 'Norman, he's trying to get the words right.' Because he would pronounce a word one verse and the next verse he would pronounce it different, because he didn't have a dialect of his own. And he asked me more than once what was the meaning of a line in a ballad."

Kennedy pauses a moment, then adds, "I mean, I like the man—he was a holy terror to some folk, but him and Peggy [Seeger, MacColl's wife], they were always nice to me."

Though he was rubbing shoulders with professional performers, Kennedy still had no aspirations to a musical career. As traditional singers had done for centuries, he worked a day job and just sang for his friends. Then one day the American musician and folk song collector Mike Seeger came to perform in Aberdeen, and Kennedy went down to the club to hear him. "I was getting fed up with being trotted out as a tame traditional singer," he recalls. "So I paid my money at the door. They said, 'What are you paying for? You're gonna sing.'

"I said, 'No, for once I want to sit and listen.'

"They said, 'Oh, you can't be like that.'

"I said, 'Just watch me.'

"So the fella come up at half time with a double glass of whiskey. He never give me whiskey, and I said, 'I should try this oftener.' Well, after drinking the whiskey I would have stood on my head and whistled 'Dixie' to the Queen of England."

Kennedy sang a song, and at a party afterward he sang some more, and a few months later word came that Seeger wanted him to come to the United States: "The fella from the folk club, he comes and says, 'I have a letter for you from America,' and here he was asking would I come across, and they would pay my way and things like that. But my boss wouldn't let me. I was working in a dentist's office, and they wanted me to come across for six months, but no, he wouldn't let me. But I says, 'Well, I've got two weeks holiday, I'll just go.'"

Kennedy was booked to appear at the 1965 Newport Folk Festival, the same weekend that Bob Dylan set the folk music world aflame by plugging in an electric guitar. It didn't take amplifiers and a rock 'n' roll revolution to make the visit memorable for a young Scottish working man: "I woke up in Newport," he recalls. "A gorgeous place, I'd never seen the likes—all those yachts. And I walked to the moor, and I smelled it and I said, 'Christ, I'm gonna try and come back here.' Because I smelled freedom. I'd been born and brought up in a very tight place, you know, where you find your place and you stick to it and you've very few options. Even now, when I go home, I hear, 'Well, you cannot say that,' or 'You cannot do this.' It's like going into a little closet and shutting the door."

Kennedy managed to make it to Newport for the next six festivals, and in 1974 decided to emigrate to the United States for good. "I come across, honest to god, just like some of the old timers," he says. "With the equivalent of about two hundred fifty dollars and two wooden chests with my spinning wheel and my shuttles and a couple of blankets. But folk have been good to me in this country. Damn sight better than they could afford to be in the old country."

Kennedy worked in a crafts shop in Cambridge, Massachusetts, then took a job at Colonial Williamsburg, Virginia, before finally settling near Burlington, Vermont. He always worked as a weaver, only singing in public if someone pressed him. "It takes a lot of effort," he insists. "And I'd rather be using what breath I've got left to teach folk the skills of the weaving."

And that is why one of the world's finest ballad singers lives only a few hours from one of America's most active folk music centers, but has never become a regular performer. It is the scene's loss, but as usual Kennedy is doing what he cares to do rather than what some people think he should. "It's the freaks in this world that keep things going," he remarks, with finality. "We're goats, the Kennedys. A lot of folk are sheep, but we're goats, and goats go their own way."

Dick Gaughan

If Norman Kennedy represents the roots of the Scottish traditional music world—and in a broader sense the deep strain of song that connects the British Isles—Dick Gaughan is a member of the modern generation. He can sing a cappella ballads in a traditional style, but is as likely to turn up with a solid-body electric guitar and play a set that ranges from ancient fiddle tunes to the Rolling Stones. He is intensely political, and intensely attached to the idea that both his politics and his music are part of a Scottish heritage that has been perverted by capitalists and bourgeois romantics. He is also a magnificent musician and one of the most powerfully moving and intelligent singers on the European folk scene—the original *Rough Guide to World Music* devoted two of its five paragraphs on the Scottish folk revival to his work, noting that "his passionate artistry towers over three decades."

A small, scrappy man who started playing professionally with the Boys of the Lough in the early 1970s, Gaughan went on to form a group called Five Hand Reel, then went solo, mixing medieval ballads with original songs and the work of friends like the anarchist songwriter Leon Rosselson. This combination is more common on the British scene than in the United States, where the folk world has tended to polarize into traditionalists on one side and singer-songwriters on the other. British artists like Gaughan, Martin Carthy, and June Tabor have managed a comfortable blend of old and new material, and Gaughan says he finds the separation of categories rather silly.

"I have this problem with the use of this word *traditional*,'" he says. "I grew up in a family of traditional singers and musicians, and to me those are just songs. This idea of dividing things into 'this is traditional' and 'this is not traditional,' I don't understand those concepts. I know what other people mean by them, but I don't accept them myself. There are songs I sing now that I've been singing since I was a kid, and I didn't make any real distinction between them and rock and roll. I mean, I was aware that I hadn't heard them on the radio, but they were just songs that nobody else sang—they were our songs, you know?"

That possessive feeling is a key to Gaughan's work. He sees himself as carrying on the musical tradition of the Scottish working class, and by extension the working class of Britain and of the world. He grew up in the era of the skiffle craze, and his father sang songs by American left-wing folksingers like Woody Guthrie and Leadbelly along with the old Scottish ballads. While the music was different, the themes and outlook were similar and fitted Gaughan's perception of the world around him.

"To me, the politics and the music are inseparable," he says. "It doesn't make sense to me that any human beings could be singing about what they see, what they experience, and what affects their lives, and ignore politics—to me that's ludicrous. Scottish and Irish traditional music always had a very large part of itself which would nowadays be regarded as political. Folk music is dangerous stuff."

Gaughan laughs, then catches himself. "In its own way it *is* dangerous," he says firmly. "It's subversive to admit that ordinary working-class people have actually got a culture and artistic merit. This flies against the vested interests of those who would have us believe that the poor are poor because they are stupid."

Gaughan's politics have been a factor in his American obscurity, leading to years of visa problems. Despite the seriousness of his commitment, however, his concerts do not feel like musical lectures. He has the black humor of his Celtic forebears, a tradition that produced comic songs about massacres and famine, and his work has a bite and directness that is a long way from the sentimentality of much topical songwriting. He is also a superb musician, one of the finest and most original guitarists in the British Isles (Carthy has called him the best player on the folk scene), and a brilliant all-around entertainer.

Indeed, Gaughan is a craftsman in a world where too many performers separate themselves from their listeners by invoking the secular talisman of art. Asked what keeps him going despite his somewhat limited commercial success, he uses the language of a workman proud of his abilities, an unalienated laborer.

"This is my trade," he says. "It's the set of skills I have spent my lifetime learning. I want to put them to use, and I want to do that in such a way that I am contributing something to somebody else rather than just doing a job—if I was just doing a job I would play some other kind of music and make a lot more money than I am doing. Basically, what I'm trying to do is to stand up and say, 'Look, this is how the universe appears to me and to my people over the last thousand years.' And to do that in a way that is musical."

France

Alan Stivell

Alan Stivell is among the most influential musicians of the continental European folk revival. A harpist, piper, singer, and bandleader of Breton French descent, Stivell was inspired by the American and English folk scenes of the 1960s to experiment with fusions of tradition folk music with the new sounds appearing in the rock world. He went much deeper than most of his models, though, studying medieval instruments and becoming deeply involved with a pan-European revival of Celtic languages and culture. In the 1970s, Stivell-inspired groups swept Europe, mixing ancient instruments with electric ones to create new styles that at their best sounded completely organic. These days, fewer players cite him directly as an inspiration, but it seems fair to wonder what bands like Spain's Radio Tarifa would sound like had Stivell not done his groundbreaking work. And that is not to mention his roles as a pioneer of New Age and European folk-rock music.

Stivell's work has been extremely varied, from the acoustic sparseness of his groundbreaking *Renaissance of the Celtic Harp* to a full rock band sound that recalls Steeleye Span, or even Jethro Tull. The unifying thread is Stivell's devotion to the Celtic heritage of his native Brittany.

"Even when I was a child I have been impassioned with all the Celtic civilization, and I wanted to help it survive," he explains in thickly accented English, speaking from his summer home in Carnac, the French equivalent of Stonehenge. "I felt it was so nice, so beautiful that it was too much pity that it would disappear and die. So I studied everything about the culture, from the languages to the arts or the mythology or the ancient history. I began to learn the Breton language at the same time as I began to learn the harp, and at the end of the fifties I put myself more into the study, because I knew many things in Breton and even words in Irish Gaelic or Welsh, but I was not able to speak in fact, to have a conversation. So about when I was fourteen or fifteen I worked much more on the language, and a bit later it became a second language for me. But as I was a musician, I felt the best way I could help this culture was through the music."

Stivell's father was a leader of the French Celtic revival, and the first to attempt a reconstruction of the medieval Breton harp. Stivell explains that in the early Middle Ages there were harps in all the Celtic regions—which, like the countries around the Mediterranean, were joined by sea passages that in those days were more easily traveled than overland routes. By the end of the Middle Ages, though, the harp had disappeared from Brittany, for reasons that are far from clear. It survived a bit longer in Scotland and Wales, and harps were still being made in Ireland in the nineteenth century, but by the time Stivell's father began his research, there had been no Celtic harp built for decades. Eventually, after studying surviving Irish harps and old manuscripts that described the Breton variety, he built an instrument on which Stivell made his concert debut at age nine.

At the time, the family was living in Paris, and Stivell says that his fascination with the Celtic past was balanced by an equally strong fascination with the modern world: "I decided I would try to make a fusion of the Celtic cultures and open on the world, open with other cultures and with other times, coming from the past and going as much as possible to the future. It was the time of the first arrival of rock 'n' roll in Europe, and I was feeling that in Brittany we should do music from our own time, but at the same time go on with our culture."

This was in the late 1950s, and Stivell says that at first it was no more than a dream: "It was not possible even to imagine—I didn't know any guitar player or anybody else who could do this experiment with me, so I had to wait till the mid-sixties. At that time, I was doing many things: I was playing Celtic harps and playing in a Breton pipe band, studying the Breton dances and the Scottish bagpipes and things like that. It was when the American folk wave came, with Bob Dylan, Joan Baez, that I realized I should try to be professional. And I was helped also by the evolution of British and Irish pop music, which was beginning to use ethnic instruments against guitar, for example, or sometimes even some medieval instruments. So it was around that period, the mid-sixties and a bit after, Fairport Convention and Steeleye Span, then it was really helping to make it more easy to find the answers for the evolution or the sensibility of people. So in fact, my first real experiment with the fusion of Celtic rock was only in '71."

Stivell became a star the following year, when his live recording, *At the Olympia*, topped the French album charts. It featured a band that would become something of a training ground for French folk progressives, including the singer and guitarist Gabriel Yacoub, soon to form the band Malicorne, and the Breton guitarist Dan Ar Braz.

While American audiences were treated to Stivell's folkier side, and remember his haunting a cappella renditions of Breton ballads or the gentle lilt of his harp, at home he is at least equally noted for his rock edge. Indeed, when folk purists see him in an electric band setting, they are startled not only by Stivell's music but by his instrument. "My father wanted mainly to make a reconstitution of the old Celtic Breton harp," he says. "But myself, I've always been very much enthusiastic into the conquest of the cosmos and science fiction. When I was a child I was already dreaming and making drawings of futuristic harps. I had my first electric harp in 1980, and after [that] I had the harp I'm bringing with me, a Plexiglas and aluminum harp with pedals on each string, and I think it's maybe the harp of the next century."

Despite the modernist trappings, Stivell concerts typically show-case his full range of styles, from the early harp instrumentals to pieces from his most recent albums. "I am starting with the Celtic folk music," he says. "But what is very interesting is that there are infinite possibilities from this base, from something which is just a song to something close to the hard rock or something more influenced by jazz rock. There are an infinity of possibilities and so, in a way, with my different albums I tried these different possibilities.

"I'm interested with a very large panel of expressions. I love to do music which is very meditating or relaxing, but I love also when it's very warming up or exciting. In fact, I need both. And sometime I'm a bit more classical or traditional, because at the same I time need to prove to myself that I still have the real roots."

Afro-European Music

Les Nubians

Europe is currently undergoing the most profound cultural upheaval it has faced in hundreds, maybe thousands of years. The very meaning of the term *European* is up for grabs, with the disappearance of internal borders and the arrival of hundreds of thousands of immigrants from other continents. These changes have provoked a wide range of reactions, from enthusiasm at the possibilities of a new Europe to fears that precious traditions are on the verge of extinction. In music, the new mix of populations has spawned a broad array of fusions. Some of these must certainly be considered part of the world music scene, but it is hard to decide how to categorize them geographically. Lucien Bokilo's *soukous*, for example, has clearly been affected by the fact that he lived in Paris, and one could argue that he belongs in this chapter rather than the one on Africa. Meanwhile, Les Nubians are dark-skinned and work within a multitude of African and Afro-American styles, so some people may bridle at the idea that their music is European. But what else could one call it? A youthful pop style that has absorbed African rhythms and hip-hop, their work clearly reflects the reality of present-day France.

In the last few decades, France has become a hotspot of multicultural pop music innovation, spawning a range of artists from MC Solaar to Manu Chao who elude any sort of easy categorization by continent or genre. Les Nubians are an obvious example—starting with their name, which bows to Africa, France, and English (in French they would be called Les Nubiennes). Their debut album, *Princesses Nubiennes*, featured a jazzy R & B sound interwoven with African samples, orchestral strings, and even a snippet of interview with the American jazz singer Abbey Lincoln.

A pair of French-Cameroonian sisters, Les Nubians started performing in their teens. "We used to sing at home together," elder sister Hélène (written "LN" for American fans) Faussart remembers, speaking in delicately accented English. "And some friend was like, 'Wow, you have to share your music, you have to share your experience.' So he programmed us on a festival and that's how we began. We used to propose to people a voyage into black music, from the roots to the leaves. We started with African traditional music from our village; Wolof songs from Senegal, or Xhosa songs from South Africa; and also modern music like songs from Lokua Kanza, Miriam Makeba, and Kofi Olomide; some Makossa tracks from Cameroon—and then gospel songs, blues, soul, reggae, R & B, hip-hop, jungle . . ."

Considering that range of taste, it should not have been much of a surprise when *Princesses Nubiennes* broke outside the "world" scene, placing a single at number 36 on *Billboard* magazine's R & B chart. Nonetheless, their hit track, "Makeda," was a far cry from normal American pop fare: its soft-soul instrumentation might be familiar, but it was sung in French and paid tribute to the fabled Queen of Sheba.

Faussart says that this overlap of ages and cultures is typical of Les Nubians' self-defined mission: "The more we are getting into the third millennium, things are going so fast, we are traveling a lot, we are working a lot, we are in a kind of speedy wave, and finally you arrive at the end of the line and you're like, 'Oh, but where I'm from?' And then it's maybe too late to go back and take care of your roots. So we talk a lot about history, and also, we discovered when we came back from Africa that a lot of people were so ignorant about the African culture. They were living with only clichés. And another thing very important is that I think that a lot of people don't realize how powerful can be a mixed couple, and children from a mixed couple."

Faussart explains that she and her sister Célia (sometimes written "C. Lia") were born in Paris, of a French father and a Cameroonian mother, and raised between Paris and Chad. Their formal schooling was in French, but at home their mother would tell stories and sing songs of her native village. "I thank my parents because they did it well," she says. "We know as much our French culture as our African culture, and you are able to see the good in both of those cultures, and the bad sides, and you just try to get everyone together to create harmony all around you."

The Faussarts found an early musical model in the Afro-Belgian group Zap Mama, whose a cappella blend of Arab, Central African, European, and American styles took the world music scene by storm in the 1990s. "They are the Afropean band," Faussart says. "And they really succeeded in such beautiful way. Their voicing is just wonderful, their vision of music is incredible and when we used to do our shows a cappella we used to cover a lot Zap Mama."

While that influence is still audible in their work, Les Nubians hit the international stage not as an a cappella duo, but as pop singers, part of a new wave of European, hip-hop-flavored R & B. Faussart feels that the sampling and fusions of hip-hop, and its worldwide impact, have made it an ideal cross-cultural bridge. "Hip-hop is getting bigger and bigger in Africa every year," she says. "In West Africa and Central Africa and I won't forget of course South Africa. So I think that more and more we're gonna have more connection and more cooperation between the African continent and France."

Though their debut album had only brief moments of rap, and sounded closer to Sade than to early favorites like Public Enemy, Faussart insists that hip-hop is still the most logical category for their work. "We really did this album in a kind of hip-hop process, with a lot of samples," she says. "Our music is urban music, and for me hip-hop is a way to take mud—urban mud, street mud—and turn it into something beautiful. Of course, at the beginning of hip-hop, French people and people of the world were completely influenced by American production, but now they are really doing a French production, with their own style, their own vocabulary, their own attitudes, and without copying America, which is a very, very, very good step."

Nonetheless, she says that she does not want the genre label to become a musical straitjacket: "We are very close to this new wave of socially conscious hip-hop, but sometimes people have the assimilation and just get stuck on it. So when we did this album we didn't want it to be classified. To be a part of hip-hop is very nice, but I think that we are a part of world music and a part of Afropean music, and also a part of soul music, a little jazz music. So, I just call our music *music*."

Nonetheless, that idea of mixing disparate elements fits perfectly with the hip-hop ideal, and Faussart feels the links are deeper than most people realize. On her African side, she relates rap to the West African griot tradition, the musical storytellers who were oral historians of their cultures. As for her French side, "I'm sorry," she says firmly, "but at this moment of French history of music, rappers are the only ones who are really writing. If France is a country of literature and poetry, here are the new poets. 'Cause when you listen to contemporary adult music in France—oh my God, the lyrics are near nothing. It's just stupid, it's horrible."

Of course, the hip-hop connection has also provided a bridge to the United States, but Faussart says that this was a happy accident. After all, Les Nubians are only one among many modern French groups, and they had no expectations of blazing a trail across the Atlantic.

"We did this album thinking about French-speaking countries," she says. "And when we heard that the album was doing well here in America we thought it was like French-speaking people who bought it. Then, when we arrived and we realized that it was everyone from seven to seventy-seven, and especially the Afro-American community, we were like, 'Wow!' Because we never thought about succeeding in America. I mean, it was always a kind of a dream somewhere in your head, in a little cupboard, but you don't think about it. Just a dream, but it's a beautiful dream coming true. And more than that, it's a blessing."

5

FLAMENCO

Napoleon Bonaparte famously said that Africa begins at the Pyrenees, and while there are plenty of reasons to disagree, the remark still has some truth. For almost eight hundred years, while the rest of Europe was cut of from the outside world in what are remembered as the medieval dark ages, Spain was linked to Islamic empires that reached from sub-Saharan Africa to deep within Asia. Urban centers like Cordoba, Seville, and Zaragoza were meeting grounds for musicians, philosophers, and scientists—and Muslims, Christians, and, Jews—from throughout the Islamic world, and the country's architecture and music remain deeply influenced by that period. Above all, the country's most famous music, flamenco, retains the blend of Gypsy, Arab, North African, Jewish, and European cultures.

Flamenco is far from the only traditional Spanish music, and indeed it is something of a world unto itself. Andalusians, Basques, Castillians, Catalans, and Gallegos all have their own folk music traditions, and in the thirty years since the fall of the dictatorship of Francisco Franco there has been a flowering of regional music revivalists: Milladoiro and the bagpiper Carlos Nuñez in Galicia, Euzkadi and the accordionist Kepa Junkera in the Basque country, Altao in Valencia, La Musgaña in Castilla, and dozens more.

Very little of this music has been heard in the United States, however, and to most Americans, Spanish music is flamenco, and vice versa. Flamenco certainly deserves the attention it has received, but it is important to understand that it is neither a national style, nor is it folk music in the normal sense of the term. It is southern and Gypsy music, and at a professional level it involves a degree of full-time commitment and technical skill that invites comparison to the most elevated virtuosity of the classical and jazz fields. Even flamenco amateurs tend to devote a time and attention to their music that is very different from the casual pleasure of village players who accompanied dances as a respite from their daily work.

Flamenco is thus an anomaly. It is not a court or concert music like the classical traditions of Africa, Asia, Europe, or the Islamic world. Its masters have generally come from poor families, and their music has often been disrespected, so it is in some ways logical to compare it to blues, *fado*, and *rembetika*. And yet, in musical terms it can very reasonably be grouped with the classical styles of the old Islamic empires, both for its complex rules, legendary artists, and high emphasis on virtuosity and for its form of improvisation within set patterns. In recent years, new styles and fusions have emerged, and while some flamenco artists have pursued links to jazz and European classical styles, many have looked south to Algeria and Morocco, Mali and Senegal. So it makes some sense to treat this music separately, and place it in the borderland between Europe and North Africa.

Mainstream Flamenco

Carmen Cortés and Manuel Soler

At its best, flamenco rests on three pillars: dance, song, and guitar—all of these supported by a solid foundation of rhythm, supplied by clapping hands. Coming to the style for the first time, outsiders are often perplexed that a young, brilliant guitarist (for example) will be accompanied at concerts by a couple of old men who only clap the rhythm for him. One thinks, "Surely the guitarist is more important than the people keeping time—wouldn't it be better to see an older, experienced guitarist, and let young guys stand back and clap?" When I was living in Malaga in the 1970s, I had exactly that reaction at the concert of a sixteen-year-old guitar sensation. It was only when I went over to talk to one of the old men that I learned that he was the young man's teacher, though he did not play guitar. The way he explained this apparent incongruity was to argue that a guitarist must spend so much time practicing his technique that he can never really master the essentials of flamenco.

That is an extreme position, but it suggests the problems surrounding a music like flamenco in a commercial world of nonaficionados. Outsiders are dazzled by fast guitar runs, and don't notice if a rhythmic rule is broken. A musician trying for mass acclaim—and flamenco artists are as eager for applause as artists in any other form—will constantly be tempted to give the audience what it wants, and in the case of flamenco this is flash, be it speedy guitar, stamping feet, or vocal pyrotechnics. There is also the temptation for all the members of a group to try to show their best stuff on every tune. Guitarists in particular are now going into the field with dreams of stardom. In the old days, the singers and dancers were the stars, and all but a handful of guitarists where known as great accompanists rather than soloists. It was often said that a flamenco guitarist should spend twenty years accompanying dancers, and then if he was good enough he could graduate to singers, and after twenty years of that, he might possibly attain a knowledge and depth that would justify hearing him as a solo concert artist. Today, when a hot eighteen-year-old can make more money than an aged master, few guitarists care to submit themselves to this sort of apprenticeship.

All of the flamenco people I have interviewed talk about the dangers of losing the music's essence—indeed, it has become something of a cliché, and even the young, hot stars tend to pay it lip service. But the more flamenco one sees, the more one comes to understand the value of soul, experience, and grounding in the form. Great flamenco, like great blues or great Indian classical playing, is a very subtle thing, and is becoming harder and harder to find.

Over the years, music and dance audiences in the United States have had the opportunity to see plenty of flamenco-oriented shows, but very little straight flamenco. With the world boom, though, a few promoters have seized the opportunity to put together packages that showcase deeper, more traditional performers. One example was a festival featuring the troupes of two of Spain's most respected dancers, Carmen Cortés and Manuel Soler. It may seem odd to treat these performers as musicians, but dance and music are inextricable in flamenco: in a world governed by rhythm, it makes little difference if you perform with your mouth, your hands, or your feet.

Soler is a master of the *zapateado*, the percussive footwork that he demonstrated to world audiences during fourteen years with Paco de Lucía, and a bastion of flamenco purism. "My specialty is percussion," he says.* "And we know that dance is percussion. And all the people coming with me are very highly qualified and respected by the true flamencos. They are a marvel, the very best, and flamenco *flamenco*."

Most Americans are at least tangentially familiar with flamenco's image—the soulful passion, the fierce grace, the bullfighter's calm, the lightning guitar runs, the spectacular footwork of the dancers— but few forms are as consistently misunderstood. The most famous flamenco artists in the world are the Gipsy Kings, who do not even play flamenco (their music is a French and Catalan pop variant called *rumba*), and Paco de Lucía, who is a flamenco master but devotes most of his time to fusion music.

Flamenco dance is particularly ill-served. Films and touring companies have tended to present flamenco ballets, featuring richly choreographed troupes of dancers twirling and stamping in unison. These can be very fine in their way, but are the antithesis of traditional flamenco, which lives and dies on the unique magnetism and intelligence of an individual performer, improvising in the moment. The most respected flamenco virtue is not technique, but *duende*—that unquantifiable magic best translated as "soul."

Of course, there are difficulties in bringing this sort of dance to a large stage—just as one will never hear really first-rate jazz at Lincoln Center or in Symphony Hall—so some compromises are necessary. "One tries to make sure that one keeps this sense of improvisation in the moment," Cortés says. "You have to protect that, because flamenco comes from an inner expression and feeling. So you professionalize yourself and try to present that same thing that you had at family gatherings and later in the *tablao* [flamenco club], and bring it to the larger frame of the theater, while somehow keeping that feel. You add choreography, you have to have something defined, because not every night is good. But one always leaves a space, a part of the dance, for improvisation, because that is what makes it a valiant flamenco."

---

* These interviews were conducted in Spanish.

Cortés is one of the best-known contemporary flamenco dancers, or *bailaoras*. While she is known for large shows that explore the boundaries of the genre, including two ballets based on the work of the poet Federico García Lorca, she often tours with only a male partner, two singers, and two guitarists. In this context, she says, "I will be dancing flamenco. It is of today's world, with my own approach, but I am not going to mix it with anything. It will be orthodox flamenco, the typical flamenco *palos*."

The palos (literally, "staffs" or "posts") are the basic forms that make up the flamenco style—*soleares*, *bulerías*, *alegrías*, and so on—each defined by a certain rhythm and mood. Traditionally, the singers, guitarists, and dancers would not play a particular song or piece; they would just agree on a palo and improvise within that form, much as jazz players jam on, say, a blues in D.

This lack of defined compositions was not a problem in the old days, when musicians and dancers grew up in a flamenco culture, surrounded by the style from birth and learning the palos as they learned to walk and talk. Today, though, young virtuosos are likely to be formed in schools, or by practicing scales and footwork in their bedrooms, and they are often more comfortable playing set pieces than taking part in an improvised conversation that includes singers, dancers, guitarists, and a clapping crowd of aficionados.

"Many of the young guitarists have formidable technique," Soler says. "But they can't play for dancing and they don't have *aire* [roughly, 'style']. People tend to imitate Paco [de Lucía], which is normal, but with Paco one has to look at where he came from. He played a long time for singers and for dancers, and that's necessary. Afterward, you should study technique, but you need roots. The young people are not used to listening to the singing; they don't know how. For example, there is a young dancer who, when they are singing him an alegrías, he wants them to sing a certain lyric that he knows. If they change that lyric to another that's just the same, in the same meter, he can't dance."

It is not that Soler wants to live in the past. He is quick to insist that his work remains thoroughly contemporary: "Flamenco has kept advancing, of course. We can't keep doing a zapateado from forty years ago. It's like with doctors: in the old days there were sicknesses that couldn't be cured and today they can be cured. We respect the old ways, and we use that, but to improve on it, to enrich it musically. The technique they had before was limited by what they could do, and now it is open. For example, any singer today can perfectly master ten or twelve different palos, and in the old days no. In the old days they sang two or three palos, they were satisfied there, and that was that.

"But many dancers, they have added ballet, for example, and flamenco dance isn't that. With [my troupe], all that is real flamenco is respected—a guy who dances a *soleá* dances a soleá."

In keeping with this respect for tradition, Soler describes his current singers, Juan José and El Estremeño, not as wonderful soloists, but as "the best that exist for singing for dancing." As with guitarists, many young singers in the flamenco world are not primarily interested in serving as accompanists. "Singing for dancing is very different," Soler says. "Because when you sing for listening you can sing freely, you don't have to submit yourself—though there are certain rules and limits you have to respect—but for dancing, you have to sing for the dancer. Aside from the rhythm, you have to sing squarely. It is very difficult; some of the greatest singers, they are very good for a festival or whatever, but they cannot sing for dancing."

Soler's attention to such details is a testament to his essential classicism. Both he and Cortés have been dancing since childhood, and while the two are quite different, they speak well of each other—Soler describes Cortés as "phenomenal"—and both are acutely conscious of not only the power but the vulnerability of the flamenco tradition.

"It's fine to be a star," Soler says. "But you have to start with the roots, and prepare yourself very well, in the right atmosphere. Then, if you have quality, everything comes in life. But with the way people are learning today it is very hard to find anyone who can do this."

Paco de Lucía

In 1964, when the Society of Spanish Studies published D. H. Pohren's *Lives and Legends of Flamenco*, the youngest artist included was a sixteen-year-old then known as Paco de Algeciras. Together with his brother Pepe, he had taken the flamenco world by storm two

Paco de Lucía. Photograph © Jack Vartoogian/FrontRowPhotos.

years earlier, winning a major contest and releasing a first album as Los Chiquitos de Algeciras (The Algeciras Kids).

By the end of the 1970s, Paco de Lucía had changed the course of flamenco, and become the only serious flamenco artist who is widely recognized outside the genre. His innovative ensemble, which mixes the traditional voice, guitar, and clapping hands with saxophone, electric bass, and the Peruvian *cajón* (a wooden box that a percussionist sits on and uses as a drum), has added harmonies and improvisational approaches from jazz and set a pattern for three decades of flamenco modernists. This has made him somewhat controversial—while many feel he has given flamenco a new lease on life, purists protest that his influence has led to an adulteration of the classic tradition—but no one questions his technical prowess, or his ability to play the deepest, most traditional flamenco when he chooses.

While his musical explorations have taken him a long way from Algeciras, de Lucía has never lost touch with his roots. He always travels with first-class singers and dancers, and for his 1998 album *Luzía*, he set aside his jazz-tinged sextet in favor of a solo guitar format and revisited the classic flamenco *toques*, the rhythm patterns that

define the traditional style. Since that album arrived just as he turned
fifty, it was natural for fans to see it as a sort of career summation,
a taking stock at the half-century mark, but de Lucía says that the
birthday was merely coincidental to the recording.

"Hombre, I was not waiting to reach five-zero to take account," he
says.* "That is something that you do day by day, as your mind and
your body grow older. Imagine how horrible it would be to feel like
you turned fifty and suddenly changed from being young to being old.
No, what happens is that you go ahead, accustoming yourself to the
changes and balancing your energies: what you may lose in power you
compensate for with experience. For me, there is a natural equilibrium
in aging; I am not one of those guys who says 'Ay, fifty!'"

The subject puts de Lucía in a somewhat meditative mood, though,
and sets him to musing about the state of current flamenco, the delicate line between purity and innovation, and music in general. Speaking of the choice to record again in a solo format, he says, "I have
to do a record like this every so many years for the flamencos, my
people, and above all for myself: playing solo, and playing flamenco
toques, not rumbas and things like that, but purely flamenco themes
like siguiriyas, soleares, bulerías. I have to do these records to show
where I am, and where I am going. This is what marks my evolution
as a flamenco guitarist, and shows me which way to go next, how to
evolve in flamenco."

Along with playing the guitar, de Lucía surprised longtime fans
by singing on two of the album's tracks. One was dedicated to his
mother, who died in August of that year, and the other to his sometime partner, the legendary *cantaor* (flamenco vocalist) Camarón de
la Isla.

"I wanted to dedicate a lyric to my mother, and the most direct way
to do that was with my voice, rather than use a singer who would be
like an intermediary," he explains. "And for the piece to Camarón, it
was the same thing. I have always loved song and singing, but I always
felt a great respect for the *cantaores*, and I was ashamed to sing myself.
But in this case, there was an important excuse to do it. And I just
sing a very short lyric at the end of each piece."

---

* This interview was conducted in Spanish.

As de Lucía points out, in flamenco as in blues it is not so much the technical brilliance of the voice that counts; it is the emotion conveyed by the singer. And, though he has done more than any modern player to redefine the guitar as a lead instrument, he insists that singing remains at the music's core: "For me, the essence of flamenco is the voice. As a guitarist who started out in traditional flamenco, I have always felt that when a singer sings you have to be at his service. You must listen to him, sense what he is doing, and help and empower him, not wait for the singer to finish a phrase so you can show your virtuosity, so you can shine. There are many people who, when they play for singing, are thinking continually of their guitar, but that is wrong. You should fall in love with what the singer is singing, not get in the way, and just do what is appropriate to make that voice come across as well as possible."

De Lucía is one of the few contemporary virtuosos who is also a master accompanist. Indeed, to some fans his greatest recordings remain those he did with Camarón in the early 1970s. These records, imbued with deep traditional roots and rock 'n' roll passion, were the opening salvo in the modern flamenco revolution, and remain among the most exciting of modern times.

De Lucía had a classic upbringing, raised in Algeciras by a father who was a guitarist and aficionado, in a family of singers, dancers, and players. Though *payos* (non-Gypsies), they were deeply immersed in the world of Gypsy flamenco, and, though born Francisco (Paco) Sánchez Gomez, he followed the medieval Gypsy tradition of taking his mother's first name for his artistic name, Paco de Lucía, or "Lucía's Paco." (The divergent spelling on the album suggests the Spanish word *luz*, or light, though de Lucía says he used it because his mother was Portuguese and originally spelled her name that way.)

De Lucía spent his youth at in the *juergas*, or late-night flamenco gatherings, and firmly believes that this informal schooling is vital for a flamenco artist. Unfortunately, he says that such training is becoming difficult to find in modern Spain: "It still exists, but less every day. In my teenage days, the artists had parties, we got drunk together, we played and sang. Today, there is more of the artist who stays in his house, studying and growing musically, but with less communication.

"There are young guitarists who respect song, and who play with intuition, in the traditional way, but now there are many who are concert guitarists. To be a concert artist, in my opinion, should be a consequence of having played many years for dancing, many years for singing, and, with this base, to play solo. But now they have instituted the guitarist as soloist—from childhood they shut themselves up in their house and practice, learn music and develop technique, but they have lost something important, which is the fiesta, the juerga, to play for singing, to get drunk with the flamencos.

"Because of this, it seems to me they lack something. The school of flamenco is to have lived with the flamenco people, to have spent the early hours of the morning, entire nights, in fiestas, and to feel the music in a way that is much more rooted, emotional and not purely intellectual. In a small room, whether it is a jazz club or a tablao flamenco, there is an emotional communication; one is always confronted by other artists.

"These days, people are more and more self-sufficient; they shut themselves away to study, to compose, and we don't have that interchange. When you play in a party, with other people, then you are aware of another dimension that you don't feel when you are alone. Thinking by yourself is not like thinking with other people around, and talking and communicating. Communication is very important, to create a contrast with what you understand or create when you are by yourself. It gives equilibrium to your thought, to your attitude."

The irony behind de Lucía's observations is that he is to a great extent responsible for the new generation of *concertistas*. Building on the work of Ramón Montoya and Niño Ricardo, he elevated the guitar soloist to the pinnacle of the flamenco world, as well as bringing in new instrumental styles from samba and jazz and infuriating a previous generation of purists.

"Of course I feel a bit responsible for the way people are playing," he acknowledges. "In part, this is why I have done this record of just guitar: to mark the path that I think needs to be followed. But I do this with some doubts and insecurity, because this music is moving very quickly and I don't want to impose a criterion. I am afraid of purism, I am afraid of becoming like the old people were when I was young.

"There is always this line where all your knowledge can become dangerous, because suddenly you don't understand what is happening—the evolution has overtaken you. That is why I have this insecurity. I do not want to be the voice of authority, to say, 'This is flamenco and this isn't flamenco.' I am pretty open about this, because a person can't say where that line is; and if you try, then suddenly your ignorance puts you in a posture that is retrograde, castrating, negative. So I try to be liberal, to understand everything. But, within the margin of my insecurity, I do have criteria which I try to make concrete when I make a record or when I perform."

In keeping with his rejection of restrictive conservatism, de Lucía emphasizes that the solo record was a step forward rather than a step back. "It is traditional, inasmuch as it is basically solo guitar, but it continues the line of evolution and change to which I have always dedicated myself, respecting the tradition but incorporating new concepts, new harmonies, and creating new music.

"Since I was very young I have had a kind of obsession to keep growing," he continues. "Because I have always had the feeling that really what makes you old is to limit yourself, to fence yourself in, whether you do it at twenty or thirty or at sixty. There are people who are born conservative, who never want to go beyond where they feel secure. For me, that is to be dead, or to be old. But as long as you continue with a desire to grow, a desire to learn, a desire to create surprises in your music and to keep evolving, that is what makes you alive."

Carmen Linares

Duende literally means a familiar spirit or demon, but in flamenco it is used to designate the indefinable quality possessed by certain great artists, bullfighters, people with a unique depth and magic to their work. Next to the section on duende in the flamenco chapter of *The Rough Guide to World Music* is a picture of Carmen Linares.

Like Paco de Lucía, Linares was a leader of the generation of flamenco innovators that revolutionized and reinvigorated the style in the 1970s, and like him she seeks both to preserve and to expand the tradition. For instance, she devoted much of the 1990s to perform-

Carmen Linares. Photograph © Linda Vartoogian/FrontRowPhotos.

ing flamenco-styled settings of songs collected by the poet Federico García Lorca. "This is the centennial of his birth, so I wanted to pay homage to him," she says.* "I wanted to do something special, so I put together this program. They are songs of the people, which do not have an author; they are anonymous. And García Lorca collected them, because he liked them very much, and as he was a musician as well as a great poet, he brought them to piano and harmonized them and wrote them down in sheet music. So, thanks to him, we still have them."

García Lorca did his collecting in Andalusia, the region of southern Spain that is the homeland of flamenco, but his collection does not consist of flamenco songs. Linares makes a point of saying that although flamenco is related to the Andalusian folk style, they are quite different—though, pressed for specifics, she insists that the subject is far too complex for her to explain in a short conversation, and it would take a full lecture with musical examples. She will say that, despite the songs' background and the fact that she is backed not only by guitars but by violin, flute, and acoustic bass, her approach remains flamenco.

"We based ourselves in the melodies of the García Lorca songs, but our conception is completely different," she says. "They are still folk songs, but, as I am a cantaora, I have brought them to my terrain. There are rhythms of bulerías, tangos, a guajira, petenera. It is not the deep, traditional flamenco, but it has its inspiration in this tradition."

Though Linares was at the forefront of the flamenco generation of the 1970s, she notes that de Lucía is the only performer of that time who has truly captured an international audience. Flamenco singing has never reached as many people as the guitar style, and she naturally finds this regrettable: "I think the voice is the most authentic instrument," she says. "It can express so many things, and also it has words, which is very important. It is something human. And there is not a school for it, like for guitar or dance, where you go to a teacher who teaches you the technique. Singing is much more anarchic; you have to do it all yourself, all by ear. There is not a technique to learn how to sing. You have to be born with this condition, God has to give you this ear and this voice, a cantaora's voice."

---

* This interview was conducted in Spanish.

Linares began singing as a young girl, in her home province of Jaén. "My father played guitar and was a great flamenco aficionado. He was not a professional, he had his regular work, but he played very well and I always sang with him, and my artistic inspiration comes from him.

"I learned by living the art with my companions, and by listening to older people in Andalusia. Then when I came to Madrid I was lucky enough to be able to hear some very great singers in person, and also there is a stupendous discography of flamenco—many, many very good older recordings that allow us to hear cantaores of another time, another century. At first, I listened and I learned; I was like a sponge. But then I came to have my own personality, to stop imitating other people, and to sing as I feel."

Linares went through the traditional apprenticeship, first singing for dancers, then beginning to perform as a soloist in the tablaos. She made her professional debut in 1968, but it took time before she had any major success. "A flamenco career, whether you are a guitarist, a singer, a dancer, is very hard," she says. "Because flamenco is something very authentic. It is very difficult, very beautiful, and you have to like it very much; if not, it is impossible. You have to be very devoted to it, to have *muchísima afición*."

Where a few decades ago many aficionados feared that flamenco was a dying art, Linares says that since the 1970s it has undergone an astonishing renaissance: "Flamenco now has taken a place that it did not have before. It was very beautiful before, and whenever anything evolves it gains many things and loses others, but I think that, on the whole, we have gained. Flamenco has been opened up to the world, and now it is on a level with any other music. We sing in great theatres, and flamenco artists are not so scared to make fusions and try new things. I think this is very important, that we have more liberty. Paco de Lucía, Camarón, Enrique Morente, Antonio Gades, who did the movies [a trio of flamenco ballets directed by Carlos Saura], they have opened up many new paths which have permitted us to reach other publics. Now there are many young people getting into flamenco, and this is very important, because young people are the future."

Linares has been involved with various broader projects, from theater pieces to performances with orchestras, but she insists that all share one thing in common. "Everything I do is flamenco," she says. "Whatever I may attempt, it will always have to do with that. Because that is what I know how to do, and it is what I do best."

And, bit by bit, she hopes the rest of the world will gain a deeper sense of the music she loves. "I understand that it is harder for singers than for musicians," she says. "Perhaps the biggest problem is the language. Music is universal, and if Paco de Lucía plays guitar the whole world understands, but singing also has words. But sometimes I listen to someone sing in English, and I don't understand what they are saying but it absolutely goes to my heart. I listen to Barbra Streisand, for example, or Ray Charles, and I like them very much. I think that everyone has their heart in the same place, and when you give people something authentic, they have the same sensibilities in the United States as in Spain or anywhere else."

Rumba

Gipsy Kings

While flamenco fans applaud Paco de Lucía and Carmen Linares, a far larger and more varied audience of concertgoers and record listeners have acclaimed the Gipsy Kings as the world's most popular flamenco group. Purists argue that what the Kings play is not even flamenco, but the band has had a huge effect on the music scene, not only in their native France and internationally, but also within Spain. Hearing the group onstage, with its French backing musicians almost drowning out the acoustic guitars, it is easy to join the detractors. On the other hand, when you see all the people dancing and enjoying themselves, it is hard to deny that the music—flamenco or not—has a vibrant, infectious energy.

When I asked de Lucía what he thought of the Kings, his response was measured: "You can't ask that people know everything. Flamenco is something you might call elitist, of a particular people, a particular country, and not even of a whole country, but of one part of a country. If you go to the North of Spain, you find people who are like Americans, who don't have any idea of what flamenco is. So flamenco is a sort of cliché for them, just as Brazilian music is a cliché or African music. To really get into flamenco, you have to be an aficionado.

"So I think the success of the Gipsy Kings is logical, because people know what gets promoted, and the Gipsy Kings is a product that has been promoted very well. They are French, and there is a very good infrastructure in that country; it is richer and has more impact on the world than Spain, and it is more original to have a flamenco group in France than in Spain, because we have so many. But, in any case, I am grateful to the Gipsy Kings for their work, because after all they have opened doors so that people are discovering flamenco, through them, and those people can then investigate and find a flamenco that is deeper and more authentic.*

As for what the Kings themselves might have to say about these issues, the group's lead singer Nicolas Reyes is surprisingly straight-forward. He is thrilled with their success, but also well aware of the differences between their music and the deeper tradition. After all, their defining hit, 1987's "Bamboleo," was reworked from a Ven-ezuelan song, and featured a barrage of rumba guitars and Reyes's flamboyant vocal along with a rhythm section that turned it into an international dance-club rage. On tour, they draw an astonishing mix of young and old, world music fans and nightclub scenesters.

Reyes considers the breadth of their audience a tribute to the Kings' uniqueness in a world dominated by American styles: "Many people, since they were born, they have heard nothing but rock 'n' roll, and I think they are fed up. They want to hear something else. That is why they come to see us. They discover a new music, and for them it is another way to see things and to live."

He adds that the Kings' own world was virtually unknown to out-siders before their rise to stardom. They are Catalan Gypsies, raised in Southern France by families that had emigrated from Northeastern Spain. Their language is a mix of Catalan, French, and Romany, and their music is similarly blended, including flamenco flavors, but quite distinct from the southern Spanish style.

---

* The interview with the Gipsy Kings' Nicolas Reyes was conducted in French; Paco de Lucía's comments were in Spanish.

"In Andalusia, flamenco has a dancer, a guitarist, and a singer, and it is listened to seated," Reyes says. "The people watch, like a performance. While with us, it is a performance and an activity at the same time. People don't stay seated. The rhythm is fast, and people dance and enjoy themselves.

"It is *rumba catalana*, which is a music that opens people up. It warms their hearts, and they use it for parties, birthdays, marriages, wherever. They need this music. You know, the way of life today is job, work, sleep. The work is hard, and sometimes people have health problems, sometimes money problems, all of that. And by listening to this music I think that they forget and enjoy themselves again, they smile for a moment. *Voila*."

Reyes grew up in one of France's foremost flamenco families. His father, José Reyes, sang for many years with the guitarist Manitas de Plata, and the Gipsy Kings have included a half-dozen Reyeses over the years. The rest of the group is drawn from another Catalan Gypsy family, the Baliardos, supported by a rock-flavored, non-Gypsy rhythm section. The stars are Reyes and lead guitarist and composer Tonino Baliardo, but the group's trademark sound is based less on their individual talents than on the thick strum of the massed acoustic guitars.

It is a sound that is instantly recognizable, and quite distinct from the stark, soulful poetry of hardcore flamenco. After "Bamboleo," the Kings wandered even farther afield. For example, their *Compas* album, which on some tracks approached a more traditional flamenco, also featured the Moorish-flavored "Ami Wa Wa." Reyes says that his intention on that disc was to go back to the group's roots, while also exploring some allied forms: "We wanted to do a record like the first ones, which were really in flamenco. This is our way of playing, our way of singing. We wanted to return to that feeling, but at the same time different, with a bit of Brazilian, a bit of African, a bit of jazz from Tonino, some sweet, romantic songs, and then the *rumba gitana* [Gypsy rumba]. It is a purer sound, but with something for everyone."

While Reyes loves the bright rumba sound, and is proud of the Kings' success, he is well aware of the criticisms his group has received from flamenco purists. However, he feels that the mainstream flamenco world is not in great shape either. "Real flamenco singing is very hard, more so than the guitar," he says. "There are lots of great

guitarists in Andalusia, many, many, who are unknown. But not singers. Because anyone can play a guitar, but to sing the *cante jondo* [deep
song], it is not for everybody. There are only maybe five or six good
singers—not the greats, but they sing well. These days, the greats
don't exist. There are little singers who sing rumba, who sing tangos,
bulerías [the lighter flamenco styles], but not more than that."

And where does Reyes see himself in this picture? "I can do it," he
says, firmly. "But I have not been able to, because the guitarist has to
come from Spain, and has to know from A to Z—the soleares, the
tarantas, the fandangos, siguiriyas. I would like to do this someday,
with a good guitarist. Because the singer needs to have confidence in
the guitarist, that he really knows what he is doing."

For the moment, though, Reyes seems comfortable resisting that
challenge. "I'm not unhappy," he says. "It's fine to play rumba, and then
once in a while just take two chairs, the guitarist and me, and another
who plays the cajón, and do the cante jondo. I think that is nice."

And he is proud of the Kings' accomplishments. Their music has
become not only an international pop sound, but the living style of
their home region. A generation of Gypsy musicians has grown up in
their shadow, playing their potently lighthearted fusions.

"There are thousands and thousands of them," Reyes says. "I will
tell you a story. The *Compas* disc had only been out about one week,
and we went to a restaurant, to eat dinner, and there were Gypsies
playing. What did I hear? 'Ami Wa Wa.' And the record was out
hardly four days. This is crazy to me, unbelievable. It's a dream."

Arab Fusions

Radio Tarifa

While it has not had the commercial success of the perky rumba
groups, there is another approach that has become more and more
common on the borderlines of the flamenco scene: the exploration of
the music's roots in Arabic Andalusia. From the folk revivalist Luís
Delgado to the flamenco singer El Lebrijano, Spanish musicians have
been getting together with their North African peers, sometimes just

adding a percussionist or *oud* (Arabic lute) player, but in other cases collaborating on large-scale concerts and recordings with the Andalusian court orchestras that still survive in Northern Morocco and Algeria. The most consistent and popular group pursuing this direction is the Madrid-based band Radio Tarifa.

Radio Tarifa's albums explore the shared cultures of the western Mediterranean, filtered through centuries of Spanish history and a quirkily contemporary sensibility. On a typical album, one track will be utterly traditional and on the next a Medieval crumhorn will be accompanied by electric organ and Moroccan drums. The group's 1993 debut *Rumba Argelina* (Algerian Rumba) was a sort of blueprint for their later work—an apt metaphor, since at that time the group didn't yet exist.

"In 1992 I wanted to move to Germany," says Faín Sánchez Dueñas, speaking in heavily accented English. "And, before I left, I wanted to record some music that I was playing with my friends. So we did it at home in my bedroom, with very bad equipment, and I moved to Germany. We did not expect it to sell, we used to joke that maybe we are able to sell two hundred records. Then, one year and a half later, it seems that the record had some success. So I decided to come back in Spain and we looked for musicians and we started a group. It made me very happy, because I was an architect, and this has allowed me to do what I really like to do. And I can say the same things about my colleagues: they all had different professions, so the music before was just a hobby, and now we are able to be professionals."

Radio Tarifa's music is surprising, earthy, and immediately accessible, but it was born from complex historical and musicological roots. The core artists are Sánchez, who plays various percussion and string instruments; Vincent Molina, a French specialist in Arabic flutes; and Benjamín Escoriza, a flamenco cantaor. Sánchez met Molina when they were both members of a medieval music group, and he says that much of Radio Tarifa's inspiration comes from the modal approach of that period—the idea that music can be based on scales rather than chords.

"In 1984 we made a group to play medieval music, from France, Italy, Spain from the twelfth, thirteenth, and fourteenth centuries," he recalls. "There was also Vincent and another musician called Ramiro Amusategui, an Argentinean, who is on our records playing oud. We were around five, six years playing ancient music and that was the start of learning how to make modal arrangements, in the way that they did in the ancient times. And at the same time I was working as a musician with flamenco companies and was also playing jazz. So we had many different origins, and finally we found this singer called Benjamín Escoriza, and we decide to work to join all those styles together."

The band's name evokes a mythical radio station broadcasting from the closest point between Spain and Morocco, and its approach is rooted in Spain's centuries as an Islamic outpost in Europe. "The music in the North of Africa is very close to the Spanish music," Sánchez notes. "The Arabs were in Spain for more than eight centuries, so that means that the influence that this music had in the old folklore is very big. For us, it's not the music from the north of Africa, but is our own ancient music."

While Radio Tarifa's work is often described as a fusion of Spanish and northern African or Arab styles, Sánchez says that in a way it is just the opposite: "It is like an antifusion, because flamenco is a fusion between ancient melodies from the Mediterranean, from Arabs, and the harmony coming from Europe, and what we try to do is to take off those chords—which is the modernization of the last five centuries in Spain, to put chords on any kind of music—and to try to understand the origin of the music. And then, to try to actualize this concept, to make it real in the present day."

That may sound confusingly technical, but the basic idea is quite simple: For the last few centuries, European music has stressed harmony, the idea of finding groups of notes that sound good when they are heard in unison, which are called chords. In other musics, from Irish traditional playing to the Indian classical schools, melody, tone and intonation are what count. Different voices or instruments may play together, but they dance around one another rather than blending in harmony. This can be every bit as complex as harmonic playing, but it has a starker, more primal sound, without the warm security of a strummed guitar or a rich piano chord. (The most famous attempt to play a normally chordal music with this approach is Miles Davis's *Kind of Blue*.)

Radio Tarifa's blend of flamenco vocals and innovative instrumental choices has led some writers to group them with the "new flamenco" movement that has produced such fusions as the flamenco-blues of Pata Negra and the flamenco-African combination of Songhai. Sánchez, by contrast, says that he would not presume to call the group a flamenco ensemble of any kind. He points out that he is from Valladolid, in the central region of Castille, and came to the southern music as an outsider.

"Flamenco is much more intense than the music of my land," he says. "I remember when I was twenty-five years old, I was a guitarist and I began to be interested in flamenco through Paco de Lucía. And flamenco, it's something like a drug—you start and suddenly you are addicted to it, and that's what happened to me. But I am not a flamenco musician. We want to work in all the different cultural traditions that we have in Spain. We want to make some flamenco, some Arabic music, some Jewish Spanish music, or whatever."

Sánchez arrived at his broadminded approach through a circuitous apprenticeship. He came of age in the rock era, and started out as an electric guitarist. (A couple of Radio Tarifa's more extreme experiments include his distortion-heavy guitar leads.) Then he spent years as a jazz musician, before making an about-face to concentrate on medieval European traditions.

Asked if his background in modern American styles influences Radio Tarifa's sound, Sánchez grows pensive. "Improvisation is very important for us," he says. "Because, for musicians, it is the only way to find something new every day. So, if you want to call that jazz, okay, this is a kind of jazz that we play. But, I think improvisation was in every music, in every style, for the whole of history. It was only the classical people after the seventeenth century, they started to stop making solos and improvisation.

"Of course, we are musicians in the twentieth century. Most of us have played jazz, so maybe we have this influence, and maybe also the energy of the rockers—but we're not so much interested in playing rhythms like in America, because we have a lot of different rhythms here, a lot of different tastes right here. We're much more interested now in playing in those thousand different rhythms that you can find in the Mediterranean. So we accept jazz and rock as a part of our influences, but now we want to play this music of ours."

6

NORTH AFRICA AND
THE ARAB WORLD

Any mention of the "Arab world" will tend to provoke contention. Africa, Asia, and Europe at least are places—though Europe could more fairly be considered the western tip of Asia than its own continent—while the Arabs are a once nomadic people who have for centuries formed a minority in most of the world that bears their name. The Arabic-speaking world is roughly the central and western reaches of the medieval Muslim empire. Especially in North Africa, this includes regions where the Arab cultural influence was relatively minimal, and where many people—though they may be deeply religious Muslims—view the Arabs as outsiders. Moroccans, Egyptians, and Saudi Arabians all speak, read, and write in Arabic, but in much the same sense that the people of medieval France, Italy, and Spain all spoke, read, and wrote Latin—that is, the formal written language is the same in all, and all speak dialects of that language, but the versions spoken in the street have diverged to the point that without effort they are no longer mutually comprehensible.

Even within the western region of North Africa, the Maghreb, the Andalusian classical music of Mohamed Tahar Fergani bears virtually no resemblance to the music played by the Master Musicians of Jajouka, and neither of these styles has a close kinship with the modern pop style sung by Khaled. And those are only the musics of one region—from Morocco to Iraq is twice as far as from Spain to Norway. All of which said, the Islamic Empire was a powerful unifying force, and the armies, court functionaries, and other emissaries from its western Asian heartland disseminated a musical style marked by microtonal subtlety and expert melisma (stretching a single word over multiple notes) throughout their area of influence.

In the intervening centuries, that essential unity has been maintained both by religion and by an entertainment empire centered in Egypt, which has dominated the Arabic film and recording industries. Whatever they may choose to play, all musicians from Morocco to Iraq have heard Oum Khulthoum and the Egyptian pop orchestras. In that sense, the Arab world is more unified than Europe, and it does make sense to group the following artists together—but if I had done a lot more pieces on musicians from this world, I would have ended up dividing them into eastern and western blocks.

As to why I did not interview more Arab and North African musicians, the fact is that for a while I firmly believed that Arab music would be "the next big thing," and I was promoting these styles with all my power and energy, but very few people seemed to be listening. There was certainly some anti-Arab prejudice involved, which has grown far worse in recent years, but also an apparently insurmountable musical barrier that continues to baffle me. When Ali Hassan Kuban's *From Nubia to Cairo* album came out, I thought it was the perfect crossover disc. It mixed Arabic touches with propulsive African percussion and a horn section, and several of my rock and soul fan friends went wild over it. But when I played it for the *Boston Globe*'s previous world music writer, a modern jazz composer and broadminded critic, he found it "too weird." I still don't understand why it struck him that way, but I have found the reaction to be surprisingly prevalent among Westerners faced with Arab styles. This is all the stranger when one considers the wide appeal of flamenco, which in many ways is more like an Arab than a European form, and the fact that Arab and European styles share such common roots in earlier Mediterranean musics. There is a natural affinity there, and I trust that the crossover will eventually come. Maybe it is just a matter of waiting for the right time and the right ambassador. The music is certainly as rich, soulful, and inventive as any on earth.

Andalusian Music

Hadj Mohamed Tahar Fergani

Arriving from Spain, a logical entry to the musics of the Islamic world is provided by the Andalusian orchestras that followed the Moorish courts into exile in the fifteenth century. These orchestras and their offshoots remain popular throughout northern Morocco and Algeria, and in many cases, the musicians still trace their styles back to specific cities in Spain: In Algeria, for example, Tlemcen has the style of Granada and Constantine the style of Cordoba, while in Morocco the school of Valencia now resides in Fez and a Granadan offshoot in Tetouan. Andalusian music is the region's classical style, the conservatory and court tradition, but it is by no means limited to an elite audience. It underlines popular forms like Algerian *hawzi*, and Andalusian musicians often play for dances and parties. Few Andalusian ensembles have toured in the United States, but in 1997 an Algerian cultural group brought one of the masters of the Constantine school, Hadj Mohamed Tahar Fergani. It was after midnight when Fergani and his orchestra arrived at a welcoming dinner in Boston, and he had been traveling steadily for the past two days, first overland from Constantine to Algiers, then by plane via Paris and New York. The band looked exhausted, but the seventy-year-old Fergani appeared fresh and relaxed, as if he could pull out his viola and play all night.

As heir to the court ensembles of Cordoba, the Constantine school is arguably the most direct link not only to the old Andalusian orchestral tradition but to the source of Arabic classical music. It was in ninth-century Cordoba that the classical style was formalized by the legendary Ziryab, a black former slave who had arrived there from the Baghdad court of Haroun el-Rashid (of *Arabian Nights* fame). Driven out of the capital by his envious competitors, Ziryab went to Andalusia, where he composed the twenty-four *nuba*, the extended suites that form the core of the Arabic classical tradition.

Moorish Spain was an unmatched cultural melting pot. A meeting place of Arab, North African, Jewish, and European traditions, it nurtured a poetry and music that formed the basis of much of what is now considered Western culture, from classical music to troubadour verse.

Indeed, Fergani's son Selim explains that Constantine still preserves the original troubadour style: "We have the classical troubadour songs. It is an Arab word, *tarab idour*, meaning 'the music-making which goes around,' because they sang it outdoors, while they walked."[*]

His father adds that *flamenco* is also an Arab word, from *ana fallah minkoum*, "I am a country person among you." Flamenco experts would argue that this is only one of several possible derivations, but an Arabic source certainly makes some sense, considering the stylistic similarities and the music's roots in Andalusia.

Whatever their shared origins, both the European and the Andalusian court styles have changed over the years. While conservatories strive to preserve the nuba in something like their pure form, there has also been a steady evolution since the exile to North Africa, with new compositions and instruments entering the tradition. Any classical style has a strong strain of conservatism, but while its European counterpart survives primarily as elite, high culture, the Andalusian tradition has continued to act as accompaniment to everyday social situations. Along with giving concerts, Andalusian musicians regularly perform at weddings and celebrations, and remain a vibrant part of the popular culture, playing lighter melodies along with the more formal compositions.

Fergani, who is known as one of the finest singers and viola players in Algeria, says that his concerts typically include both the nuba and other Andalusian songs. "The nuba is special; you must follow the norms as they were prescribed in the old days," he explains. "You have a prelude, the music without words, then you have the *m'cedder*, the longest movement. After that, it speeds up progressively to the end. But we play a variety."

Fergani's traveling troupe includes seven musicians, including two of his sons, and combines relatively modern arrivals like violin, guitar, and mandolin with traditional instruments like the *derbouka*, a metal-bodied drum, the *tamboura*, a hand drum related to the tambourine, the *juwwak*, a wooden flute, and two different kinds of *oud*, or lute (the latter word is just a Europeanization of *al oud*). "There is the Eastern lute, with twelve strings," Fergani explains. "That is played

---

[*] This interview was conducted in French.

everywhere in the Arab world, but it is not the oldest. The oldest lute, which I play, is used in Constantine, and it has eight strings, four doubled pairs, made of gut, and played with an eagle's feather plectrum." (Selim adds that a similar lute is still played in the Languedoc, in southern France.)

Fergani began performing as a flutist when he was sixteen years old, and has since mastered all the Andalusian instruments. He says that his whole family plays music, joking that he has himself raised an orchestra. Selim, whose French is better, elaborates: "It's a gift we have. My grandfather played already in 1907, and in 1926 he made records with Pathé Marconi. My uncles are all musicians, and my aunts are musicians, in the feminine style. My sisters are music teachers."

"We are trying to preserve this music," his father adds forcibly. "What we do is all to preserve this music, and to transmit it to the young people. This music will endure, because it is part of history."

When it is suggested that, to most American listeners, the most familiar Algerian music is not the Andalusian nuba, but *rai*, the modern pop sound of the coast, Fergani just snorts and waves his hand dismissively, murmuring "*passage*," a passing fad.

"That is not our music," Selim says. "It has no culture. The great music researchers, they know what is fake and what is real. If you listen to just anything—I am not criticizing rai, it makes people dance, but this is something else."

"It is a fad," his father breaks in. "With lots of noise. Ooh, la la." He shakes his head from side to side in mock agony. "For the nuba, you don't want electric lights, you want candles. You need silence. With that ambiance, the singer gives everything. It is our classical music, and sometimes people cry. Truly."

"Ours is a universal music," Selim says. "Like the music of Beethoven. It is immortal."

Morocco

The Master Musicians of Jajouka

At the other end of the traditional spectrum from the Andalusian orchestras, musicians from the Moroccan hill village of Jajouka play a wild, celebratory style that predates the Islamic expansion. William S. Burroughs once described them as "a four-thousand-year-old rock 'n' roll band," and their overpowering horn fanfares have attracted such varied collaborators as the Rolling Stones, Ornette Coleman, and Sonic Youth.

The Master Musicians of Jajouka were "discovered" in the mountains of Northern Morocco by the beat expatriates Brion Gysin and Paul Bowles in the 1950s and came to the notice of a broad international audience in 1968 when the Rolling Stones' Brian Jones produced a psychedelically remixed recording, *The Pipes of Pan at Jajouka*, which became a drug-culture classic. Success brought squabbles and splits, and Jajouka virtually disappeared from the international consciousness, the Master Musicians only resurfacing in 1991 with their definitive album, *Apocalypse Across the Sky*, produced by the American musician and composer Bill Laswell.

The group's renaissance is largely due to Bachir Attar, who took over its hereditary leadership a few years ago. A young player with experience in Paris and New York, Attar combines impeccable musicianship with worldly savvy. He remembers Brian Jones's visit—and the excitement it caused among the musicians—from his childhood, and has set out to bring the group the acclaim Jones once promised them. "Jajouka music is one music in the world," Attar says proudly, his English flavored with a thick Moroccan accent. "I can say nobody can copy, nobody can touch it."

Attar is speaking from a town near Jajouka, because the village itself has neither telephones nor electricity. The musicians returned there in the 1930s, after the dissolution of the old Moroccan court, where they had lived and worked for centuries. "Like six hundred years ago, we are in the palace of the king of Morocco," Attar says. "They play in the morning and the evening and in the parties of the king. But later, when Spanish and French was coming to Morocco,

Bachir Attar (center) and The Master Musicians of Jajouka. Photograph © Jack Vartoogian/FrontRowPhotos.

then Jajouka go back to the village. We have only these papers given by the kings of Morocco, from the holy people, signed to the musicians and blessing them. It was a great paper, but—*dommage* [it's a pity]—the Spanish they heard other people say, 'This musician they have the papers of the kings.' Then they put the musicians in a jail, and they take these papers—which is very important for us, like half of our blood."

Attar explains that his family is a hereditary clan, with roots reaching back to the thirteenth century Persian poet Farid al Din Attar (author of the epic *Conference of the Birds*), and that their musical tradition was brought to Morocco from Asia by their ancestral saint, Sidi Hamid Cherq, who still has a shrine in Jajouka. "To play this music, you have to be from the family Attar," Attar says. "Because this music is a magic gift, like the ring that you turn it and you blow up, you fly.

"You have to study this music when you are a child, like three and four years. At most you are to be five years. If you grow up more, it's no. Me, I never been in school or work. Only music. I was born and I open my eyes with my father playing, and I grow up with this music and I learn all my life. Now I'm thirty-two years old and I get it all in my blood."

Some scholars have suggested that the musicians' traditions reach back far beyond medieval Persia. During Jajouka's annual festival, the blare of the horns provokes the frenzied romp of Bou Jaloud, a dancer dressed in fresh goatskins. Attar connects this to the biblical story of Abraham—"Abraham sacrificed the son and the sheep comes, and from that time we have this festival with the man who dance inside of the skin"—but others believe it to be a survival of the cult of Pan, the last gasp of the Roman festivals of Lupercalia, which in turn appear to be recastings of pre-Roman animist beliefs.

Be that as it may, Jajouka's music is unique and fascinating. All of the performers are multi-instrumentalists, playing the *lira*, a reed flute, the four-stringed, banjo-like *gimbri*, and the *ghaita*, a sort of shawm or oboe, which is their most striking instrument. Like the ancient snake charmer's pipe, the ghaita is played using the technique jazz musicians call "circular breathing," in which the player breathes in through his nose while keeping a steady stream of air flowing through his horn. On the Laswell recording of "Bujloudia," the music of Bou Jaloud, nine ghaitas create an awesome swell of sound, the aural equivalent of a tornado.

Attar explains that bujloudia is not a single piece but a whole genre of music. "We say *bujloudia* like you say *blues*, like you say *rock and roll*," he explains. "Each name has many, many pieces of songs, hundreds. Because we have hundreds of songs." They also have a variety of styles, from the wild festival music to introspective flute pieces and village dances featuring vocals, gimbri, and violin.

Attar has sometimes ventured outside the tradition, making a solo album with ex–James Brown sax master Maceo Parker and encouraging other collaborations, but he says his heart is still with the ancient styles. "I keep this the first for me," he says. "And I'm doing other things, new compositions, to build a bridge with other artists from the Western world. We keep the real, our family music, but because other people they are good musicians, they say 'Hi, let's jump to do something,' and then I say, 'Yes, me too.'"

He adds that he recently brought a generator and satellite dish to the village to keep him apprised of current trends. "I love to see something in the world, what's going on." But he is keeping the global media in perspective: "Everybody goes and forgot them culture, but me not. I keep the spirit and what I see in my eyes, what I dream. When I go somewhere out of Morocco, always I am thinking, 'I have to go back.' But now is the time to make this idea of Brian Jones, to be Jajouka now in the whole world."

Algeria

Khaled

Of all the musics of the Arabic-speaking world, Algerian *rai* has probably drawn the largest international audience. Rai became the reigning pop style of urban Algeria in the late 1970s, but its roots are considerably older. It was a sort of North African equivalent of tango or *rembetika*, the sound of the sailors' dives in the western port city of Oran. The defining voice of early rai was Cheikha Remitti, who made her first recordings in the 1950s, shocking the country with the

Khaled. Photograph © Jack Vartoogian/FrontRowPhotos.

directness of her language as she talked of love, sex, alcohol, and life in the streets and nightclubs. Women ruled the scene for a quarter century before a generation of male challengers appeared, but while women like Chaba Fadela remain a potent force in Algeria, it is men who have been most popular abroad. The music's foremost ambassador is a charismatic singer and songwriter named Khaled.

"Though surrounded by friends in the midst of a party, I am alone with her beauty," Khaled writes in a typical lyric. "Let everyone drink till they're as drunk as I, drunk on the promise of her kiss and of her touch." It doesn't read like the voice of rebellion, but then neither does, "You ain't nothing but a hound dog." When rai hit the North African pop scene, it aroused the same ire as early rock 'n' roll. In place of a gyrating Elvis Presley, the revolutionary figure was the slim young singer then known as Cheb Khaled, whose emotional voice soared over an irresistible dance rhythm and drove the teens wild.

Khaled (he dropped the Cheb, which means "young man," when he turned thirty), was one of rai's first male stars, and he remains the music's king. He arrived on the scene just as the good-time music of Oran was getting revamped, adding electric instruments and full drum kits to the older violin, accordion, and derbouka. "Before, it was a music of older people, the musicians were forty, fifty years old," he recalls.* "We heard this music at weddings, but it didn't appear in the media, on television or radio. One only saw Egyptian music, French, English, but one saw no rai."

Handsome and energetic, Khaled was the standard bearer for a new generation. Not only did he use modern instrumentation, but he was one of the first male artists to write in the language of the street. "It's like rap," he says. "I use the language young people normally use when they are outside their houses. The old songs didn't do that. It was a sort of hypocrisy: Someone who wanted to sing about love wouldn't sing about a girl; he couldn't. They would sing about nature, about a gazelle, an animal. But me, when I sing, I say it directly. If I sing of Fatima, I say her name. I sing about nature if I want to sing about nature, but if I want to sing for a woman, I sing for a woman."

The result was national fame, the title of king, and the proud achievement of taking rai from the streets of Oran to the top of the North African music world—but also threats, censorship, and eventually exile. Though Khaled describes the possibility of performing in Algeria as "my only wish," he has not been able to do so for many years because of Muslim extremists who see his music as the work of the devil.

Khaled describes himself as profoundly religious and has nothing but contempt for the censors. "These people say they are Muslims," he says. "But they are not Muslims; they are terrorists. In Algeria, there are many interdictions, many taboos. I wanted to break down the barriers, to have a little bit of liberty. When I was young, we lived always shut up in our houses; one couldn't permit oneself to go out to clubs, especially if one was a woman. And there were many people who didn't want this music because they were bothered by the fact that the songs were about love. It's not exactly like rock 'n' roll, because that music speaks of drugs and rai doesn't speak of drugs, it speaks of love, of being drunk with life. But I think it is the same prejudice, the same story."

---

* This interview was conducted in French.

Like rock, rai was not a completely new sound, but a traditional music in overdrive, made by young artists who were listening to all the various styles coming in over the radio. Khaled cites the influence of flamenco, the Egyptian pop of Um Khulthoum, the French *chanson* of Edith Piaf and Jacques Brel, and the French rockers Johnny Halliday and Eddie Mitchell. But he adds that he was always careful not to lose the essence of rai. His groundbreaking international hit "Didi," produced by Don Was, was anchored by the rhythm of the derbouka, and Khaled's vocals showed few Western inflections. Nonetheless, it captured an unprecedented audience of non-Algerians, taking the album *Khaled* to gold status in France and huge sales in India. Khaled's next album, *N'ssi N'ssi*, used swirling Egyptian strings to emphasize his Arabic side even as Was weighed in again with pounding basslines.

"I didn't leave my old music behind; I improved it," Khaled says. "I never got rid of certain instruments which are the base of the music, like Eastern percussion, the derbouka, the acoustic violin, the accordion—I cannot leave those behind. To add something is not to betray a music. It is very good to preserve the tradition, but one must also know how to give the music a living color.

"It is like reggae, which existed for a long time, but then Bob Marley came along and improved it and brought it out of the ghetto. In rai, it's the same thing. It was there and it was improved and made known to the whole world. Because people are curious now, old and young, to hear new sounds, new melodies."

Khaled says that wherever he goes he draws a large Algerian audience, and despite his problems with the censors, he insists that they are not representative of the Algerian public. "In Algeria there are lots of musicians, artists, plenty of evolved people," he says. "Everyone lives with music, everyone is born with music. So one cannot forbid music."

Many Algerians feel exiled from their homeland, whether for political reasons or from economic need, and Khaled says that he sings to bring them together and to make them feel as if they are back home— "*au bled*," in his French-Arabic phrase. "When I play in France, in Boston, in Japan, in Scandinavia, there are always Algerians there, there is always a party and we forget our cares," he says. "Luckily, we have music, because if we did not have music we would collapse. If there was no music in the world, it would be very sad."

And he says that his non-Algerian listeners have a similar experience: "They don't understand what I say, but music is universal. This music, people can dance to it however they feel. There is no official dance, there is a freedom in it. The word *rai* means 'opinion,' and I think people give their own ideas, their opinion in their dance. Because music is the only international language, and when they listen to the melody the people can understand what I am singing."

The Classical Tradition

Simon Shaheen and
Nassir Shemma

Moving east, one comes to the heartland of Arab culture—roughly the group of countries south of modern-day Turkey and west of Iran. Here, perhaps more than in any other region of the world, classical and popular traditions routinely overlap. Classical musicians perform on pop records, and popular musicians are often devoted students of classical styles. There has been far too little Arab music available in the West, but a few musicians are trying hard to change that. Among

Simon Shaheen. Photograph © Jack Vartoogian/FrontRowPhotos.

the most energetic is the New York-based Palestinian oud and violin player Simon Shaheen, a virtual one-man embassy for Arab music in the United States. Meanwhile, the Iraqi oud virtuoso Nassir Shemma, while far less well-known, is a brilliant and innovative player whose music seems ideally suited to cross cultural divides and bring a new audience to the Arabic tradition.

Shaheen and Shemma have both given a good deal of thought to the relationship between Arabic and European classical styles, and like most people familiar with this history, they note that the Arabic tradition was the source of much that Europeans consider their own. In music and poetry, as in philosophy and science, Islamic culture can lay good claim to having nourished the roots of the artistic flowering we call the Renaissance.

Eurocentric historians sometimes grant all of that, but argue that since that time the Arab world has stood still, while Europe has continued to flower. Musically, at least, such views reveal more prejudice than perspicacity. It is true that, as European music evolved through the baroque and classical periods to twentieth-century modernism, Arabic art music has remained closer to its roots, but by the same token, a contemporary European musician playing a baroque composition is essentially presenting a museum piece, while an Arabic musician playing a composition of the same era is to a great extent improvising a modern variation on the traditional theme.

Shaheen would add that even those distinctions have far less weight than they used to. "Before, the bulk of Arabic music began as vocal music," he explains. "Then, in the turn of the [twentieth] century, we started to see some experiments with instrumental music, and in the fifties and sixties this concept came to take the interest of many composers. With the existence of good performers on the oud, the *kanun* [a sort of zither], the violin, the *ney* [a reed flute], these people began not only to compose vocally, but they composed for the instruments."

The result has been something of a new golden age of Arabic music, boasting a seamless mix of tradition and innovation that is utterly different from the iconoclasm of modern Western art music. "In European music of the twentieth century there has been a deviation and the establishment of new theories and rules of composition," Shaheen says. "We didn't have this, because what happened in European music is that the premise was to compose harmonically, depending on a few scales and structures. You had major, minor, and a few other modes, and after a time they felt that they can't move anymore, and they needed to find different formulas to compose, to make it sound different, otherwise it will be redundant. So they went into the twelve-tone scale and all these things.

"In Arabic music, we don't have this problem, because we have the concept of microtonality, and the *muqam* system, which allows a huge tableau of scales and a melodic richness, so we don't need to look for other formulas to compose. As a matter of fact, I don't think we have yet utilized the potential of our system to even a quarter of its possibilities."

The muqams are modal scales, in some ways related to the Indian ragas, though there are far fewer of them and the Arabic tradition has not reached the ethereal extremes of North Indian classical playing. Indeed, while it is an oversimplification, Arabic music can to some extent be thought of as part of a musical continuum, matching its geographical location in a cultural belt running from India through Persia to Europe.

Shaheen, who was born into a family of musicians in Galilee and grew up in East Jerusalem, plays both the oud and the Western violin (by now a common instrument in the Arab world), and performs with Arab classical ensembles and in experimental interchanges with Western players. Shemma, by contrast, plays and records alone, and the bulk of his concerts consist of his own compositions. Born in 1963 in al-Kut, Iraq, he is one of the most exciting of a new generation of oud virtuosos, working to explore and expand the limits of the instrument. His principal innovation has been to replace the flat plectrum that other oud players use to strike the strings with an intricate fingerpicking style that at times gives his playing the flavor of flamenco guitar or Baroque lute. This makes his work particularly accessible to Western listeners, though Shemma is quick to point out that it has very deep roots in the Iraqi tradition.

"In the museum in Baghdad, you can see manuscripts from the Assyrian era," he says.[*] "And you will find people playing on the oud

---

[*] Simon Shaheen spoke in English, and the interview with Nassir Shemma was conducted through a translator.

using the fingers, probably a millennium before the introduction of the *arreesha*, which is the feather, or the plectrum. When I saw these manuscripts, I began to investigate this, and I confirmed that this was done way before even Ziryab's time. Ziryab used both these methods, with the pick and with the fingers, and took them with him to Andalusia, to Spain, and after that they were played on the mandolin and the guitar. When I found out all of this, I liked the idea very much, and I revived this whole method of playing, composing with it and trying to use it in the original way." (He celebrates this journey, and the connection to flamenco, in a composition called "From Ashur [Assyria] to Seville.")

The use of fingerstyle technique is only one of Shemma's departures from the standard classical playing styles. "I have tried to bring current subjects into the music, current concerns, in a way that has not been adopted before on the oud," he says. "This has been very challenging, and there has to be some technical development that goes along with that, mastering a variety of older techniques and even inventing new techniques."

Shemma demonstrates the emotional and technical power of these new techniques on pieces like "It Happened at al-Aamyriyah," which programmatically illustrates the bombing of the Aamyriyah air-raid shelter in Baghdad during the first Gulf War. A fearsome flurry of strums and arpeggios recalls the battering explosions, followed by a long, lovely melodic section evoking the grief of the survivors, and ending with a funeral march.

Shemma studied at the conservatory in Baghdad, and says that he formed his style in a sort of parallel to what was being done by the city's new generation of painters—using old motifs but presenting them in new ways. "I'm not very strict in one area or style," he says. "I am definitely in favor of a variety of influences or winds, the give and take—for music with no limitations. The music that I play and compose, in general, I think that it is neither Eastern nor Western. It is music for all of humanity, trying to bring or give a message, more than following a certain direction or a school."

Shaheen's group also demonstrates the adaptability of the Arabic tradition. In a Boston concert, they included classical compositions alongside a segment of Lebanese folk songs, and an Egyptian piece composed in the 1940s that adapts European harmonies and Latin American rhythms. Shaheen hopes that such fusions can provide Westerners with a bridge to the more traditional styles. He points out that until recently most Americans were only exposed to Arab music through the counterfeits presented in Hollywood films. "They composed things that mostly have a visuality that reflected the harem scene and the belly dancers and the camel and the desert," he says, wryly. "It wasn't Arabic music actually; it was a kind of mish-mash of Greek and Turkish and some Arabic together, and the composers weren't Arabs, they were Americans. When I came to this country, there was almost no real Arabic music, but I took New York as my center and I contacted Jihad Racey [a multi-instrumentalist based in California] and we began performing and people began to discover that this was a fantastic, complex music."

There is now a substantial American audience for their work and that of other Arab performers, but Shaheen says that it still has a long way to go: "This music was misconceived and misinterpreted, and you can't expect that to change between day and night. But we are doing more and more, putting out recordings, appearing on radio, and also collaborating with good performers in the jazz world and musicians who are interested in world music. And we are reaching more people all the time. It will take time, but we are doing whatever we can to give this music exposure to as many people as possible."

Iraq

Mahmood Anwar

While Arabic classical music has a small but loyal audience on the world scene, the modern pop styles of the Arabian Peninsula remain almost unknown. During my years covering international music, I occasionally heard of an Arabic pop star appearing in the Boston area, but to a great extent this scene was closed to outsiders. Most concerts were given for intimate audiences in private homes or banquet rooms, and there was no way for someone outside the circle of cognoscenti to hear about them. Even if I had known, there was no purpose in writing about them for a mass-market newspaper, since the small size of the audiences was offset by ticket prices that often soared well over a hundred dollars. The people who attended such concerts were typically businessmen and students from wealthy Arab families, who considered a few hundred dollars a relatively modest sum for a special evening among their peers, eating a fine meal and hearing a familiar star.

A 1995 concert by the Iraqi pop singer Mahmood Anwar was supposed to be an exception, but that is not how it worked out. He was to be presented by a local Iraqi who hoped to draw an audience from both within and outside the community, but the fifty dollar ticket price scared off the outsiders, while the fact that the concert was to be held in an uncomfortable church setting made it unappealing to well-heeled Arab fans. The result was that it was canceled at the last moment, but I was still glad to have done the interview. This was shortly after the first Gulf War, and I thought American readers would be interested to hear about another aspect of Iraq—especially when Anwar began talking about the government's support of the arts. In hindsight, it is interesting to note that neither that war nor the sanctions imposed on Iraq in its aftermath led the United States to significantly limit visits by Iraqi musicians—though ten years later, threats of Islamic terrorism would serve as an excuse to cut off tours not only from the Arab world but from such unrelated countries as Cuba.

Anwar says that he had been touring regularly both before and after the war, and when asked if tensions between Iraq and the United States were causing any problems for him, he sounds surprised at the question: "A singer can go anywhere he wants; it's a very normal thing. People in Iraq welcome the idea that an Iraqi singer tours around the world, and in the United States I have not encountered any reactions that are annoying or strange. I think because art is a human tool, is the food for the spirit; it doesn't much get confused with politics."*

Anwar is part of a new wave of Iraqi musicians who have added electric instrumentation to traditional melodies for a youthful fusion sound. "The Iraqis resisted Western instruments for a long time," he says. "We adopted them much later than other Arab countries. It is only in the last ten or fifteen years it changed. The modern music

---

* This interview was conducted through a translator.

began to take a more lively and dancing tune. It is considered lighter and you can dance to it more than the traditional or classical music."

He adds that Iraqi music received an exceptional degree of official support, with state-funded festivals and educational facilities nurturing young artists. For example, while singers historically learned their art informally, by spending time with older performers in cafés devoted to music, he was formally trained at the Ma'had Al-Dirasat Al-Naghamiyya, a Baghdad music academy.

Modernization affected not only education and performance options, but also the artists' place in the larger society. In many Middle Eastern countries, musicians are still regarded as second-class citizens, but Anwar notes that although his family was not musical, his parents were thoroughly supportive of his career choice. "These days I know many families who encourage their children to be in the media, in the arts," he says. "I think this is something which is happening to many societies in the world, an evolution, questioning the past and working to change the present. And of course there are also many influences coming from outside the country."

Anwar stresses that music plays a central role in Iraqi society: "It is not just something for parties. The people have a lot of interest and are very choosy in what they listen to." There is a reciprocal role between listeners and performers: musicians are expected to provide the best performance they can, and the audience has a duty to respond in a process known as *tarab*: "This is a word for listening to a tune and remembering, so you start feeling sorrow or happiness. It is your reaction, either by clapping or moving your body as you're sitting, or by sighing or crying. All these emotions are part of a tarab. The Iraqis are very emotional, and this is what they like in music, in addition to dancing."

Anwar's band includes an electric organ modified so that it can play not only the twelve tones of the Western scale but also the quarter tones that lie between those notes, and a rhythm section of bass guitar and two percussionists, one playing the *tabla*, a double kettle drum, and the other the *khashaba* or *dumbug*, a long, thin Iraqi drum that is played with the fingertips.

The audiences for which they perform have remained overwhelmingly Iraqi, but Anwar notes that each of his American tours drew more people from other Arab countries, and sometimes even a few curious Westerners. "It is definitely a new style of singing, a new color for them," he says. "And also the rhythms are completely different. Even for those who are accustomed to Arabic music, this is again a unique style, not what you hear from Egyptian or Lebanese music. But it is very interesting, because it is a very emotional, very lively music, with dancing tunes. The only thing which they probably cannot understand is the lyrics."

7

WESTERN AND CENTRAL ASIA

Moving east toward India, one traces the longest trade route of the ancient world. Usually called the Silk Road, in its broadest expanse this route linked the Atlantic Ocean to the Pacific, moving goods, people, and ideas from China to Europe and back, and connecting all the points along the way. It is impossible to make neat cultural divisions along this route. The separation of the world's largest landmass into Europe and Asia is a fiction that conceals as much history as it preserves, and any listener tracing musical styles will find infinite areas of overlap and few clear lines of demarcation.

The region in this chapter, which extends from Turkey to India and Bangladesh, is defined less by cultural cohesion than by the fact that it is east of the Arab world, and yet within both the known world of Alexander the Great and the area of Muslim influence. A necessarily loose definition, this recognizes the reality of a musical culture that had Persia roughly at its center and extended both east and west. This is the culture Arab musicians cite when they call the roots of their music "oriental," and Indian musicians when they note the arrival of instruments like the *santoor* from the West. Unsurprisingly, Persian music often sounds like a bridge between Arab and Indian music. The Indian classical style reached a level of intricacy and virtuosity that is in some ways unequalled anywhere in the world, but it is clearly the high point of a broader style, and there is a degree of musical as well as geographical logic in approaching it slowly, in the migration lightly traced below.

Turkey

Cinucen Tanrikorur

Turkey was long a meeting point—and a battleground—between Asia and Europe, and it reflects this in its music. Today, Turkish groups like Barbaros Erköse's ensemble play music that is closely tied to village styles of Greece and Hungary, while artists like Cinucen Tanrikorur play a classical form related to the formal schools of Persia and the Arab world. Whether the differences between these performers are more a matter of geography and ethnic background, or of class and musical history, is an open question. All of these factors have played a part, and one could as easily explore their similarities as stress the divisions.

In any case, like Erköse, Tanrikorur was destined for music from his childhood. "I was born and grew up in the ancient part of Istanbul," he says. "My mother used to play the lute, which was a tradition for young girls in Ottoman society; my uncle sang classical music; and I was surrounded by *ezan*, the call to prayer, which was coming from the mosques. I started my musical education by singing when I was only five, I was nine when I learned musical notation, and I started composing when I was fourteen."

Tanrikorur also became an expert performer on the *ud*, the fretless Turkish lute, and a master of both Turkish classical music and the ceremonial music of the Mevlevi order of Sufis, the so-called whirling dervishes. In a parallel to Western orchestral music, the Turkish classical style originated as the court music of the Ottoman Empire. Although Westerners note similarities between it and Arabic music, and many of the instruments are similar or identical, Tanrikorur says that the two traditions are quite different: "In Arabic music there is not a very clear distinction between classical and folk music," he says. "It is all mixed up. And since Arabic music is not written down, like Turkish music, the so-called classical pieces don't go before the last century."

Tanrikorur is a leader of what might be called the Turkish "early music" movement, a return to the instruments and smaller ensembles of a previous era. In Turkey, he is best known for his solo performances, singing accompanied only by his lute, in emulation of the *ozans*, the medieval minstrels. "In Turkey it is very unusual for a musician to play and sing at the same time," he says. "One of my teachers, who passed away last year—he was ninety-four years old—he was the only one of the twentieth century to play and sing by himself. And for thirty years now, I am, very humbly speaking, the only representative of this very old minstrel tradition. I do not play the traditional repertory of the minstrels, because this has become more part of the folk tradition, but I play the classical repertory in the minstrel way."

Tanrikorur says that the minstrel tradition died out in the fifteenth century, surviving only in folk-song styles, and that other classical music has suffered in the last century from ill-conceived attempts to emulate European performance practices. The contemporary Turkish scene has been dominated by large choirs and elaborate orchestras using Western instrumentation, which Tanrikorur considers an inappropriate approach to a music that in essence is monodic, based on single melody lines without the Western conception of harmony.

"It doesn't have any reasonable musical explanation," he says. "It is only a very poor imitation of a Western orchestra or choir. Because Turkish music is so delicate, its nuances get lost in a group of eighty people, or even fifteen. So I am fighting against this by insisting on playing and singing by myself or in very small groups, with one instrument of each kind."

This is not to say that Tanrikorur is a strict traditionalist. "I am trying to revive the classical tradition of the old composers," he says. "But in a contemporary musical setting. The presentation, the technique, and the feelings are contemporary, because I live in the twentieth century—and I received, like others, many, many influences from surrounding cultures, like Western influence or Eastern influence, which it is not possible to be free of. But the substance is classical."

Tanrikorur's touring ensemble includes three other instrumentalists, on the *ney*, a seven-holed reed flute, the *tanbur*, a long-necked, fretted lute that can be plucked or bowed, and the *kanun*, a sort of zither. It also features Ahmet Calisir, a Muslim religious singer, or *hafiz*, who sings Koranic verses to improvised melodies.

Calisir's contributions show the religious aspect of Tanrikurur's work. One could make an analogy to European music, where composers like Johann Sebastian Bach created pieces for the entertainment of royalty but also a great deal of church music, often of a quite different character. In Tanrikorur's case, he says that his religious music comes from a completely different source than the classical style: "Sufi music takes its origin from the Central Asiatic shamanistic ceremonies," he explains. "It is musically different and the texts are different and the rhythms are different. Sufi music is musically much simpler, because it is addressed to the mass public level, and it is based on what is called *dhikr*, which means remembrance of the ninety-nine beautiful names of God.

"This is mostly vocal music. In Mevlevi music, most of the classical instruments participate, but in the ceremonies of other dervish orders, only a few instruments, like reed flute and *bendir*, percussion instruments are allowed."

Tanrikuror says that the combination of religious and secular court music, and the variety of instruments in the ensemble, mean that his concerts are more accessible to non-Turkish audiences than his solo performances might be: "I sing and play as always, but I will also be accompanied by the other musicians," he says. "I'll give an example of one instrumentalist, the tanbur player, and then I play a duet, and then three musicians and four. So I give the different feelings and the colors of Turkish music."

Iran

Kayhan Kalhor

If there is one country that is constantly in the American news without being in any way familiar to Americans, it is Iran. While mention of ancient Persia conjures up images of phoenixes and carpets, modern-day Iran is often confused with its Arabic-speaking neighbors or demonized as a hard-line Islamic state leading the surge of Muslim fundamentalism. Kayhan Kalhor, a master of the *kamancheh*, a Persian cousin of the violin, is a musician, not a politician, but in conversation he doubles as a one-man cultural ambassador.

"As a Persian musician, as an Iranian actually, there is a major part of our culture that has been unknown to the West," he says. "It has either been categorized as Islamic art or Middle Eastern art, neither

Kayhan Kalhor. Photograph © Jack Vartoogian/FrontRowPhotos.

of which is true. This is a separate civilization and culture, by itself, and it's totally misunderstood because of its political situation. This is a culture that was very influential, in terms of social, philosophical, and ideological materials—as well as music and especially poetry—and was a distributor of all of these to the world. There was a time when the Persians and Greeks kind of formed a prehistoric era together. But for some reason the Western world forgot the influence of Persian culture, and it was really brutally integrated into what is called Islamic culture. I always had a problem with that, because Islam was brought into so many different cultures, and it is not fair to put all of this in one set. And so much of it, the architecture for example, was part of Persian culture long before Islam."

Kalhor first came to the attention of a broad American audience through his work with Ghazal, a project he put together with the Indian sitar player Shujaat Husain Khan. Ghazal's album titles—*Lost Songs of the Silk Road* and *Moon Rise over the Silk Road*—evoke the medieval trade route that connected China to the West, and spread Persian inventions like chess and the hammer dulcimer to both India and Europe.

As well as showcasing the kinship between two ancient traditions, Ghazal was an attempt to explore the possibilities of a cross-cultural interchange that avoided the more typical "world fusion" pattern. "Usually in this kind of project, there is this famous Western guitarist or pop group employing three, four musicians—famous, or second-rate—from other cultures," Kalhor explains. "The Westerners use these musicians here and there, and dictate what to do and how to do it, and it's basically because of the famous person that the project gets exposure. I never wanted to do something like that, because obviously you cannot get your music across in that situation. I wanted to do a project in which I'm a hundred percent involved, where I can have a say artistically, can cook it a little, get it to go somewhere, and put a lot of effort and heart into it. I did not want to do this just so I could say, 'Well, I did a fusion project too.'

"Really, we never thought of this as a fusion. It's just two musicians playing together. We share a lot of common ground in personality, and if I would do the same project with another sitarist, or him with another kamancheh player, it wouldn't be the same. We have respect for each other and as a result of that we give each other room to play and to be comfortable. Our characters match, and the music is created by these two characters."

Of course, that musical camaraderie is facilitated by the kinship between the Persian and Indian classical styles, which share instruments and are both based on improvisations within set rhythms and scales. "I've been listening to Indian music for a long time," Kalhor says. "So I knew some basic ragas that I proposed, that have scales that we share—the major scale from G, from D, and the minor scale from D—and we just started from there. For each piece we compose a little phrase, and we start with this, and in the middle we improvise and have a dialogue, and then we come back to it."

The North Indian classical tradition is far more familiar to Westerners than its Iranian counterpart, having been promoted by artists as varied as the Beatles and Yehudi Menuhin. Kalhor points out that India's status as a British colony created a link as early as the nineteenth century, and that today many of the greatest Indian musicians—Ravi Shankar, Ali Akbar Khan, Zakir Hussain, and Shujaat Khan's father, Vilayat Khan—live mainly in the United States. "They've been giving concerts here for more than forty years, and that's not a joke. We didn't have those conditions, and Persian musicians only got out of their country after the revolution—before '78, you couldn't find a single Persian record in stores here."

Despite Indian music's head start, Kalhor believes that in some ways the Persian tradition has a natural advantage: "If I just put myself in the Western listener's position for a moment, I would say Persian music is probably more accessible or more comprehendible than North Indian music, and less obscure or abstract. North Indian music can be very abstract to *me*, as an Eastern musician. Persian music is more melodic, the melodies make more sense, and the way it's performed is closer to what Westerners are used to. And there are reasons for that—basically, our geographic place between Europe and India."

Kalhor also points out that what he and Shujaat Khan play in Ghazal is in some ways more accessible than the more formal classical music they play on their own: "It is not traditional; it's a development that we created for ourselves. The way we develop our material in the classical music is very different. For example, if I do a classical solo, I might do a forty-minute, fifty-minute piece and there's a certain traditional rhythm and meter, and a certain way that you develop the material. For me, in a way, Ghazal just brings the nicest parts of both musics out—and since we cannot take a deep turn in our classical music, this is somehow more appealing for Western listeners."

Having reached that Western audience, Kalhor has continued to branch out, working on Yo-Yo Ma's "Silk Road" project and teaming up with a Turkish *saz* player, Erdal Erzencan, but he also has used his new stature to promote the mainstream Persian classical tradition in which he grew up, recording and touring with a quartet billed as the Masters of Persian Music. The group includes two of the older musicians who inspired him, Mohammed Reza Shajarian, Iran's most respected classical singer, and Hossein Alizadeh, who plays the *tar*, a Persian lute whose name links it to the sitar and guitar.

"I've known Shajarian's music all my life," Kalhor says. "I was brought up with his voice on the radio, and Hossein Alizadeh is considered a revolutionary figure in composing and tar playing. These two people were touring separately, and I was touring on my own; we were all doing our own things. But everywhere I would go, people would ask me, 'Why don't you play with Shajarian, or with Alizadeh?' And they were asking them the same question. So it was actually other people that made us decide to do this."

The Masters of Persian Music have been astonishingly successful, filling concert halls both with Iranian expatriates and with Europeans and Americans hearing this music for the first time. While the newcomers cannot understand all the subtleties, they do indeed seem to find something accessible about the style. As Kalhor has pointed out, to some extent this is a natural consequence of Iran's geographical location as a middle ground between East and West. But lest anyone take him for a purist who is claiming that Persia was always the source, and the West a follower, he adds that his music reflects an ongoing interchange.

"In the old times, the Eastern cultures affected the Western cultures, but in the modern world it's both ways, and mostly West to East. In modern history there was a lot of interaction and a lot of fascination for the West, and a lot of promotion for Western culture. For example, in the beginning of the twentieth century, the violin and the piano were introduced to Iran and the Arab and Middle Eastern countries. So, whether we want it or not, we have been influenced, and I'm not ashamed of saying that. It's not bad to be influenced by any other elements that we respect."

After all, artists are part of an ever-changing world: "I don't think a musician is allowed to lock him or herself in a cage, in a kind of tradition. Traditions can be very vague things that we depart from and belong to, and what we present today is certainly not what we presented five hundred years ago, or a thousand years ago. Traditions are not entities that we carry. Any living tradition breeds and changes according to the ways of life. It is like the English language that we speak now is not the same English language that Shakespeare wrote his text in. In the last century we have experienced many, many changes, of technology, ideology, philosophy, and how can we not be affected by that? Change is inevitable, in culture, in languages, in music, in everything."

Kalhor's personal evolution reflects a desire to balance past and present. A prime example is his choice of instrument. Before studying kamancheh, he played the Western violin, and he still speaks of it with respect and a degree of affection. "The violin was the only Western instrument that took over the world," he says. "Everybody loved it, because it's so handy, it's got a huge range, and it sounds beautiful, and Iran wasn't an exception. When it was introduced to Persian music, a lot of kamancheh players started to play violin and adapt it to Persian classical music, because there was this big notion of Westernization, and it was chic or something like that. So it totally destroyed the kamancheh. Up to this day, there are a very small number of kamancheh players, and at one time during the forties and fifties, there was just one kamancheh player left. This was the motive for me to go after it and research what was there before, working with old recordings and the people who were playing kamancheh at that time, seeing what their material was like.

"The violin is very capable, but I have my criticisms too, because there are certain techniques that you cannot do on violin. I never thought it was well adapted to Persian classical music; I always felt a kind of disappointment. I think the sound of kamancheh matches Persian music, the soul of classical Persian music."

As he talks, Kalhor regularly comes back to words like *soul*, and the division between traditional and experimental music is clearly less important to him than the quest to find forms that satisfy his own passion to grow and express his musical ideas. "You always go through these different phases in your career," he says. "You want to do different things, and your tastes change. So I do each of these things, and if I'm satisfied with the result, that means musically I'm happy. If you're not open-minded enough to try different things, or if you have fear of what people say and what the critics say, nobody can work. As a musician, you have to be courageous enough to experiment, and if you are happy with your experiments, that's enough. For example, with Ghazal, it's interesting that so many other people share what we feel about this music, but in a way it is not so surprising. I strongly believe that any project, any kind of music in any part of the world, if the musicians believe in it and put their hearts in it, it's going to be understood by people."

Pakistan

Nusrat Fateh Ali Khan

Nusrat Fateh Ali Khan was one of the most startling successes of the world boom, but at least in the United States his story was more complicated than the press releases indicated. He packed large halls, recorded with rock stars, and did Hollywood film soundtracks, but his crossover audience was never as big as it appeared. I learned this when, after two or three major concerts for Boston's World Music production company, he was booked by a mainstream promoter to do a summer show at the pavilion on Boston Harbor. When I saw the announcement, I called Maure Aronson, the head of World Music, to ask why his company wasn't booking this appearance. His response was, "That show will never happen. You can't do Nusrat in the summer, because all the Pakistani and Indian students have gone home." I pointed out that it was a double bill with Eddie Vedder, and in any case Nusrat had become an international star. Maure was having none of it. "There's a lot of press, but sixty or seventy percent of the tickets are still Indians and Pakistanis. Just watch: when they see what sales are like, that show will be cancelled." And indeed, within a month Nusrat was off the summer schedule and only reappeared at Symphony Hall that winter, on the World Music program.

Which is not to say that Nusrat only reached his own community. Simply the fact that there were almost as many Indians as Pakistanis in the audience was a miracle. When other *qawwals* attempted to duplicate his success, the Indians stayed home and the tours were financial disasters. And there were plenty of Europeans and Euro-Americans who were caught up in the power of his music and became devoted fans. Still, they numbered in the thousands, not the hundreds of thousands. As with many apparent "world" stars, Nusrat's core audience was always made up of homefolks.

All of which said, it was amazing that his music reached as wide an audience as it did. A traditional *qawwal,* or Sufi religious singer, he would sit Buddhalike on a carpet spread at center stage, surrounded by a dozen musicians and backup singers, weaving a sound that was utterly exotic and yet completely accessible. The *Boston Globe*'s Fernando González described his local debut as having "the energy of a rock 'n' roll show, the loose attitude of a house party and the spiritual power of a religious event all rolled into one," and his later visits confirmed this judgment—the ushers were always hard put to control the crowds of young fans who danced in the aisles and sought to overflow the stage.

Nusrat's first New England concert was at Harvard University's Sanders Theater, an intimate, acoustic masterpiece of a hall, ideally suited for his performance. The excitement it generated was such that he had to be moved to a larger venue for future visits, and as a result, all his later concerts were in Boston's Symphony Hall, a strange setting for music that traditionally was sung for small gatherings of worshippers at the tombs of Islamic saints.

"Qawwali is a religious institution, invented to spread the religion of Islam," Nusrat explains.* "The message is unity of God, praise of the Prophet, and other mystical and spiritual themes. We recite mystic poetry, and in this poetry our elders have said that a human being can reach the state of God. Because God is in us, and if we can cleanse ourselves from inside, through the *qawwali* medium a human being can travel through all those stages and reach that elevated stage which

---

* This interview was conducted through a translator.

we would probably not be able to reach even through years and years of worship."

Though his family have been quawwals for over six centuries, Nusrat says that his father tried to discourage him from continuing the tradition: "He was a master of music, but in those days it was a very hard life, so he did not want me to be a musician. He wanted me to get an education, to become a doctor or an engineer."

Nusrat had other ideas. "I would learn from his students, sneak to their lessons and learn from them in a sneaky way," he recalls. "Then one day I was practicing, and my eyes were shut, I was very much absorbed in the lesson, and he came and stood by me. When I saw him I was shocked, and I was very worried. At first he rebuked me, but then he smiled. He said, 'Okay, if you don't want to stop it, come on, I'll teach you.' And he started teaching me, but unfortunately soon after that he died. But then I started learning from my uncle. And, practicing every day, God has blessed me with this art."

There was more to the educational process than simply singing. "The qawwal has three or four types of training," Nusrat explains. "First of all, he has to know the literature. He has to inherit literary texts and he has to know the literature and poetry. And he should know how he can improvise from his verses. He should have education of literature, and then he should have education of music. Then, he should know singing, and he should know ragas."

According to Nusrat, this last requirement was what set his family apart from other quawwals. The classical tradition, with its complex system of *ragas*—roughly, set scales on which one improvises—has apparently been quite separate from the quawwali devotional style, but his family created a blend of the two genres. And beyond the special traits of this family school, he made his own innovations: "Every new person has to make some individual contribution," he said. "Just as the poets all have their own styles. I introduced *sargam* [the classical scale] and also included *fayal* [a wordless expansion of the melodic line]. And I introduced rhythm, which is very important, because if someone does not understand the words, rhythm will tell what is being said."

Nusrat's unique style, and the power of his performances, gave qawwali singing a broader audience than ever before and made him a national star. "He has revived the popular interest in this music" says Siddiq Abdullah, president of the Pakistani Association of Greater Boston. "He is more broad-minded, and he appeals to the younger generation by improvising and deviating from the pure tradition. Also, this music is a sort of way of getting high, without any drugs. It really takes you to a higher plane."

In the 1990s, Nusrat proved that his music could reach far beyond his home country, touring Europe and the United States, collaborating with Western musicians, and receiving a reception no other Asian singer has approached. "The Europeans and Americans have appreciated my music, and I am very happy with that," he says. "I thank God for that. When we present a program here, we make it slightly different from in our country. Because in our country we know that people are also understanding the words, but here we know that people don't follow the words. Therefore we use the classical music to express our message, and they understand my rhythm, and the meaning of what we are singing gets home.

"As I said before, our message is religious, about Islam. But it is not purely Islamic. There is a big part of our message that is for everybody. It is for Hindus, for Sikhs, for Christians. Our elders created this medium that goes beyond religion—it is basically regarding the relationship between a human being and his god. If a human being is trying to reach God, it is not necessary that he be a Muslim. Anybody can strive to reach God, and qawwali is a medium to do it."*

India

Purna Das and the Bauls of Bengal

From the other side of the subcontinent, the *bauls* of India's eastern state of West Bengal perform a music that is like a mirror image of Nusrat Fateh Ali Khan's devotional song. Indeed, as one listens to them describe their art and beliefs, it is tempting to wonder whether Nusrat's tradition is a fusion of Islamic teaching with earlier, pre-Muslim traditions like those the bauls keep alive. There is certainly

---

* Nusrat Fateh Ali Khan died in 1997.

The Bauls of Bengal: Purna Das Baul (left), with his son Manju "Bapi" Das and wife Subhendu Das. Photograph © Jack Vartoogian/FrontRowPhotos.

a similarity in the way they describe their mission, though the bauls are more lighthearted and down-to earth, as befits a tribe of wandering minstrels. Their music is likewise less complex, without classical adornments, but with the exuberant pleasure of a village celebration. If Nusrat's music invites comparison to the Mevlevi devotional style of Cinucen Tanrikorur, the bauls seem more like distant cousins of the village musicians of Jajouka—which may be why they likewise attracted the attention of the 1960s rock world.

Few Americans have heard the music of Purna Das and his family, but folk-rock fans will find his face familiar. He and his brother Luxman flank Bob Dylan on the cover of the *John Wesley Harding* album, Das smiling out from under a cowboy hat that Dylan had just plunked on his head. The year was 1970, and Das and Dylan shared the same manager, Albert Grossman, who had gone to India to meet the bauls on the recommendation of Allen Ginsberg. "Allen Ginsberg came and is staying in our village house several days with our family," Das's son, Manju "Bapi" Das, explains. (Bapi is the family's English-language spokesman, as his father speaks only Bengali.) "He learned some philosophies, ideas, and when he came back he said [to Grossman] 'Bring him here, I think it is a joyful philosophy and a joyful music.'"

The bauls' music is indeed supremely cheerful. Propelled by a variety of percussion and two obscure string instruments, the one-string *ektara* and the four-string *dotara*, it is a celebratory sound, befitting their unique lifestyle.

For over six centuries, the bauls have been a sect of humanist philosophical travelers. Bapi explains that, when the Indian caste system evolved, the bauls were left out: "We are not in any caste, and we don't believe in any gods. We believe that if we satisfy humans and if they are happy for that, that is our pleasure and that is our love and that is our worship. In Sanskrit, baul is meaning *batul* [insane], it is meaning someone who is mad for *moner manush*, inner soul. Like how you know yourself inside, what is in you. Because if you don't know what is in you, if you don't love what you have, then you can't love anybody else and you can't know anybody else. But if you know yourself very well inside, then you can know everybody who is around you—you know very well what is the flower, what is in the small animals, everything. So we are just moving around to find this moner manush wherever we are traveling."

In the old days, the bauls roamed Bengal on foot, and in each village there was a special house set aside for them. They would arrive, and the villagers would supply them with food and the necessities of life for as long as their visit lasted. "Some people come to give the rice, some people come to give their vegetables—whatever they have and they can give them," Bapi explains. "That is the responsibility of the village people. And [the] bauls' responsibility is to make them happy, give them a clear message of life, how they can go on with their happy soul."

Unfortunately, Bapi says that modern India can no longer support this nomadic lifestyle: "Now is totally different. Before, people have respect for many things, and now those things are gone because the time is changing. People are much more poor and they don't have food themselves, so how can they give to baul?

"Bauls are trying to continue that same thing, but without having food they can't go far. So now they have to go to sing to have some money to have the food. Now bauls have their own house and they are staying in one place, not moving around. Baba [Father] has a house in

Calcutta, and he is very famous for this type of music and this tradition and philosophy. People respect him and they are making lots of concerts to him, and that's how the life is going on."

Purna Das can trace six generations of bauls who came before him, and he is trying to find a way to preserve the core and spirit of the tradition despite societal changes. He has concluded that one solution is to reach beyond India, to try to spread the bauls' mission around the world, and says that if he had known how important people like Dylan and Ginsberg were, he would have tried harder to collaborate with them.

At that time, though, Europe and America seemed unbelievably foreign. "When he came in San Francisco, Baba is thinking, 'Where is the heaven I came here?'" Bapi says. "Because it's strange for him to see such a long street going on, lots of cars going on, and the people are so mad for music. Those things struck Baba at that time."

The reaction to his performances was also a bit disconcerting. Trained by the Beatles and Ravi Shankar, American audiences thought of Indian music as the deepest, most spiritual tradition on the planet, and treated it with great seriousness. "When they are listening this music, they are like doing a meditation, cool and calm everywhere," Bapi says. This was quite different from the reaction the bauls get at home, and Purna Das says that his recent visits have been much more gratifying. "Now, people are clapping, shouting, and dancing so much. He [Purna Das] feels it is better now, because public are coming with him and that fills him with much more influence to go through. He thinks, 'What I am giving, they are taking; they follow it and I feel good.' And he is enjoying so much."

Bapi now lives in France, and says that his father is encouraging him to collaborate with Western artists. "We don't think that music has to be all in one bottle; you cannot keep it like that," Bapi says. "He want to spread his music, his idea and joy, and share with everybody. Because this is not only music, it is a meditation, it is yoga. When we sing like this, then we realize the beauty of God's grace. We see God in human beings, and when we satisfy the human needs with music, we feel we are worshipping God."

In keeping with their universalist philosophy, Bapi and his father have had a number of Western students, and while some are simply interested in the music, others hope to become full-fledged bauls. Bapi notes that this is quite possible, but that it is not just a matter of choice: "We have to find out, actually recognize the people who are capable of doing that," he says. "Not everybody can be a baul in true sense. If you just want to learn music, that's a different story, but if you want to be a baul in true sense, from heart and within, then it's a different way of learning."

Still, the bauls are well aware that if they want to see their tradition continue into the future, they are going to have to adapt to the modern world. "We are trying very hard to make it survive," Bapi says. "In this situation that is going on in India, with the Western influence and people changing for modern things, it's kind of hard. But we believe if the baul is in somebody's inner strength, they will come out, and they are trying to spread it all over the world. It is not a religion or a caste or something, it's inside of a person, it's a feeling. And if a person has that, they will always be a baul."

North Indian Classical Music

Ali Akbar Khan

Indian classical music has never caught on with a broad Western audience.* Ravi Shankar is the only musician who has widespread recognition outside the genre, and more from his associations with the Beatles and Yehudi Menuhin than because many people actually buy or listen to his albums. The usual reason Westerners give for ignoring the Indian classical tradition is that it is too sophisticated—which is often a polite way of saying that we admire it in theory, but in practice find it boring. I was lucky, because before anyone had told me I would not be able to appreciate the subtleties of the Indian classical masters, I had seen Ali Akbar Khan.

---

* As is common in the West, I am using the term *Indian classical* to refer to the North Indian classical tradition. South Indian, or Karnatic, music is a closely related but quite different style, which to my ears should be more accessible but has had virtually no penetration to Western audiences.

Ali Akbar Khan. Photograph © Jack Vartoogian/FrontRowPhotos.

The first time I saw Khansahib in concert I was twelve years old, and it was one of the most exciting shows of my life.* I had never seen anyone play with such depth, such speed, such power, such grace. It was not that I loved Indian classical music in general—on record, I found it difficult and monotonous—but on stage, Khansahib is among the greatest musicians on the planet, and I did not need to be an aficionado to appreciate his work.

"Oh, yes," Khansahib agrees, when I tell him this story. "For the good music, you don't need to understand. It's like for fresh air you don't need to understand. It goes to inside you, and makes you healthy."

Born in 1922 in the region that is now Bangladesh, Khansahib has been performing since the mid-1930s. Today, he is regarded by many as the dean of Indian classical musicians, but he insists that in some sense he will always remain a student. "There is so much to research in this work that one life is not enough," he says. "There are so many beauties you can bring in, that every day you can improve. The improvement is endless—but if you want to destroy, you can destroy in a second. If you don't do it the proper way, if you play out of tune or

---

* Khan is an honorific title, and Khansahib the respectful form of address.

out of *ragas* and out of rules, then you lose the beauty of that particular melody, and that is a kind of destroying."

Indian classical performances consist of improvisations on *ragas*, set scales with a certain series of notes ascending and often a different series descending. The artist improvises within these scales, including key phrases associated with the particular piece, in several sections defined by tempo and time signature. Each player thus has great freedom, but within very strict boundaries.

Khansahib says that all classical musicians must start out as singers: "Everything is very similar to singing at some stages. You start with singing and then go on to the different instruments. Every instrument has got different technique, but they all can say the same thing, like the same word in different languages."

Khansahib began his apprenticeship as a singer at age three. His father, Allauddin Khan, was a master multi-instrumentalist, and developed a form of notation that allowed him to write down pieces that had until then been preserved only in the oral tradition. He was also a famous teacher, his protégés including Khansahib, Ravi Shankar, and Khansahib's sister Annapurna Devi, a legendary *surbahar* (bass sitar) player who has not performed in public since the early 1940s.

"My father knew two hundred instruments," Khansahib recalls. "And he used to play Western music, too. So I learned many instruments from him, and then when I was seven years old, he chose that I should stick to one."

That one was the *sarod*, a relative of the sitar (and, more distantly, of the lute and guitar). The sarod has four strings on which one plays the melody, four drones, two rhythm strings, and fifteen strings that provide sympathetic vibrations. Unlike the sitar, which has frets, it has a wide, curved neck covered with a sheet of metal. This allows for sharp, clear notes, and also slides worthy of a steel guitarist. "It is the only instrument on which you can play any kind of instrument sound," Khansahib says. "Other instruments have got limits, but sarod is really limitless. You feel sometimes like many people play together; in one instrument you feel like a whole orchestra is going on."

The sarod is also famously difficult, and even with his unusually early start, Khansahib says that mastering it was no easy feat: "I had to practice and learn from my father for over twenty years, eighteen

hours a day—it's a lot of time. And then, performing thirty-five programs a month for many years. To become a top, top-class musician,
that is God's gift, luck, good teachers, and hard work."

However, he adds that once the technical barriers were sur-
mounted, playing became so natural that he ceased to think of it as
work, and these days he does not even bother to practice. "Once you
really understand the music, then it becomes more easy than making
tea," he says. "So I just practice inside. Inside, always some music is
going on. I'm always busy—in my sleeping also or while I'm talking
to you, the music is going on, nonstop."

So, one wonders, what is this internal music like? Is he hearing
sarod pieces, or songs, or what?

"According to old theory, there's two kinds of sound," Khansahib
answers. "One sound without making sound, that is only for the yoga:
you don't make sound but you can make inside sound. And the other
sound, if you use an instrument or singing then you make a sound that
others can hear. The inside sound is many different kinds of sound,
and when I play music then also I sing inside, so there is one sound
I can feel without an instrument, and when I play I can hear them
bothly, inside and also through my instrument."

To many Westerners, this sort of talk is almost as difficult to follow
as the intricate raga forms, ethereal and removed from day-to-day life.
However, this is the last thing Khansahib intends. "People have all
kinds of wrong ideas, even in India," he says. "That is why I became
a musical director of many films, because the film audience never
wanted to go to any classical music. I hoped that at least they would
go to see the film, and through films they can get a little idea and hear
the real classical music. I have done that for ten years, and then after
that I have seen that all these taxi drivers and rickshaw wallahs, the
shopkeepers, they all started buying tickets for the music festivals."

In a way, this same process brought Khansahib to the United States.
He was one of the first serious classical artists to perform here, the first
to record a Western LP or perform on television, and he went on to
duet with Ravi Shankar in front of rock audiences, most famously at
George Harrison's Concert for Bangladesh. Today, he has colleges of
music in San Rafael, California, and Basel, Switzerland, as well as

in Calcutta. His mission has always been to spread his music to new audiences and new generations, and to make sure that it is carried on.

When it comes to the latter aim, he is only limitedly optimistic. He still believes in the power of "the good music" to reach any willing audience, but the world that produced the older players has vanished, and there is virtually no way for new artists to get proper training. Traditionally, classical artists were supported by the courts, so they could devote their lives entirely to playing and teaching disciples, who in turn spent virtually every waking hour in study. "In the old days, the great musicians did not have to worry about money or food," Khansahib says. "Nowadays, musicians are earning more money, but they have to tour all the time. Therefore it's very difficult to concentrate themselves and to teach in the proper way to many students.

"There are many music schools in India nowadays, but it is like a routine work, like a hospital. Before, it was like an ashram, where you go to a guru's space and the atmosphere and attitude and whole system was like a haven. Today, there are very many young musicians, the younger generation is more talented and more intelligent, very good at picking up things, but then they come up to one stage, you see, and the philosophy has become that you should have box office."

The old system was more highly specialized than the modern market will allow: "Someone who played fast things, with drums, he practiced only that section for his whole life. If you wanted to hear slow music, you'd have to go to another one. If it's morning melodies you wanted to hear, then you go to so-and-so, evening melodies to someone else." Today's players are far more versatile than their predecessors, but one result is that they cannot present any particular style with the depth and knowledge of the old specialists.

What is more, musicians now perform for a general audience rather than a select company of aficionados. Khansahib worked hard to create this broader public, but he is aware of its drawbacks. He recalls that the old masters used to sit in the front when young artists were playing, and publicly correct their mistakes: "If they were doing anything wrong in the raga or style or composition, the musicians always used to shout. Now, the old masters are not alive, there's nobody left like that, and the younger generation has no one to show them what is wrong."

As a result, many players are dumbing down their style, trying to find tricks that will dazzle inexpert fans: "People are not really serious to learn or understand or perform real music. They are mostly involved to please others or make a show with it. They don't care so much about the purity of the ragas, they even don't follow the time; sometimes they sing a morning raga in the evening or anytime. These kinds of changes are not good for music and not good for the listeners—and also not good for your health. Because this sound is created by God. This sound can purify your soul and mind."

One does not have to be intensely spiritual to notice that the flashy new artists have not developed anything that can grip an audience with the power of Khansahib's work, keeping it enthralled for hours at a time. Great art is not only deeper but, in the end, more exciting and satisfying than hot licks and empty entertainment. "This kind of music is not for show business," Khansahib says quietly. "Because if it is right music, then you get the effect of that. It's not the performance or even the instrument. When you play real music, the totally real music, you don't need to explain to anyone. The sound goes to everybody's ear, and through their ear to their soul."

That emphasis on soul and musicality over virtuosity means that the great Indian musicians can keep performing long after they reach an age when most of their Western peers would be in retirement. Khansahib says his father lived to be 110, and played into his last decade, so he considers himself to be in his musical prime: "I am still improving, and I'm trying to get the right feeling of the melody, which can make me happy and also those people that listen. Music is the only thing that you can share with a million million people and you don't lose, you only gain. It helps you to get energy and to live long, because if your soul is very happy then you don't want to die."

And, whatever the problems of the current marketplace, Khansahib is convinced that somehow the music he loves will endure. "It will continue, because all the good things remain," he says. "Many good people are dead and many are still here, and many are born. My father always used to tell me that the real music sound, God created. And if you can play it properly, then maybe one day you can see the God. Our religion is to play in tune. And that makes it so you can love all the people, and it will help your heart and mind change to help others."

Ravi Shankar

To most Westerners, Ravi Shankar exemplifies the Indian classical style. Through collaborations with Yehudi Menuhin and Jean-Pierre Rampal, associations with John Coltrane and, most famously, George Harrison, and half a century of tours and recordings, he has acted as an international ambassador of Indian music and a symbol of cross-cultural communication.

Nonetheless, the sitar master is quick to correct the impression that he ever wanted to create a fusion of East and West. Though he has performed with jazz and classical players, used synthesizers and Western instruments, and composed orchestral pieces, he insists that he has always played pure, Indian music.

"The name *fusion* is very disturbing to me," he says. "Because it means more or less mixing two things like a cocktail, and that is something that I have never done. All I have done is use non-Indian musicians and non-Indian musical instruments, but everything has an Indian root. I am never trying to do something which I'm not. I listen to a lot of different music, but I don't try to play Western classical music, or rock or jazz or any of these musics."

Shankar pauses. "But sounds, yes." Unlike Western classical compositions, Indian ragas are not linked to any particular instrument, so it is not necessarily a departure from the tradition to use a keyed flute or slide guitar rather than a sitar or sarod. "I have really experimented with sound, and I love to do that. I love the range, the quality, the dynamics, and the color elements in many of the non-Indian instruments."

Shankar had an unusual background for a classical musician. When he was eleven years old, he started performing as a dancer in the Paris-based troupe of his brother, Uday Shankar. Most of his teen years were spent touring the West, including a visit to the United States in 1932–33, and it was only at the age of eighteen that he returned to India and began seriously to study the sitar. He became an apprentice of Allauddin Khan, giving up the worldly life he had enjoyed and immersing himself in the classical tradition.

For seven and a half years he lived in Khan's house, practicing fourteen hours a day alongside Khan's children, Ali Akbar Khan and Annapurna Devi, who became his first wife. During this time, he also began to be known as a concert artist, making regular radio broadcasts. In 1944, he went out on his own, performing and composing film scores, including those for Satyajit Ray's *Apu Trilogy*. His radio and film work accustomed him to Western instruments and musical approaches, and in the 1950s he set his sights on the European and American concert world.

"My main objective was to bring Indian music to the West," he says. "My childhood experience in the West gave me a wonderful insight to the Western mind, to understand the way they listened to our music formerly. They couldn't accept it, because they thought it was too monotonous, not changing the tonic and no modulation, no harmony, and it goes on and on." Shankar laughs quietly at his list of stereotypes. "It used to make me very sad, and sometimes angry, that they don't understand the greatness of our music. And that was my motivation, which made me come back to the West from 1953 onward, first in Eastern Europe and Western Europe, and then by '56 I started coming to the States."

Shankar soon developed a devoted, if relatively small, following in classical and jazz circles. Then, in 1966, George Harrison became his student and he suddenly found himself a rock idol. He appeared at Woodstock, Monterey Pop, and the Concert for Bangladesh, where, in a landmark moment of cultural misunderstanding, the audience applauded his tuning, thinking it was the first raga.

"Everything happened almost simultaneously," he says. "That pushed me into an area as a cult figure, and I became popular in the pop sense. Let me tell you, I'm glad that I was around forty-seven, forty-eight. I was quite mature, and very deep into our own music and our own tradition, and spiritual, so I didn't go crazy and become like a raga-rock king. And I didn't take advantage and start talking of high philosophical things and become a guru or a swami or something like that. I've been called, like, a "godfather of world music," but that was George [Harrison] saying that, not me. I was doing something that was very natural to me. I love to try out new things, new sounds, but not to do some gimmicks and to sell the record. Of course, it would make me happy when the record sells, but that was not ever my motivation."

In fact, in the 1970s Shankar returned to India and his classical roots, once again immersing himself in the pure tradition. He has continued to experiment on record, but in concert he is a classicist, playing the traditional ragas to the accompaniment of the *tambura* drone and a tabla player.

At least in part, this conservatism seems to be a reaction to the disappearance of the society that nurtured the classical style. "The world has become so small, with all this media and everything," he says. "Now the differences between East and West have become so much less, especially when you consider the elite class, rich, upper-middle-class people. If you go to Lisbon or Calcutta, you won't find much difference in the living, talking, business, making money, pollution, and all those negative aspects, along with the old Coca-Cola and the hamburger and everything. It is becoming very common all over the world, and it's all stress."

Shankar adds that, when it comes to music, it is particularly hard for young players to get the personal contact that they used to have with older masters. "Our music has always been something that has been very personal," he explains. "It was passed on either from guru or father or both together, and that made not only the music but the whole philosophy which is connected with our tradition. Now, most of them are learning by listening to tapes and to video and different things—which is very good, and they are picking up very well, but I worry if they can sustain it. Some people are lucky to have the traditional way of learning, but very few."

Nonetheless, he says that the current classical music scene seems to be quite healthy: "There are wonderful upcoming musicians, really mind-boggling talent, and I am very hopeful for many, many of them. The young people, they have much quicker ability to adapt something in every field. The only thing is, we have to wait and see. Because it is not the dexterity of the hands, not only the neatness in performing and to dazzle people—all that is fine, but our music has something which is deeper. That depth, call it aesthetic or spiritual or whatever, does take time. And also the attitude of humility, which is so much connected with our music. But I am an optimist. I believe that our music will continue and will have really wonderful musicians."

Shankar himself is still going strong despite two heart attacks, and he has no plans to retire. He continues to tour with his daughter and protégée Anoushka, and he feels that he is playing better than ever:

"Our music is not a written-down music; it's all improvisatory. So what we do, we mature in our music and we become better. In our music, if one doesn't retire or give up or become handicapped with some physical disability, a musician always improves. Because it's a constant quest, an adventure and we're always gaining new ideas. It's really a fantastic experience."

8

EAST ASIA

The underrepresentation of East Asia in this book is due first to the vagaries of the world music scene. There simply are not as many musicians touring from the "Far East" as from other parts of the world—or rather, most of the musicians touring from this region are playing Western classical music. Beyond that, it is often difficult to interview the musicians who do come through. Many are in large touring companies, such as Peking Opera troupes, and the company spokesman is usually a director or cultural attaché rather than a musician. There is also a linguistic problem. Once one gets east of the Indian subcontinent, there are relatively few musicians who are comfortable doing interviews in English, French, or Spanish, and in my experience the translators provided by troupes and promoters are almost always amateurs, and tend to have only a limited grasp of one or the other language.

There has also been relatively little acceptance of Asian music by Western audiences. The Indian classical world gained a cachet through its acolytes in the classical and rock worlds, and Japanese *taiko* drumming has become popular on college campuses, but in general there seems to be a feeling that Asian music is difficult and weird. This is to some extent a matter of prejudice and stereotyping, but it is true that for the average American music listener, Peking Opera is harder to understand and enjoy than an African pop concert or a flamenco show. Of course, the United States has large Asian immigrant communities, and each has its music. Chinese, Korean, and Vietnamese concerts are common in many American cities, but most of the performers working on these circuits are lounge and pop singers, backed by electric keyboards or simply a taped instrumental track, and of little interest to outsiders.

There are exceptions to these rules—traditional artists who play at cultural events both within their communities and at the growing number of small, locally sponsored international music festivals, and the occasional showcase troupes sponsored by Asian governments—but this remains one of the imbalances of the world music market.

China

Wu Man

The first time I saw Wu Man, she was appearing as a guest artist with the Kronos Quartet. They were performing an avant-garde composition that frankly left me cold, but her playing was superb, and her involvement highlighted the genre-spanning curiosity that has made her by far the most visible Chinese traditional musician on the American scene.

When we met, she was practicing for a collaboration with the Ugandan musician James Makubuya, and I found them in the Endicott World Music Center at the Massachusetts Institute of Technology. It was in a way the perfect setting. Surrounded by the brass gongs and painted wood frames of a Balinese *gamelan*, three students sat on the floor in their stocking feet, playing Ugandan *adungu*, or bow harps, while Makubuya coaxed tuned rhythmic patterns from five variously sized drums. Meanwhile, sitting on a low stool, Wu Man cradled her *pipa*, a pear-shaped Chinese lute, and searched for ways to enter the unfamiliar arrangements. She listened to each tune for a while, then began to pick out a note here and there. Eventually, she would get the basic melody, then begin to improvise, her fingers plucking quick trills and arpeggios, or strumming fierce rhythmic counterpoint.

Such collaborations are quite a stretch from the Chinese traditional music Wu Man was trained in since childhood. Born in the southern city of Hangzhou, she was plucked from her elementary school to become a conservatory student. "My family not musician family, but artist family," she explains, in strongly accented English. "My father is painting, and my mother is teacher. But during eighties and seventies, the Chinese system is very much like former Soviet Union system.

Wu Man. Photograph © Jack Vartoogian/FrontRowPhotos.

They went to schools looking for kids, at very young age, and they find their talent and they choose them and they train them. So, I'm one of the musically sort of talent kid, and when I was nine they just picked me out of normal school and I went to a special music school."

Asked if the school was specifically for classical music, Wu Man says that the curriculum was actually quite broad: "Any sort of traditional Chinese music—court music, folk music, and also local opera, and of course piano and music history, Western music history, and all kinds of ear training."

Wu Man concentrated on the Chinese tradition, becoming one of the most promising young players on the pipa. She explains that there are various kinds of pipas, and if one goes back far enough her instrument is not actually Chinese in origin: "This kind of a pear-shape pipa, where the body looks like a lute or *oud* from the Middle East, was introduced from Central Asia to China through the Silk Road. That's why when you see it, it seems familiar, like a guitar, maybe."

At the conservatory, many of Wu Man's fellow students were specializing in Western styles, and as possibilities opened up for them to travel abroad, they began leaving in droves. "During the eighties, the Chinese government opened the door to the West," she recalls. "It was closed for, like, forty years, so my generation was very, very curious about what's happening outside of China. Especially musicians. So in my school a lot of schoolmates, they all gone: 'Bye, I'm on tour, I'm going to America.'

"'What?'

"'I'm on tour, I'm going to Europe.'"

Naturally, Wu Man was tempted to follow their example: "It's kind of influence: they go, and I want to go, too. But everybody told me, 'Well, you play Chinese traditional music. Pipa is not a common instrument. Nobody knows this instrument. What are you going to do if you go to States?' So I prepared a kind of joke; I said I maybe become a computer scientist. And I really thought about it, because many schoolmates changed their major. But I loved my instrument, so I took four pipas with me that first trip here. I want to try if I can survive as a musician. And I'm lucky."

Indeed, Wu Man's success in the United States has exceeded that of any other Chinese traditional performer. In part, this is simply a tribute to her instrumental skills: even before leaving China, she was being hailed as one of the finest players of her generation. Beyond that, though, it is a tribute to her phenomenal versatility. As well as working with Chinese traditional and modernist ensembles, she has performed with jazz, Western classical, and "new music" groups, recorded with the Kronos Quartet and the New York New Music Consort and appeared at the White House with Yo-Yo Ma.

She seems particularly excited with her discovery of jazz: "I have no idea what is jazz in China. Not allowed to play jazz in China; they thought this is bad music. But to me it just come naturally. I just immediately love it."

Historically, improvisation had been part of the Chinese classical tradition, but by the time Wu Man began her studies it had disappeared. "During the sixties a lot of things became written down," she says. "So we lost the improvising, and I have no training for this. But it is just natural to me. That's why my father said to me, 'You can't do anything else besides music.'"

Continuing to expand her horizons, Wu Man was preparing her first acting role in an opera to be staged at the Charleston, South Carolina, Spoleto Festival, and also a theater piece with artists from Japan and Korea. However, she has always maintained her connection to the Chinese classical world, and has also been back to tour the People's Republic. "They really enjoyed, because they never saw a pipa player like me," she says happily. "I went back to my school, and my professors were very appreciate and very proud. Because I have opened this instrument. I found a different way to present it, a different voice. And there is now an international jazz festival in Beijing and also in Shanghai, and I played the two. They went nuts! They were yelling, like, 'Wu Man, we love you!'

"I said, 'Oh my God, I'm a star!'"

Yoshikazu Fujimoto of Kodo. Photograph © Jack Vartoogian/FrontRowPhotos.

Japan

Ondekoza and Kodo

One of the most surprising developments of the world music boom has been the spread of Japanese *taiko* drumming. Though still not as common as African drumming or salsa dancing, taiko has attracted enthusiastic amateurs on college campuses across America—one website lists over two hundred groups—and is the only Asian performance style to have attracted a large Western following.

The modern taiko style emerged in the 1950s, pioneered by Daihachi Oguchi, a jazz drummer who conceived the idea of taking the ancient taiko (literally "fat drum"), which had traditionally been played to accompany festival celebrations, and using it as the basis for a new kind of ensemble. The style's international acclaim, however, is due to the vision of Tagayasu Den, who in 1969 brought together a group of young musicians for a sort of musical retreat on the island of Sado in the Sea of Japan.

Den named his group Ondekoza, or "Demon Drummers," and under his leadership the members lived together, played together, and also began to run together, routinely doing a full marathon to warm up for the day's practice. "Running in the late sixties was something very unusual, especially in Japan," says Marco Lienhard, a Swiss musician who joined Ondekoza in the early 1980s. "But on the Island of Sado, there wasn't much to do. I mean, we could practice all the day, but they decided to start running. So for about five years the group just stayed on the island, no performances outside, and after five years they made their debut in Expo at Kyoto, and then they went to Boston for the Boston marathon. Seiji Ozawa [then the conductor of the Boston Symphony Orchestra] saw them perform at the finish line of the marathon, and then he had a piece ordered for orchestra and taiko that was performed at Tanglewood [a long-running summer music festival in western Massachusetts]."

The combination of marathon running with intense drumming made for catchy publicity, but Ondekoza was always more than a novelty act. As Lienhard explains, "Mr. Den used to be the student of a famous ethnologist in Japan that kind of rediscovered the different festivals and customs in each part of Japan, discovering new areas that people were not very well aware of. So then he traveled around Japan to discover more about it and he saw all those different festivals, so when he started the group he had in his head already what he wanted to pick. Then he sent some members to that area to try to learn the drum routines from the local people."

Den himself was not a performer, but Lienhard describes him as "the choreographer, or the person who sets the ideas of the songs that we do." One of the ideas was to combine and reorganize folk traditions to fit a concert stage. "Most of it is inspired by traditional songs, or folk songs," Lienhard says. "But we have restructured, reworked them. Like, some rhythms are what you could hear at a festival, but the festival would last four hours or even the whole night, so we decided to do something a little bit shorter, a ten-minute song, and instead of using one drum use several drums, or give each drum a solo."

In 1981, Den's original group split, the musicians reforming as Kodo (a name that apparently has the dual meanings "heartbeat" and "children of the drum"), while Den assembled a new version of Ondekoza including some Europeans, Americans, and women. While Kodo is seen by some fans as a purer, more classically Japanese group, the company manager, Takashi Akamine, echoes Lienhard's comments about the need to reshape the tradition to fit a concert environment: "Once you put it on the stage, of course, you have to be different," he says. "Because it involves many theatrical things, like lighting, and you ask people to pay for the show; therefore, you have to come up to their expectations."

Kodo has earned international acclaim for the intensity of its concerts. For example, it will open with a line of six drummers kneeling at the front of the stage, as still as statues, all staring straight ahead. Then, with no apparent communication between them, they very slowly begin to raise their right hands, each holding a thin wooden stick. The drummers do not have any way to see each other, and the room is utterly silent, but the sticks rise over their heads in perfect unison over the course of what seems to be nearly a minute, pause, then fall so precisely that the six drums sound a single note.

Given this incredible precision, it is a bit surprising to hear Akamine say that the biggest change in the newer ensemble is the space it has provided for individual initiative. "In this group, individuals are more involved with the creative work," he says. "In Ondekoza time, the company director was very much in charge and the performers were told what to do. We encourage the musicians to contribute their ideas, then the artistic director listens and he blends their creativities into one."

Akamine stresses that he is speaking about the old Ondekoza, and does not know the current group's rules, but says that after the first few years the musicians found the original regimen oppressive: "In Ondekoza time, members lived in a kind of monastic lifestyle: no drinking, no smoking, no TV, radio, papers, boyfriends, and girl-friends. Kodo, we like to respect their individuality. We don't run together anymore, except for the apprentices. Outside the performance, the performers do what they want. If they want to smoke, they may; if they want to drink, they can. But they are professional people, so they know how to look after themselves. Because our performance requires physical strength and stamina."

Akamine adds that the more democratic approach has allowed Kodo to take advantage of the varied skills and experience of its musicians, whose backgrounds range from classical music to jazz and rock. Instrumentally, they stick to Japanese folk instruments, and their concerts remain firmly rooted in traditional styles—for example, in the 1990s they sent three members to a small island to learn a special type of drumming that is played only by women—but the group has also tried to stretch the boundaries of the ancient forms.

"It is important to understand traditional performing arts," Akamine says. "But it isn't really our priority to preserve all. We are performers and creators, and if you are artists, then I think there is always the urge to create something new. It's a challenge to do new things, staying with our identity, and that's what we are doing now.

"So it's changed quite a bit. If you are familiar with Japanese traditional music, then perhaps you will hear some different flavors. Because we tour a lot and we encounter with artists from different musical backgrounds and those people influenced us in certain ways, so perhaps you recognize African rhythms or other Asian musical sounds. Then we blend that in the kind of form that we play."

As part of its outreach, Kodo has hosted an annual Earth Celebration festival on Sado with guests like the Drummers of Burundi and jazz great Elvin Jones, and has recorded with the Peruvian folk group Kusillaqta. "Changes in our lives cause musical change a little bit also," Akamine adds. "Individuals try to express their thoughts and feelings, and the performance will change."

Nonetheless, he emphasizes that the core approach remains constant: "The music work may become less traditional, the rhythms are a little different, but the way we play is a very traditional way: how we stand, how we place the drum. And the drum itself is the old Japanese taiko."

Indeed, whatever the differences between the two groups, both Ondekoza and Kodo always end their concerts with a piece played on the huge *o-daiko* drum. The o-daiko is so large that it has to be wheeled onstage in a cart and is played by two men, one at either end, stripped to white loincloths and headbands, and glowing with sweat as they wield drumsticks the size of baseball bats.

This is the image that has made them famous, and Lienhard clearly is a bit concerned that they will be seen simply as showy drummers. To counter this impression, he emphasizes that Ondekoza also uses other traditional instruments: "There is the *shakuhachi*, which is a vertical flute," he says, "and another one which looks like a piccolo, but made of bamboo. We also play the *shamisen*—not the classical shamisen, but a folk shamisen, which is a string instrument with a body like a square banjo. You play it with a big plectrum that looks like an ice scraper, and you hit on the strings and the body, so it's like a percussive instrument. And we have also learned the Noh theater flute, which is interesting because the teacher didn't consider it as melodies or music—it was like a word or a phrase, and we had to learn it by a song before we would take the flute and start playing."

He adds that even the drumming has a vocal basis: "To teach it in the traditional way, there's basically two sounds, right and left hands, and you could, through the song, know which. They make it longer with an N ending, like dokodokodon, dokodokodon, and you learn the rhythm by learning the song. The rhythm will be in your head, and then you'll be able to play on the drum. Each instrument would have its own words or phrases: shamisen has a different type; shakuhachi also has a different type. Basically, what the musicians in Japan used to do is not write it down; you play with the teacher and try to pick up the phrases little by little, playing over and over, and try to remember like that. Still today, a lot of teachers don't like to give you notes. They give you the melodies, and you work on one song for months and build up your repertoire."

With the intensity of its performances, Kodo has become the most famous and acclaimed taiko group in the world, while Ondekoza has attempted to keep more of a grassroots approach. For example, the latter band did a tour of the United States in the 1990s during which the musicians ran more than nine thousand miles, from New York down to Florida, across to California, north to Seattle, then back to New York via Montana and the Dakotas. Kodo's Akamine describes this feat as "wonderful and amazing," but adds that "at the moment [Ondekoza's] presentation is very much suited for Western audiences. We try to bring something that we think more, 'This is ours.'"

Lienhard says that Ondekoza has not lost its Japanese roots, but he agrees that the group is trying to broaden its appeal, reaching not only outside the country, but outside the concert world: "We wanted to do something different, to expose as many people as possible to this music, not just in the large cities, but also smaller towns, and to spark an interest in Japanese music, or different music, or just music in general. And also, by the running, to interest people in doing something about themselves."

9

THE UNITED STATES

In at least one sense, the United States can be considered the birthplace of "world music." The early years of recording overlapped the great wave of immigration that peaked around the turn of the twentieth century, with the result that many of the most important Chinese, Eastern European, Irish, Italian, and Latin American recordings of the first decades of the twentieth century were made in New York and Chicago and marketed primarily to ethnic communities in this country. In the assimilationist fever that gripped these communities during the two world wars, people changed their names and customs, and lost their native languages, but the music often held on. In St. Genevieve, Missouri, flocks of Christmas revelers still sing medieval French wassailing songs; Irish bars in Boston echo with the sound of fiddles; and polka festivals thrive throughout the Midwest.

Should we think of these musics as "world" styles? The question is as interesting and contentious as it is unanswerable. Louisiana's Cajun and zydeco musics are as homegrown as blues or country and western, but often sung in a language that few Americans understand. Salsa was exported to Latin America from the streets of New York. Tex-Mex fused German and Bohemian rhythms and accordions with Mexican *ranchera* styles. None of these could have emerged anywhere but in the United States, and yet most Americans continue to think of them as foreign. Meanwhile, new immigrant communities are both preserving traditions from abroad and creating new fusions every day.

An entire book could easily be devoted to international music as it has evolved in the United States. Rather than taking such a broad approach, this chapter focuses on the music of several communities whose roots reach back before the first Europeans arrived. That does not mean that this music necessarily is older or more genuinely

"American," but it is roughly the same standard applied in the other sections, and hence the only one that seemed logical here.

Hawaii

Raymond Kane

Everyone in the United States has heard some version of Hawaiian music, though many may be unaware of that fact. The first Hawaiian troupes began touring the mainland around the beginning of the twentieth century, and were so popular that early slide guitarists, whether hillbilly hotshots or Mississippi Delta bluesmen, referred to their styles as "Hawaiian." However, much like Mexican music, the Hawaiian tradition tended to reach outsiders through tourist stereotypes rather than through its finest artists. The islands' blend of cozy familiarity and Polynesian exoticism proved irresistible to generations of travelers, and these twin appeals were distilled into the lounge schlock of Don Ho and a thousand tiki bar bands.

Ry Cooder shifted the balance somewhat in the 1970s, recording with respected older players like Gabby Pahinui and Atta Isaacs, and along with the folk-rock of Keola Beamer, this attracted some mainland listeners to the islands' fingerpicked "slack key" style. (The name derives from the custom of retuning the guitar, "slacking" the strings to get a variety of harmonic textures.) Less obviously distinctive than the slide guitar, slack key has a mellow lilt that fit with the "New Age" styles that emerged in the 1980s, and the New Age pianist George Winston made it his mission to bring it to the world. In 1994, he issued the first of what by now are some forty CDs in his Dancing Cat record label's Hawaiian Slack Key Guitar Masters Series, which showcases many of the finest living players in the style, and also sponsored tours and concert appearances by many of the artists. Of all these performers, the grand master was Raymond (Ray) Kane.

Ask Kane how he learned to play slack key, and his story recalls Isaac Newton's discovery of the law of gravity: "I sat under a tall pineapple tree, about twenty feet tall, and all of a sudden a pineapple fell and hit me on the head. My hand went down from the bass string to the last string, and I thought, 'Hey, we got two different sounds there.' So that is how I started to use the bass. The slack key has the bass and the melody plucked at the same time."

Or maybe it wasn't like that. "No-o-o," he laughs, stretching the word to three syllables. "My wife is kicking me in the back, so I got to tell you: There ain't no pineapple trees. Pineapples ain't no higher than two feet off the ground."

Kane is the elder statesman of slack key. He started playing in the 1930s, at a time when the style seemed to be disappearing. Hawaiian traditional music was being drowned in a flood of pop records from the United States, while the Hawaiian-flavored bands in the tourist hotels favored the louder and more distinctive slide guitar over the gentle slack key sound. The old guitar style, which at one time had even been played by members of Hawaii's royal family, was only kept alive by a handful of aging amateurs. "Those days you could count them, one, two, three, four at the most," Kane remembers. "It was a very rare thing to hear and a rare thing to see the people that played slack key guitar. The first time I heard it I was nine years old and I was staying on the beach. My father had a fishing crew, and one of his men played. So he was on the beach and I walked over and asked him, 'Would you teach me?'"

The answer was less than encouraging: "Before I got there, he slacked the strings and put the guitar down and put his foot on it. In those days, slack key guitar was very secretive and they didn't want to teach nobody unless they are family. Because there are several different tunings, and some that are prettier than others, and these tunings represent the family. So he tells me, 'Scram, beat it.' He says I'm bothering him.

"So I scrammed, and the next morning I went to him and said, 'Look, you get tired of eating this mackerel. How about me going out to catch you some other kind of fish?' That was all they had been eating, this mackerel, you see.

"So he say, 'What kind of fish can you catch?'

"I say, 'All kinds of fish. What kind of fish you like?'

"He said, 'Anything.'

"I said, 'You sure, anything?'

"He said, 'Yeah.'

"So okay, next morning I went out to get some fish, so I came in and I was dragging this fish—but it was a little heavy for me to drag. He run out and the next thing you know, he say, 'Hey, Ray! You got a whale on that line!'

"I said, 'You told me any kind of fish.' I made sure he had enough fish to supply him for a month. So that way I could get a lot of lessons."

Whether or not one believes that story, Kane went on to become one of Hawaii's foremost musicians, part of the generation of now legendary guitarists including Pahinui and Sonny Chillingworth. However, while those players were strongly influenced by mainland trends, especially Nashville's blend of hot picking and mellow vocals, Kane stuck to an older tradition. In the nineteenth century, Mexican cowboys brought the guitar to the islands, and between their influence, the "parlor" styles then flourishing in the United States, and local melodies, Hawaii developed a sound all its own. Slack key's variety of tunings are designed to produce distinctive harmonies, and while some players have developed fast and intricate picking styles, its greatest strength is its unique tonalities and languorous, evening-on-the-beach tempos, rather than speed or virtuosity.

In the last thirty years, Kane has helped to lead a slack key revival. While younger masters like Keola Beamer and Ledward Kaapana have carried the music forward, fusing it with mainland folk, rock, and country-and-western, he has taught a generation of students how to play in the older styles. He is a vibrant and funny performer, but most of his music consists of simple, traditional melodies illuminated by his lovely, rich guitar tone and subtle melodic variations.

Most of Kane's tunes are instrumentals, but his love of the older traditions comes through even more clearly in his vocals. His middle name, Kaleoalohapoinaoleohelemanu, means "the voice of love that comes and goes like a bird and will never be forgotten," and he is one of the few remaining masters of the archaic *i'i* singing style. "It's a rough style," he says. "See, the singers were old men in their sixties and seventies, and they tried to sound tough to impress the ladies." The result is a combination of gruff, low tones with bright falsetto passages, which can sound bizarre on first listening and forms a startling contrast to the sweetly flowing guitar lines.

Kane's wife Elodia also sings, and accompanies him on all his tours. "I play a little slack key music, and then I call her up and she sings the old traditional Hawaiian wedding songs," he says. "She has a beautiful soprano voice. That was what attracted me to her, her singing. It was the wedding song, and two weeks later we were married. And I never saw her before in my life, and her boyfriend was there . . ."

While many slack key artists now sing in English, Kane and his wife prefer Hawaiian—though, oddly enough, he says that they do not speak the language: "I just speak broken Hawaiian," he explains. "Sometimes I don't even know what I'm singing about, to tell the truth. But normally it is all about flowers, trees, beautiful things. Moonlight, some girl left a guy—all those things."

For Kane the real message is in the music. "Slack key is a very mellow sound," he says. "It is hard to describe it. Words can never express the feeling. You just have to be there and listen."*

Dennis Kamakahi

Like the folk revival that swept the mainland United States in the 1960s, the slack key scene benefited from the mix of older performers like Kane, who picked up the music because it was a fun way to relax after a day's work, and ardent young revivalists. As with Joan Baez, Bob Dylan, and their many heirs, the slack key players who came of age in the 1970s were not content simply to learn the older styles. Players like the Beamer Brothers and Sunday Manoa brought together soft rock, Nashville country, singer-songwriter poetry, and traditional melodies in a fusion that at its worst is sappy and forgettable, but its best has a unique blend of relaxed good feeling and profound musicianship.

Dennis Kamakahi is of that revivalist generation, and his efforts have been integral in keeping the music alive and growing in popularity both on the islands and abroad. His work, both as a soloist and with the quartet Hui Aloha, can be classed with the more traditional wing of the contemporary scene, but he has consistently striven to make it relevant and accessible to young listeners. With Hui Aloha, in

---

* Ray Kane died in 2000.

Dennis Kamakahi. Photograph © Jack Vartoogian/FrontRowPhotos.

which he is joined by his son David on ukulele, guitarist George Kuo, and bassist Martin Pahinui, he plays a loose, engaging style known as *pana'i like*. "It means 'give and take,'" he explains. "And that's the way we play. Say I take a solo, then when I finish we nod and the next guy takes it to the next level. This is the way we play back home; we call it 'backyard music.'"

Kamakahi considers the easy, good-time feel of this style a natural introduction to the deeper tradition: "What we're trying to do is get the younger generation in Hawaii," he says. "Because they're going back and rediscovering the type of music that turned us on to Hawaiian music. It's like what happened to us in the early 1970s: the old style, it's pretty simple, 'cause it belonged to the older generation, so the younger generation said, 'This is boring, let's go someplace else.' I was playing rock and country, and I'm sure George was playing something else, and Martin was a great rocker. Then this trio named Sunday Manoa came along with a new type of slack key sound, mixing in a folk-rock thing and embellishing the voicing. When we heard this group, we said 'Wow, this is really cool,' and we started coming back. So now we're trying to take it to another level, to another generation."

Despite his youthful flirtation with rock, Kamakahi is considered one of the most traditionally-oriented artists of his generation, and he clearly takes pride in that role. "One of my teachers told my mother that she believed that I lived in another time," he says. "She said I lived back in the 1860s, and was put back here to finish what I didn't finish then."

It is easy to see where his teacher got that idea. Kamakahi's solo *Pua'ena* album starts with a song composed by Hawaii's last queen, Lili'uokalani, in 1868, and while most of the other songs are original compositions, their language, guitar work, and melodies are stylistically indistinguishable from the older material.

"There's a tradition in Hawaii that the oldest grandchild, if it's a male, is given to the grandfather," Kamakahi says. "And my grandfather was musical, played slack key. That kind of music is what I remember him playing, and it takes you back to the days before electricity, when you'd sit on the porch and kerosene lanterns would be lit. I remember this when I was small. At that time my great-grandfather was still alive and he couldn't speak English; he only spoke Hawaiian. Our family would gather in the evening and the lanterns would go on and you would hear this sweet music. They'd play a couple of songs and remember the days when they were younger, and the stories would all come out. So I try to capture that in the style I play, and try to bring it up to this generation."

This is not to say that Kamakahi is narrowly focused on the local tradition. Like many Hawaiian musicians, he hears a natural affinity between the islands' music and Nashville country-and-western: "I think that country music is like what Hawaiian music is. It's the kind of music you like to turn on when you are driving on long distances, to relax and listen to. The language might be different, but I think the feeling is the same. And it's only natural it would sound alike. Country is very popular in Hawaii, especially in the areas where the cowboy lifestyle is still strong, like Parker Ranch on the big island, which is the biggest ranch in the United States."

That said, Nashville has the power of radio and the mainland recording industry behind it, and for a while its products threatened to swamp the local music. While syrupy variations of Hawaiian melodies were trotted out for the tourist trade, until the 1970s few islanders thought of their older styles as anything to be seriously studied and pursued. Kamakahi's own return to his roots happened only after exploring everything from high school brass band music to a period playing and composing classical pieces. "What made me want to come back to Hawaiian music was I was far away from home," he says. "I was working public relations for the Hawaii Visitors Bureau and that took me through Canada, and I heard this radio program, *Hawaii Calls*. And I said, 'What am I doing here so far away? I should be going back to the roots of the music I was brought up in.'"

The late 1960s had brought a surge of ethnic pride among Americans of all stripes, and a lot of young Hawaiians were feeling the same way. "It was a really exciting time," Kamakahi recalls. "Because all of a sudden Hawaiian music was making a resurgence." The most popular young players tended toward a Crosby, Stills and Nash sound, but a few were also digging deeper. Having grown up in a old-fashioned musical family, Kamakahi considers himself "one of the lucky ones." He could play the new styles, but also had a solid grounding in the traditional approach, and in 1972 he was chosen to replace Gabby Pahinui in the pioneering band of the Hawaiian music revival, Eddie Kamae's Sons of Hawaii. "It was as if I was in rock music in the sixties, and one of the Beatles said, 'Hey, fill in for so and so,'" Kamakahi recalls. "You'd just fall off the chair."

Kamakahi's position in the Sons gave him a unique stature: he was young and could play rock music, but had also received the mantle of the older generation, with the result that he was appreciated by both purists and crossover players. Over the years, he has assiduously nurtured young musicians, teaching them the traditional ways while encouraging them to find their own voices. He is also one of the few songwriters who continues to compose in the classic forms, and to write in Hawaiian rather than English.

"The language is very important," he says. "Because the words that are chosen will dictate whether the song is a right song or a song that is not going to be right. We call that *pono*, if it's right. If it's not pono, the song will not convey the spirit to the person that hears it. So we have to choose our words real carefully. It's a lot harder composing in the Hawaiian language, because we have all these ancient traditions to follow.

"The modern writers, they have no taboo, which are the limitations. They do not use the poetic images like how I learned; it's more literal, so they've lost the beauty of the language. The Hawaiian language is very, very poetic; you can use one word to mean several things. Now, with the Hawaiian language immersion programs, the generation of Hawaiian speakers are more than when I was young, but the art of writing in the poetic style has dwindled with the passing of the older generation. I would like to bring that back."

To Kamakahi, the Hawaiian tradition has a strength that can only come from deep roots and a hearfelt honesty. "It's like blues," he says. "If you look past the tonality to the feeling, Hawaiian music and blues music deliver the same type of emotion. It's improvised, spontaneous music, and spontaneous music is the best type because it's the emotion of the person, and the inner soul of that person coming out at that time that he plays."

That spirit of improvisation and spontaneity balances the traditionalism of Kamakahi's approach, and keeps it a living style rather than a museum recreation. For example, "Ke Kaua Laiki," one of the strongest songs on the *Hui Aloha* album, is a piece he wrote about Hawaiian soldiers in Vietnam. This is unusual in the slack key world, where lyrics tend to be about love and the beauties of nature, but Kamakahi says that for him it is simply another way of carrying on the tradition: "My teacher, Mary Pukui, told me, 'Think about how your ancestors were writing at the time they lived.' Because it's sort of like a picture of history that was captured in the song—and once a hula is attached to it, then the song lives forever, because the movement of the hula and the song will tell the next generation what happened during that time. So she always encouraged me to write about my time."

Now that his son is following in his musical footsteps, Kamakahi is more conscious than ever of the need to pass on his traditions and history. "This is going to be important when I'm no longer here," he says. "When people sing that song, they will know it was about a time where the composer lived, and the feeling of how he felt. I can see fifty years, or a hundred years from now, they'll look at this song and say 'Vietnam, what is that?' and it will make them turn back and research about that time."

Native American Music

The Iron River Singers

Native North American music is in a unique situation. It has been going through a far-reaching revival in recent decades, both as a symbol of pride and unity among Indians, and more recently as a soundtrack to New Age spirituality—two functions that are widely divergent and often openly inimical to each other. However, it has attracted relatively little attention from the people who come to international styles simply because they want to hear interesting music.

The failure of Native American musicians to reach a broader public has a variety of explanations. One is that almost all of the traditional styles are very subtle and personal, without the intricate melodies, rhythms, or harmonies that developed in court cultures that could hire and support generations of professional performers. Traditional North American cultures had no concept of entertainment or performance in the European sense, and much of their music is connected to rituals that are not supposed to be revealed to outsiders. Even the styles that are not expressly barred from public performance are part of larger social occasions, and often make little sense outside this context. The circle of men holding a regular rhythm on a large drum and singing "hey-yah-hey" is vital to a powwow dance, but heard out of context on a concert stage it has nothing to hold the interest of a seated, uninvolved audience.

For many Indians, the powwow movement has created a new sense of identity, and a way to meet and communicate with people from other tribes and nations across the United States. This is somewhat controversial among traditionalists, since Indian cultures were extremely varied and the powwow style by no means universal. This means that in many regions young people are asserting their ethnic pride by adopting customs that their ancestors considered utterly foreign—a bit as if young Spaniards were getting in touch with their ancestral roots by learning to yodel. That said, after centuries of genocide, forced dispersion, and isolation on reservations, it is easy to understand why so many Native Americans have welcomed a shared, pan-Indian culture, and the powwows are a powerful meeting place.

In eastern Massachusetts, the powwow movement caught on in the 1980s. In a corner of the meeting hall of the New Bedford Rod and Gun Club, a large, log-walled room framed by an American flag and a stuffed pheasant, seven young guys and an older man sit in a circle around a large drum. They start playing a steady rhythm, their drumsticks rising and falling in unison, and then the lead singer, Rui Sousa, comes in, the others joining in chorus around him. Sousa's song is a piercing keen that soars above the blended voices and drumbeat like an eagle on the hunt.

The Iron River "drum" (the term comprises both the instrument and the group that plays it) was started around 1990 by Sousa, his cousin Nelson Araujo, and their godfather, Paul Levasseur. "When we first started going to powwows, we were always interested in the singing and the drumming," Sousa remembers. "Then one day we went to a gun show in Newport, and we were walking around through all those vendors, and I came across this little drum. It was only about a foot wide and it was real cheap, and I bugged Paul: 'You gotta buy it for us. We're gonna start on this drum.' So he ended up giving in to us, and we got a couple of beaters, and we just kind of listened to some tapes and started playing around with it, learning to keep in beat, and we've been singing ever since."

The Iron River Singers are typical of a broad Native American cultural renaissance. Though relatively few non-Indians are aware of it, it is a national movement and has developed an intertribal style that, even in New England, draws largely on the traditions of Western nations like the Cree, Lakota, and Ojibway.

"There's different styles that we do," Araujo says. "There's a contemporary style and an old style, and what we'll do is we get a tape, or we'll go to a powwow and record the drums that are actually there, and we learn songs that way. When we first started, we'd just hear a song and we'd do it, but we learned that that's not right at times. You got to ask permission for the song, or if you're doing a song that has Indian words in it you should know what you're saying. So it took us a long time to know what we was doing and how to do it right."

He adds that, once they got their drum in shape, they discovered that there was much more to it than the music. "It took a while for people to really like us, but then all of a sudden we were in demand.

All summer long we have powwows, and even in the winter we have socials, and not only that but you have wakes, weddings, anniversaries. People don't realize the responsibility there is in the drum."

"The drum is really the servant of the Native population in the area," Levasseur agrees. "It's a drawing point for everybody, and it keeps everybody together. People depend on you. Just recently we were called for a funeral and we only knew just a few hours before, so we had to get everybody together and high-tail it. It's tremendously important to a lot of people."

The three leaders of the Iron River Drum are all Abenaki, but the dancers, singers, and musicians they meet at powwows around New England include representatives of some half-dozen tribes, especially Wampanoags, who are the largest group in the area. Despite their local roots, most perform styles from far away: the grass dance, fancy dancing, and the jingle dance of the Plains states. In part, that reflects the fact that the western tribes, bunched together on reservations in isolated regions, have been able to keep more of their tradition intact than their more assimilated eastern counterparts.

"You have to understand that at one time in history you were not allowed to speak your language," Levasseur explains. "You were not allowed your religion, you were not allowed most anything of your culture. You had to be like the settlers, what we call the 'boat people' from Europe. And so much was lost because of that. Luckily we still have some people that speak the [Abenaki] language, and we now have a two-volume dictionary out, thank goodness, which helps out."

Along with their powwow drum, the Iron River Singers are also studying the traditions of their own nation, working to keep them alive and make sure that, having survived the European invasion, they do not get drowned in the wave of pan-Indian styles from the western plains.

"One thing I'm proud of is that we don't all do western dancing," Araujo says. "A lot of the singers and dancers on this drum have an eastern outfit, because they're people from around here. I think it's very important we don't loose that. We gotta represent who we are."

"We're a minority in a minority group," Sousa agrees. "And we have to let them know that eastern people are still alive and we're still dancing and singing and we're still doing our own ceremonies."

They add that one of the reasons that so much of what one sees at public powwows comes from the western tradition is precisely because these gatherings are a recent import and thus not bound by ceremonial strictures. For example, Araujo plays the water drum, an eastern instrument that uses water to change its pitch, but he does not bring it out at performances.

"That's not something we do as a show," Sousa says. "It's not a presentation-type thing; it's more personal. And a lot of the songs are the same way, at least according to the way we were taught. The person who taught us most of our eastern songs always taught us that this is just for Native American people at a social to have a good time. That's when you sing those songs, and you don't ever do this for money or for the wrong reasons, because you're gonna bring all those bad spirits into that drum and you're just going to ruin the whole thing."

Today, with Native American culture attracting growing attention from "boat people" as well as Indians, the Iron River drum is doing more outreach. Still, the musicians stress that what keeps their group together is not public performances, but the music's direct connection to their lives and their place in the community.

"We're like a family," Araujo says. "We might have our arguments, but when it's time to sing, our attitudes are all the same. It's a healing to us."

"It basically puts us in a trance," Sousa adds.

"In the zone," Araujo says. "It's powerful. 'Specially when you've got a good song going, and the dancers get dancing really hard. You can feel the energy there."

"Sometimes they'll all come right towards the drum and they'll dance right in front of you," Sousa says, his voice reflecting the excitement. "They're facing you, and you feel it. It just brings you right up. You have to experience it, really—it's impossible to put it into words."

Jesse Morales. Courtesy of Herminio and Jesse Morales.

Mexican Music

Jessie Morales "El Original de la Sierra"

Spanish-language music has been popular in the Southwestern United States for far longer than English-language music, and over the last two hundred years the Spanish-English overlap has created a range of fusions, from cowboy waltzes and "blue yodels" to Pachuco boogie and brass-band rap. In the last decades of the twentieth century, Los Angeles became the de facto capital for a new wave of immigrants that is unlike any other in American history: they are largely of Native American heritage, and living within easy reach of the border they have no reason to cut their ties to Mexico or Central America. In cities with names like Los Angeles, San Antonio, Santa Fe, and San Francisco, they have an obvious counterargument for any claims that English is the established local language, and with every year they are growing more conscious of their cultural and political strength, and more reluctant to be treated as newcomers or outsiders.

Jessie Morales is one of the most popular singers in the new generation of urban Mexicans north of the border. He was barely thirteen years old when he made his debut at the Mercadito, one of Los Angeles's popular Mexican markets. The Mercadito's third floor is dominated by three large restaurants, each with a live band—*norteño* duos on weekdays and full mariachis, complete with violins, trumpets, and silver-spangled cowboy suits, on Saturday and Sunday. Morales's family was there one weekend, and urged him to take the stage: "I asked [the band] if I could sing a song, and they said okay, so I went up there. I had on baggy pants, so-lows, the basic rap attire, and I know that all the Hispanics there, they were saying something in their minds like, 'Look at this *cholo* [street tough] singing with a mariachi—what's up with this guy?' But when I stopped singing, I heard some applauses. And I was like, 'Am I crazy, or are these people just applauding me?'"

Morales was hooked, and he began learning more songs and sitting in with bands at restaurants and flea markets. It was quite a turnaround for a boy who had always considered Mexican music old-fashioned. His parents were immigrants from Zacatecas and Nayarít who listened to norteño acts like Ramón Ayala and Los Tigres del Norte, but Morales was born and raised in South Central Los Angeles, and his favorite stars had been people like Run-DMC and Tupac Shakur. "I was in Washington High School, that's in the heart of South Central," he recalls. "I was around African Americans—basically that's all I was around—so I was listening to Eazy-E and everything, but they weren't going to listen to no Ramón Ayala, you know what I mean? At that time, I thought, 'Oh, my old folks are hearing all this ranch music.' If my friends came over to the house, I would be like, 'Hey, Ma, put that stuff down!' But then, with time, I started appreciating that this music was really mine."

The change came after he heard a tape with a song about the murder of his cousin Lolo Ramos. It was one of the last recordings by Chalino Sánchez, the local superstar who had himself been shot and killed in Mexico in 1992. Sánchez led a new wave of singers, harder-edged heirs to the Tigres, who were famed not only for singing corridos of the cross-border drug trade, but of themselves being immersed in the world they were chronicling. Though musically they stuck to polkas and waltzes, their attitude and themes linked them to the gangsta rappers who were emerging in the same Los Angeles neighborhoods at the same time, and their records provoked similar outrage from lawmakers and citizens groups. In Mexico, *narcocorridos* (drug ballads) are prohibited from airplay in most of the main drug trafficking states, and there has even been talk of a national ban.

It took Morales a while to get into the sound of the *corridistas*—nasal country voices, backed by mariachis, accordions, or brass bands—but their raw, real-life narratives won him over. "That impacted my life," he says. "Because Chalino was singing about someone in my family, and it was a different way for me to listen to music. I was listening to all this rap, and this was basically the same thing, dealing with a death and society and all that stuff, but it was *mis raíces*—my roots.

"There was like hundreds of tapes coming out from kids and older men who were in the *narcotráfico* and had the money to make their own CDs. So I was scoping everything out, and I would go to the swap meets [flea markets], where there was like the little norteño groups, and go, 'Can I sing this song?' Some people said no, but I think it was actually because I was getting more popularity than they were when they were playing. A lot of groups started learning about me, but they didn't let me sing with them. So that was kind of messed up, right there."

Like rap, *corridos* are often accused of glorifying a gangster lifestyle, but for Morales that was part of the appeal: "The *narcotráficos* [drug traffickers] were happening around the area. So that's how I heard the music: 'Hey, that guy has a big truck and he's bumping this Mexican music, he must be doing pretty good, he must be selling some stuff!' You know what I mean? I wanted to come out of the ghetto and bring my parents out—maybe not with that lifestyle, but with this music that they were hearing."

Morales was part of a generation of *chalinitos*, or "Little Chalinos," who mimicked the late star, but where others adopted Sánchez's look and manner, Morales concentrated on the sound: "I was hearing these tapes day and night, day and night, studying the curves, the hooks that he did, the style and all that kind of stuff." He laughs gently, thinking back to those early efforts. "I was actually sounding kind of identical, like I was faking the voice—but it was coming out pretty good."

By the mid-1990s, there were hundreds of chalinitos on both sides of the border, but Morales managed to develop his own style. Though he bought a cowboy hat and boots, and began calling himself "El Original de la Sierra" (The Original from the Mountains), he was also a hip, urban teenager with the shaved head and gangsta attitude of the Los Angeles streets. The combination caught on with other young Mexican Americans, and when he was seventeen his *Homenaje a Chalino Sánchez* (Tribute to Chalino Sánchez) shot to the number one position on *Billboard* magazine's Latin music chart and became the first Spanish album ever to make Southern California's pop Top Ten.

The pop success was particularly sweet, since Morales has never seen himself as a specifically Mexican artist, or ranchera as his only musical touchstone. Indeed, his early efforts were largely financed by the Southern California rave scene. His brother Herminio was a deejay and concert promoter, and made the money for Jessie's first recordings by staging huge, virtually all-Anglo, dances. "He was getting like twenty, thirty thousand people in a place," Morales remembers. "And they were all Caucasions. I was like, 'Oh, man!' And my ma would be selling hot-dogs and stuff, and I was doing security. It was a family thing."

Herminio took Jessie to Angel Parra's studio, where Sánchez had recorded his breakthrough records, and while they were making a demo they happened to run into George Prajin, one of the most powerful figures in the local Latin record business. "He was waiting for a mix for one of his groups and he heard me when I was inside the vocal booth," Morales recalls. "And he was like, 'Oh man, I can't believe you sing like this.' He told me, 'Come down to my record store,' and from there he wanted to sign me. He was like, 'I'll pay you whatever you're wasting for that recording, Herminio, and let me take your brother up to another level.' And that's when we started record-ing with him."

Morales's first releases were on Prajin's Z record label, but he was shortly picked up by the huge Univision Music conglomerate, and presented as a voice of the new Los Angeles. "In L.A., there's a lot of different cultures coming in," he says. "Salvadoran people, they're not from Mexico, but they listen to that music. There's a lot of people from like Ecuador coming down to the shows. Everything that's coming out is hitting from L.A. down to Mexico, and I think the people are liking it because it's a different, urban kind of style, corridos—it's a new style for them."

Morales adds that in the beginning his sound caused some con-fusion: "At first, it was hard for me to write a corrido, because my Spanish wasn't really good. When I went to Tijuana, that was kind of weird for the people, because they thought I was from Sinaloa [Chal-ino's home state and the heartland of the Mexican drug world]. There was a lot of talk like, 'His Spanish is not coming out pretty good, he must be a *pocho* [U.S.-born Mexican].' But now the people over there love me, they give me a lot of respect. Basically because I'm the son of immigrants that come from Mexico, and they like me having this *éxito* [success] in L.A., and bringing my roots, showing all these youngsters what is our music, the Mexican music."

At the same time, Morales has never forgotten his other roots, as a street guy from South Central. Once he had established himself as a corridista, he began working on his rap chops, and he managed to sneak a few of his experiments onto disc, adding a hidden rap track on one album and rapping along with a corrido by his younger brother, Jorge, on another. He says that, ironically enough, his record company has tended to discourage this side of his work—despite rap's overwhelming popularity, they fear it may alienate some of his fans. "I did a crazy rap presentation in Los Premios Que Buena [an awards show sponsored by the premier Los Angeles Spanish radio station]," he says. "And the older people were like, '*Es un cholo, no sé, esta mezclando la música*—he's mixing up the English music with the Spanish music.' They thought I was a gangster, basically. So I took some hard hits to bring this stuff out. But now I laugh, because all these guys have come out and the people, suddenly they accept it."

Indeed, on the track with his brother, Morales pioneered what has become a trademark sound of the new Los Angeles, the Mexican-hip-hop fusion known as "urban regional" or *banda rap*.

I was like, "Let's get the bass drum from the banda, hit it hard, give me the tuba to give me, like, an R & B beat, a rap beat." And these guys started hitting the *tambora* [bass drum] hard, so I started feeling that vibe, and I got a little verse from Eazy-E—in English—but the corrido was the Spanish part. My brother was singing the corrido and I rapped the English.

"I think it was only a matter of time for that to happen, because if you had people like me listening to Eazy-E, Dr. Dre, and Snoop Dogg and we're interested in the Spanish music, buying Ramón Ayala, 'Tragos Amargo de Licor' and all that kind of stuff—I mean, I think it was only a matter of time for that to mix up and make a whole different market: a regional Mexican, rap, banda, norteño mix."

The fusion has since caught on, with artists like Akwid and Jae-P getting gold records and exciting a new generation of fans by laying rap lyrics over accordion and brass-band tracks. Once again, though, Morales is bucking the trend: the banda rap hits have all been in Spanish, but while he will keep making Spanish albums for his old audience, Morales plans to do his rapping in English.

"I see that there are not a lot of Hispanics, Latinos that are making it, like the Dr. Dre status or Snoop Dogg status," he says. "I want to bring the L.A. vibe, and all my Mexican people that listen to me and banda music to follow me with this stuff. I'm gonna keep mis raíces, my heritage and all that kind of stuff, the mariachi, we're gonna use some banda, some tubas, but all in English. So that's gonna be totally apart from all my Mexican records, *mis discos de norteño*. I'm gonna keep on doing that too—keep on keeping all my Mexican people happy with these corridos and these romantic songs—but I'm also gonna do this rap music that I've always wanted to do since I was young."

Morales's goal is to reflect his own experience and that of his generation. After all, there are a lot of kids just like him, in every city in America, who have grown up bilingual and bicultural, and for whom both gangsta rap and corridos have been the soundtrack of their lives. "I'm trying to show the people where I'm coming from," he says. "I had to start from mis raíces, so I can get recognized, and I want to keep the two things together. I want all the young people that hear my Spanish stuff to hear the English, too. Because that's us, right there."

Recommended Listening

While the artists in this book speak for themselves, all are of course much better understood if one has heard their music. In the brief guide that follows, I have selected records that provide an introduction to each of the musicians interviewed. I tried to choose discs that will be easy to find, but for people like Tabou Combo or Sir Victor Uwaifo, you may have to search a bit. Many foreign-language or non-U.S. releases do not get sold through mainstream outlets like Amazon.com and Tower Records, and even for the better-known names, I strongly recommend getting out on the street and browsing. Especially if you live in a town where there are large immigrant communities, there will always be places (often grocery or convenience stores) that sell recordings, both domestic and imported, and usually at better prices than in the megastores. What is more, the owners will be able to steer you not only to discs but often to live concerts.

The Internet is also a useful resource, providing access not only to niche suppliers in the United States, but to mail-order sites around the world. Many artists have websites, and often these will include a store, as well as samples of their music and tour schedules. There are also online dealers like worldmusicstore.com and sternsmusic.com (a particularly good source for African recordings), and specialized sites like descarga.com (for Latin and tropical music).

Ladysmith Black Mambazo is a remarkably consistent group, so the main question is whether one wants to hear them on their own or with guest stars. Preferring the former, I would recommend *Classic Tracks* (Shanachie), culled from their early work in the 1970s, while their later work is well displayed on *The Warner Brothers Collection* (Rhino/WEA), which starts out with their Paul Simon collaboration, "Homeless."

Ephat Mujuru's work is not widely available, but *Journey of the Spirit* (Alula) gives a nice taste of his sound.

Stella Chiweshe has a number of offerings; a good place to start is *Healing Tree: Best of Stella Chiweshe* (Shanachie).

Ali Farka Touré is probably best known for *Talking Timbuktu* (Hannibal), his collaboration with Ry Cooder, but I prefer *Ali Farka Touré* (Mango), the album that cemented his reputation as the "Malian bluesman," with its John Lee Hooker–influenced "Amandrai," or *Niafunke* (Hannibal), an excellent, relaxed recording done at his home.

Oumou Sangaré has a superb band and a lovely voice, and her records are all excellent. *Worotan* (World Circuit) would get the nod for its collaboration with soul saxophonist Pee Wee Ellis, but is out of print, so go for the career overview, *Oumou* (Nonesuch).

Tabu Ley Rochereau has dozens, if not hundreds, of albums, but finding them in an American record store is another question. Of the easily available options, the nod goes to *Africa Worldwide: 35ᵗʰ Anniversary Album* (Rounder Select), a solid dance set.

Lucien Bokilo has one solo album available, *Africation* (Jatelo), which is hard to find at mainstream distributors but can be bought directly from him through cdbaby.com. He can also be heard and seen on CDs and DVDs by the Soukous Stars.

Fadhili William has one CD currently available, *Fadhili Williams Mdawida 1963–1967* (Music Copyright Society of Kenya). His version of "Malaika" is currently unavailable, though it will undoubtedly appear on some anthology in the near future.

Sir Victor Uwaifo's *Greatest Hits, Volume 1* (Premier Music) is an excellent selection of his work, containing most of the songs mentioned in the interview.

King Sunny Ade hit the international scene with 1982's *Juju Music* (Mango), and it remains a fine first choice. If you want to hear him at his early peak, though, check out *Best of the Classic Years* (Shanachie), with some great tracks from the late 1960s and early 1970s.

Tarika Sammy has only one available disc, *Beneath Southern Skies* (Shanachie), but the group also appears on the album that introduced most of us to Malagasy music, *A World Out of Time: Henry Kaiser and David Lindley in Madagascar* (Shanachie), which ranges from old village players to young rockers. I also enjoy *Fanafody* (Xenophile), by the alternate version of the group, which had Sammy accompanying the singers who later formed Tarika.

The **Mendes Brothers** album that best fits this interview is *Bandera*, on their own MB label, which showcases their pioneering reworkings of traditional Cape Verdean styles, and I would also recommend checking out their more recent *Cabo Verde* (MB).

Tabou Combo have changed a lot over the years, keeping pace with mainstream American trends. This interview was done shortly after the release of their *360º* (Musicrama), which ranges from a bit of rap to their terrifically danceable compas grooves.

Emeline Michel's self-produced *Cordes et Ame* (Cheval De Feu) is a lovely, intimate disc (and can be bought direct from her through cdbaby.com). *Rasin Kreyol* is the best choice in stores, and shows the range of her working band and regular concert repertoire.

The **Mighty Sparrow**'s early recordings are the easiest to find, and are among the classics of calypso. Ice Records has the hits, starting with *Volume One* or *16 Carnival Hits* (which is half Sparrow and half his main rival, Lord Kitchener). Another good choice is *First Flight* (Smithsonian Folkways), which has excellent commentary as well. Sparrow's many later records have little mainstream distribution, but they can all be found at his website, www.mightysparrow.com.

María Díaz has two widely available CDs on the Sony International label, *Que Vuelvas* and *Concejos de Mujer*. Both are somewhat overproduced for my taste, but still give a good sense of her style.

Fulanito's breakthrough album was *El Hombre Mas Famoso de la Tierra* (Cutting), which is largely standard hip-hop, but also includes accordion merengue tracks like the hit "Guallando."

El Gran Combo has been making strong dance records for so long that it is impossible to choose one. Fortunately, every five years they release an anniversary set that traces their evolution thus far, and any of these give a good taste of the group.

Yomo Toro's *Las Manos de Oro* (Xenophile) is designed to show his range. Another nice choice is his Christmas album, *Celebremos Navidad* (Ashe), which puts a salsa twist on traditional Puerto Rican songs.

Rubén Blades created what many people still consider the greatest salsa album ever, *Siembra* (Fania) with Willie Colón. He has branched out a good deal since, including a Grammy-winning "world" excursion, *Mundo* (Sony International). I still return to *Siembra*—the perfect combination of music for both head and feet—but especially for Spanish-speakers, his later work is well worth exploring.

Eliades Ochoa and **Compay Segundo** can be heard together on *Buena Vista Social Club* (Nonesuch). Of all the Buena Vista offshoots, Compay's solo albums are my favorites, and the greatest is *Calle Salud* (Nonesuch), which features the gorgeous clarinet trio he added to fill out his string group. For Ochoa, *Sublime Ilusion* (Higher Octave) shows him both with his regular band and with guests.

Los Van Van have changed quite a bit over the years, and a good overview is provided by *The Legendary Los Van Van: Thirty Years of Cuba's Greatest Dance Band* (Continental Music). For a single, thoroughly danceable and well-recorded choice, *Llegó Van Van* (Atlantic/WEA) is an excellent look at them circa 1999.

Charanga Habanera can be heard at length and at full power on *Live In The USA* (Ciocan), though if you don't want songs to run over ten minutes you may be better off with *Grandes Exitos* (Caribe Productions).

Gema 4 show off their a cappella style on *Grandes Boleros A Capella* and *Te Voy A Dar* (both Picap), though they have gone on to record with instruments.

Mercedes Sosa's classic recordings are nicely represented on *30 Años* (Polygram), and can be fleshed out with her tribute albums to Atahualpa Yupanqui—*Interpreta Atahualpa* (Universal)—and Violeta Parra—*Homenaje a Violeta Parra* (Polygram).

Sandra Luna's debut, *Tango Varón* (Times Square), captures her compelling voice and excellent accompanying musicians.

Susana Baca's first album *Susana Baca* (Luaka Bop) gives a good sense of her range and depth. To put her work in context, it is also worth hearing the anthology that brought her to international attention, *Afro-Peruvian Classics: The Soul of Black Peru* (Luaka Bop).

Gilberto Gil's disc *Gilberto Gil*, part of Mercury/Polygram's Millenium Series, has the classic early work, and *Quanta Live* (Atlantic/Mesa) gives both a good view of his later explorations and a taste of how powerful he is in concert. The Millenium series also has a strong tropicália anthology, showing Gil alongside Gal Costa, Os Mutantes, and Caetano Veloso.

Caetano Veloso has been all over the map, musically and otherwise, for forty years. The eponymous collection in Verve/Polygram's Personalidade Series gives a good overview of his classic work. The misleadingly named *Best of Caetano Veloso* (Nonesuch) is a good overview of his work since the early 1990s—more serious and less exuberantly experimental, but still fine.

Olodum has a good career overview, *A Musica Do Olodum: 20 Anos* (Sony International).

Daniela Mercury's early work can be a little formulaic, so I would start with *Feijao com Arroz* (Sony), where she broadened the samba-reggae mix to include merengue and "trash" electric guitar.

Los Tigres del Norte have several "greatest hits" packages, all overlapping and fine, but their masterpiece as the corrido-singing "voices of the people" is the double album *Jefe de Jefes* (Fonovisa).

Paolo Conte was introduced to the American market with *The Best of Paolo Conte* (Nonesuch), and it is an exceptionally well-chosen set, with text translations of all the songs.

Mísia's albums are quite consistent, with *Garras do Sentidos* (Erato) standing out for its unique collection of fados by the likes of Nobel Prize winner José Saramago.

George Dalaras has an immense discography, but a good place to start is the well-chosen anthology *A Portrait* (EMI/Metro Blue), though I personally favor his great rembetika set, *50 Hronia Rebetiko* (EMI).

Haris Alexiou has had few releases outside Greece, but there is the *Very Best of Haris Alexiou* (EMI), and she also appears on the excellent anthology of contemporary Greek music, *Dance of Heaven's Ghosts* (EMI/Metro Blue).

Barbaros Erköse has only one album that I know of: *Lingo Lingo: Gypsy Music from Turkey* (Golden Horn).

Muzsikás and Márta Sebestyén have not been lucky in terms of staying in print in the United States, but *Morning Star* (Hannibal) is a typically varied set of Hungarian folk music, while *Maramaros: The Lost Jewish Music of Transylvania* (Hannibal) is a haunting exploration of an almost vanished tradition.

Kálmán Balogh's *Gypsy Jazz* (Rounder Select), though it does not sound much like jazz, gives a nice sense of his effort to both explore and broaden the Hungarian Gypsy tradition.

Norman Kennedy's first album, *Ballads and Songs of Scotland* (Folk Legacy) is still a delight of pure a cappella singing.

Dick Gaughan is the kind of artist who makes fans want to compile their own anthologies of his work. Mine doesn't exist, but *The Definitive Collection* (Highpoint) makes a decent stab at replacing the out-of-print *Handful of Earth* (Green Linnet). *A Different Kind Of Love*

Song (Appleseed) showcases his political side, while *Gaughan* (Topic) is a stripped-down, early album for hardcore folk fans.

Alan Stivell has traveled many paths since *Renaissance of the Celtic Harp* (Rounder Select), but it's still the place to start with him.

Les Nubians broke worldwide with their debut album, *Princesses Nubiennes* (Higher Octave), and it neatly encompasses their range of tastes and keen pop sensibility.

Paco de Lucía is usually celebrated for his genre-expanding solo and sextet work, which is widely available, but as a hidebound purist I am not a good guide to these recordings. To me his most passionately beautiful playing is on El Camaron de la Isla's early albums, the finest flamenco records of the modern age, for example Camaron's *Disco de Oro* (Philips/Polygram).

Carmen Linares stakes out important historical and personal ground on *En Antología: La Mujer en el Cante* (Universal), a tribute to the great female flamenco singers. Her tribute to Federico García Lorca, *Canciones Populares Antiguas* (Auvidis), which blends flamenco vocals with the broader Andalusian folk tradition and tastefully wide-ranging accompaniments, is currently out of print, but worth looking for.

Gipsy Kings have branched out on occasion, but their forte is super-charged rumba catalana, and the hits are on *The Best of the Gipsy Kings* (Nonesuch).

Radio Tarifa wasn't yet really a band when they made *Rumba Argelina* (Nonesuch), but that gave them the freedom to experiment with varied guests and musical flavors. The personnel had gelled somewhat by *Temporal* (Nonesuch), but it still has much the same blend of European and North African traditions with well-integrated modern touches.

Hadj Mohamed Tahar Fergani currently has only one disc available internationally, *Arab-Andalusian Anthology, Vol. 1* (Ocora), and fortunately it is a fine introduction to his work.

The Master Musicians of Jajouka became international cult favorites thanks to onetime Rolling Stone Brian Jones's psychedelic production, *Brian Jones Presents: The Pipes of Pan at Jajouka* (Philips), but they still sound most powerful straight, and *Apocalypse Across the Sky* (Axiom) puts you right in the middle of their wailing ghaitas.

Khaled has two periods: his early Cheb Khaled recordings, with straight Algerian rai bands, and his international productions, starting with *Khaled* and *N'ssi N'ssi* (Cohiba). The production values are higher on the later discs, but it's a toss-up as to whether the American players toughen or dilute his sound. I'd go back and start with *Forever King: Classic Songs from the King of Algerian Rai* (Manteca).

Simon Shaheen shows his purist, traditional side on *Turath: Masterworks of the Middle East* (Times Square), and a more modern style, with Western classical and jazz players added, on *Blue Flame* (Ark 21).

Naseer Shemma is an astonishingly virtuosic, tasteful and imaginative musician, but represented at the moment by only one album: *Baghdad Lute* (Institut du Monde Arabe).

Mahmood Anwar seems to have no CDs available as of this writing, but cassettes can be found at Iraqi stores and websites.

Cinucen Tanrikorur has had only one album distributed internationally, *Turquie* (Ocora).

Kayhan Kalhor has such a varied career that it is hard to know where to begin. The two projects discussed in the interview were Ghazal, whose second album, *As Night Falls on the Silk Road* (Shanachie), is a good place to start, and the Masters of Persian Music, whose *Faryad* (World Village) is an excellent double live album.

Nusrat Fateh Ali Khan's best-known recordings in the United States are fusion experiments like *Night Song* (Real World), but I would avoid these in favor of *Shahen-Shah* (Real World) or the earlier recordings on the two volumes of *The Ultimate Nusrat Fateh Ali Khan* (Narada).

Purna Das is featured on *Bauls of Bengal* (Crammed Disc) and can also be heard alongside some of his peers on the identically titled *The Bauls of Bengal* (Empire Musicwerks or Legacy).

Ali Akbar Khan has a label of his own, AMMP, on which he makes available a range of classic and recent recordings. The first two volumes of the *Signature Series*, beautifully recorded in the 1960s, are a good place to start.

Ravi Shankar has ranged so widely that anyone unfamiliar with his work should start with *The Essential Ravi Shankar* (Private Music), which follows him from classical ragas in the 1950s to later fusion experiments. Indian aficionados prefer the recordings on which he plays only one or two extended ragas, but I don't know this music well enough to make suggestions.

Ondekoza and Kodo are live acts, as far as I am concerned. The power of their drumming will not come through on a normal sound system, and in any case the visual component of their performance is as important as the music.

Wu Man's roots are showcased on *Chinese Traditional and Contemporary Music* (Nimbus), and extended on *Pipa from a Distance* (Naxos). Her cross-cultural experiments, including the one with James Makubuya mentioned in the interview, are on *Wu Man and Friends* (Traditional Crossroads).

Raymond Kane is in fine form on *Punahele* (Dancing Cat), though if you are in Hawaii it is worth trying to find some of his earlier recordings.

Dennis Kamakahi's solo work is beautifully showcased on *Pua 'ena* (Windham Hill), while his work with Hui Aloha is on the band's Windham Hill release *Hui Aloha*.

The Iron River Singers have not recorded, preferring to make their music at ceremonies and pow-wows.

Jessie Morales is most interesting when he is most varied. *Loco* (Univision) has corridos, love songs, a Spanish version of Willie Nelson's "Crazy," and a hidden rap track.

INDEX

C